N

Praise for *Learning to Learn in Practice*

This is a deeply researched, comprehensive and authoritative book which integrates emerging knowledge, successful practice and proven strategies into a highly effective and relevant synthesis. This is more of a resource than a conventional text; the authors practice what they preach in that they help the reader to become a learner and to take control of the wide ranging strategies on offer. *Learning to Learn in Practice* has the potential to transform the lives of learners and those who enable and support learning. It has real implications for school leaders and represents an important step in the movement towards learning centred schools.

John West-Burnham, Professor of Educational Leadership,
St Mary's University College, London

If you are trying to be a more accomplished teacher, this book will help you.

If you want to try to understand so many of the developments that have taken place in the recent past in the way teachers go about their work, this book will shed light. If you want background from theory, insights into psychology or international comparisons about classroom approaches, you will find them in this book.

Learning to Learn in Practice pulls off the amazing trick of blending things together; good advice with practical steps to apply, comments on the way we do our work with the story behind them, logic on why we should adopt a different approach with analysis of why it is not always easy … and what we could do to get started.

The book is a good read. From Tony Hart, to Star Trek, to Twitter, to Damien Hirst, to Big Brother to garden sheds, there is a narrative that holds the attention and explains the logic. There is also the narrative of how one school built its learning village where staff, pupils and the wider community looked afresh at what they could do to help young people to achieve more. Couple these accounts with the endless practical examples of planning tools, organisational ideas, checklists and prompts and the teacher has a shed load of starting points both for practise in the classroom or conversation with colleagues and pupils.

Learning to Learn in Practice is an engaging book. Don't miss the chance to engage!

Mick Waters, Professor of Education, President of the Curriculum Foundation

Learning to Learn in Practice is a fresh and innovative book. It gets to the essence of learning with many accessible and grounded ideas. It provides teachers and students with many tools, frameworks and ideas for getting at 'natural' learning activites. It is well organised and multifaceted. It draws in all the key literature but does so in a way that gives practical and fundamental focus to learning. Teachers, students and parents will benefit from engaging with the ideas in the book.

Michael Fullan, Professor Emeritus, OISE/University of Toronto

Learning to Learn in Practice is the highest peak in the mountain range of 'Smith & Co.' publications. It is a mature book that distils many years of experience, research and reflection into crystal-clear analyses and exciting solutions.

For those who have been working on learning to learn for some time, this book is the 'slingshot' that will propel your thinking and practice into a more sophisticated orbit. It brings all the bits together, it offers coherent structures, it answers uncomfortable questions, it expounds compelling arguments, it asserts radical opinons, it provides insightful information, it describes a catalogue of practical strategies and gives ready-made resources. In other words, it puts into your hands all that you need to embed, at classroom, whole-school and community levels, proven practices that enable students to thrive on the journey towards independence.

For those who are new to learning to learn, or new to the profession, let *Learning to Learn in Practice* inform, inspire and guide you. The book sets out a vision, taking you well beyond current data-driven imperitives to the core purpose of every intelligent, modern school. It equips you, both intellectually and practically, to get on with the real job of teaching, the moral job, funnily enough the old-fashioned job, of letting educational insights rather than political dogma determine practice and of seeking to give students the best chance of life-long success as they stride out into *their* adult world, not ours.

Paul Ginnis, Independent Trainer and author of *The Teacher's Toolkit*

To be really effective children need to feel learning is their journey, that they can plan and invest in, not something done to them. One of the main outcomes should be young people who are motivated and capable learners, aware of the different ways they can learn, on their own and with others. This is an invaluable, deeply practical, but structured and thoughtful guide to creating a generative approach to learning which generates more learning and enabled learners as its main outcome.

Charles Leadbeater, author of *We Think,
Personalisation through Participation* and *21 Ideas for 21st Century Learning*

In the 21st century, educationalists are preoccupied with a crucial question: how can the curriculum prepare students for life in a rapidly changing world? *Learning to Learn in Practice* presents a brilliant case for placing the 'learn to learn' approach at the centre of the curriculum experience for every student. It is filled with ideas not only on 'what' the curriculum should offer but 'how' it should be delivered if it is to take young people on their journey from dependent to independent learner. The review of theory is comprehensive, the resources are exceptional and the 12 principles are clear. For those who are hesitating it is a great 'way in' and for those who are well down the road it will greatly enhance what they are already doing.

John Jones, writer, presenter and educational consultant

Alistair Smith
with Mark Lovatt and John Turner

Learning to Learn in Practice

The L2 Approach

Crown House Publishing Ltd
www.crownhouse.co.uk
www.crownhousepublishing.com

First published by
Crown House Publishing Ltd
Crown Buildings, Bancyfelin, Carmarthen, Wales, SA33 5ND, UK
www.crownhouse.co.uk

and

Crown House Publishing Company LLC
6 Trowbridge Drive, Suite 5, Bethel, CT 06801, USA
www.crownhousepublishing.com

British Library of Cataloguing-in-Publication Data
A catalogue entry for this book is available
from the British Library.

10-digit ISBN 184590287-4
13-digit ISBN 978-184590287-2

LCCN 2009936663

Printed and bound in the UK by
The Cromwell Press Group, Trowbridge, Wiltshire

Preface

Formation processes and the exploding shed

Structuralist philosophers and lovers of *Star Trek* have a certain fondness for the transporter – the device that allowed the intrepid crew of the *Enterprise* to disassemble themselves and then reappear intact on some remote planet. The transporter worked by converting Spock or Captain Kirk into tiny fragments, which would then be reassembled at the destination; same Spock, different planet, similar storyline. Trekkies loved it! When functioning correctly the transporter could, essentially, deconstruct any crew member and then put him or her back together again.

In 2002 I came across the remains of a shed which had been blown up by the British Army. The shed had been full of personal possessions, garden tools and assorted bits and pieces. It had, like many others of its kind, been someone's pride and joy. Now there were just bits of it left. It had disintegrated to such a degree that only small fragments of burnt and twisted wood, melted glass, shapeless metal, shards of clothing, torn newspaper, earth, grass and roofing felt remained. One minute it had been a shed and now it was – a former shed.

The garden shed is a bit of a British institution. It's the sort of place where, hidden away, secretive and sometimes furtive hobbies occur – model railways, woodturning, paraffin lamp cleaning – all going on undetected. Intimate places with a male atmosphere; partners forbidden, smelling of damp dog, often dimly lit. They are romantic for some, for others an escape from reality but always an expression of the owner's personality. This one had been shattered into thousands of pieces by two pounds of plastic explosive, put there and detonated by a Major Doug Hewitt of the Army School of Ammunition.

This shed had a name, a pretentious name but maybe one which was fitting. It was called *Cold Dark Matter: An Exploded View* (1991) and it was an exhibit in the Brit Art exhibition at Tate Modern. It had been reassembled by the artist, Cornelia Parker, to capture the instant after the explosion so all the pieces were suspended in air. She had persuaded the Army to help her transport it to a field in Banbury and then blow it up. Amazing! As you walked around the ragged remains of the now suspended 'shed' it seemed to move and to reposition itself. It was still in a basic 'shed' shape albeit one with an exploded viewpoint but now there was more of it. The addition of different lighting effects made the experience unnerving, with the 'shed' moving around and the shadows changing. It was like the transporter from *Star Trek* on a slightly off day!

The accompanying catalogue got me thinking. Apparently, the creation of such fragments is a process with a name. Professor Lord Renfrew of Kaimsthorn – formerly Disney Professor of

Archaeology and Director of the McDonald Institute for Archaeological Research, Cambridge University – a man with a name and a set of titles to die for–said:

> *We archaeologists have a name for the transformations by which what were once viable buildings and useful artefacts in the hands of the people who made and used them become buried in fragmentary condition below ground: 'formation processes'.*

Formation processes! That term strikes me as a great concept for some of my own contemporary experiences of education – transformations 'which were once viable but which are now buried in fragmentary condition below ground'.

Sometimes these formation processes are buried so deep that no one questions their existence. They have become what some call the 'grammar' of schooling. The grammar is everything that's inherited, rarely exploded though often reassembled: expectations about what schools can and can't do, buildings, terms, periods, curriculum, relationships, roles, accountabilities.

Formation processes and schools

Sometimes this inherited grammar has led to anomalies which, in a culture of testing and league tables, directly affect a student's perception of the value and purpose of learning: we see more risk averse teaching; teachers who teach to the test; students who commodify knowledge and dismiss anything which is not on the test; knowledge which is wrapped up in parcels unrelated to anything beyond school; question spotting by teachers in collusion with their students; exams which reward recall above anything else.

Learning cannot be usefully disembodied from understanding or from context. Out of context it's not learning. The curriculum is not an assemblage of bits. We are asking through this book that schools go beyond focusing on 'bits' and start to see the whole shed! If you must blow up your shed don't try to go back to what the shed once was!

Before we leave the shed, let's consider the human effect of taking something cherished and questioning its deeply buried formation processes. The major who had positioned his plastic explosive where the original single light bulb had dangled so carefully became a changed man. When he visited the exhibition later he said:

> *I was stunned when some months later I walked in ... The single light bulb, now in my mind representing the core of the explosion, threw out the debris that in turn projected dramatic shadows onto the stark white walls, floor and ceiling – such a powerful image. I had never considered modern art before, but if this was it, I was a convert.*

He had attempted to utilise the idea of the bulb throwing out energy and so had become embroiled himself in the artistic interpretation. He had to disintegrate the shed while distressing and distorting as many of the items as possible without destroying them. His explosive couldn't exceed the safe limit for the site, nor could he disperse the contents of the shed over too large an area as he had to collect them afterwards!

The major had experienced a paradigm shift. He had been affected by the experience to such a degree that it had altered the way he saw the world of art. So there we have it. A powerful mind-changing experience arises when just enough of an explosion occurs in a much loved, well-established edifice to expose its formation processes. This is not unlike a teacher having a breakthrough experience and seeing themselves and their profession in a whole new light.

I hope that this book plays some part in helping us to see what we do in a whole new light. We will argue that it is important for teachers and schools to be clear about the outcomes they seek. In the context of our students' world – a 21st century world experiencing an information explosion – ask the question: What do we want them to leave school with? Use the outcomes to guide thinking about what the curriculum should offer. We will also argue the importance of finding and applying fundamental principles (in our case the 12 essentials of learning to learn) to guide thinking about how the curriculum should be offered. We would say that schools should address the need to provide coherence: think in terms of students, staff, the school community, parents and carers and immerse what you do in the prevailing technologies of the age. To help in all of this find out, as we have done, what others are doing – borrow from the best and re-invent where there are gaps.

We designed our own L2 Approach described throughout this book as a means of taking learners from dependence to independence. The adoption of a learning to learn approach is a journey rather than a moment in time, a single commitment or a yes or no decision. Every context is different, so start from where you are at rather than where others would wish you were at. Sometimes to get to the deep you have to practise in the shallows and, whilst it can be exciting and invigorating to plunge in at the behest of others, it can also be dangerous. There is merit in our journey school concept of 'adopt then embed then spread'.

Finally, and without wishing to sound too far fetched, this is what we think learning to learn, properly thought through, can do for teachers and for a school. It will provide an assault on some of the more cherished processes, the everyday assumptions and ways of doing things and, as a legacy of the assault, it will prompt questions about the shape of things to come. People who are involved will be changed as a consequence as it is very, very difficult to remain a passive observer when there is so much reassembling happening so quickly.

Alistair Smith, May 2009

Acknowledgements

Alistair Smith

Many hundreds of hours have gone into this book. Some of those hours have been spent working with schools, travelling to or from schools, looking around schools and sometimes just thinking about schools. Thank you each and every one for making my time with you so enjoyable and for letting me help you make a difference.

Thanks also to my friends and colleagues at the FA and in the world of football for providing a whole new world of challenge. A big thanks to Ani for making me laugh, keeping me alert and up to date. Finally, thanks also go to the Alite team who have been with us on their own learning journey: Adrian, Andy, Angela, Grace, Heather, Hilary, Irene, Kim and Melanie.

Mark Lovatt

A big thanks to Jane, Hannah, Jacob and all at Cramlington

John Turner

Thanks to Julie. Ben and Emma who had to put up with me working long hours on the book and the inspiring teachers and students in the UK and South Australia who demonstrated to me the power of learning to learn.

Contents

How to use this book

This book is organised so that it is easy to navigate and facilitates different ways of reading. It sets out to be of use to teachers who want to boost their classroom practice, readers who have a passing interest, specialists in the field and decision makers.

Chapters

Each chapter is preceded by a short summary and a set of questions.

Topics

To read the book by topic use the contents list at the back or the tags at the beginning of each chapter.

Maps

Each chapter is represented by a visual map that outlines the main topics covered.

Tags

We have represented the weight of content in each chapter through a set of 'tags'. Stolen from web technology, the size of the text suggests the frequency with which it has been searched. Students can create their own tags for a topic – a useful review activity.

Levels of influence

We look at the impact of the 12 essentials at four levels: student, classroom, school and parent.

12 essentials

We provide a sample within a table for each essential at each level to give a sense of what it might mean.

Case studies

These can be found throughout the book and there is a concentration of them in Chapter 9.

National and international approaches

Our summary of what is happening in the UK and around the world is provided in Chapter 10.

Appendices

These include a diet sheet of different approaches, the 5R's progression overview, some outline five year learning to learn plans, and links to Personal Learning and Thinking Skills (PLTS) and Social and Emotional Aspects of Learning (SEAL).

Resources

An extensive selection of resources is available on the accompanying CD.

Summary

▓ A preoccupation with the detail of curriculum content and the need to secure coverage has disadvantaged a generation of learners.

▓ Students can become better at learning.

▓ Educationalists can design systems which help students become better at learning.

▓ We need to be more aware of the true nature of 21st century life and its challenges if we are to redesign systems.

▓ A new balance of knowledge, attributes, skills and experiences will be needed to prosper in a world where change – and rapid change at that – is the only certainty.

▓ Most learning to learn interventions have a positive effect but some are significantly more effective than others.

▓ There are well-established essentials which are consistent with a quality learning to learn approach.

▓ Any durable learning to learn approach must integrate the prevailing technologies of the age.

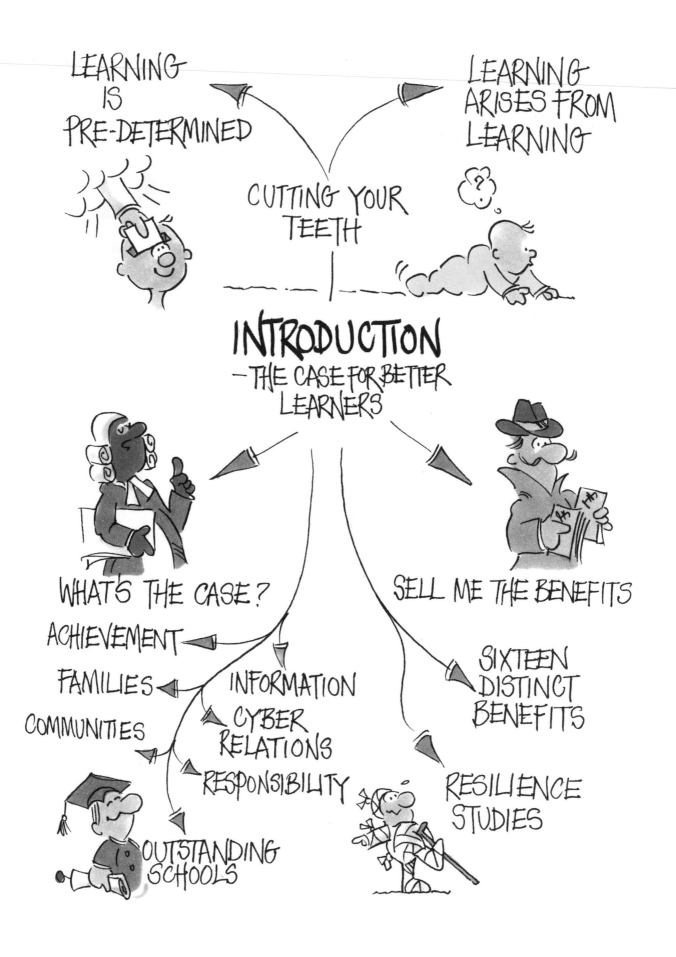

LEARNING IS PRE-DETERMINED

LEARNING ARISES FROM LEARNING

CUTTING YOUR TEETH

INTRODUCTION
– THE CASE FOR BETTER LEARNERS

WHAT'S THE CASE?

SELL ME THE BENEFITS

ACHIEVEMENT

FAMILIES

COMMUNITIES

INFORMATION

CYBER RELATIONS

RESPONSIBILITY

OUTSTANDING SCHOOLS

SIXTEEN DISTINCT BENEFITS

RESILIENCE STUDIES

Begin Parts Adopt Embed Spread
Leadership Teeth **Core Purpose** **Benefits** *Shallow* Brain *Deep*
Employment Workplace
Communique Leisure Childhood *social skills*

Introduction

The case for better learners

In this chapter we:

- Explain how and when learning about learning begins

- State the case for learning to learn

- Outline the benefits of learning to learn.

And ask the following questions:

- Is our education system fit for purpose?

- What is that purpose?

- What's the point of learning to learn?

- How can schools best equip themselves for change?

Cutting your learning to learn teeth

Learning to learn is a process not unlike getting teeth. We don't mean a new set of teeth to replace those which, through accumulated years of sweet foods and lack of attention, have dropped out. We're talking about the teeth you get when you are very young. Suddenly solids take on a whole new glamour. When you get teeth you become dramatically better at mastication. When you learn to learn you become dramatically better at learning. It can start very early.

Take the infant learn to learn class as an example. Infants at 10 months of age learn about 10 times faster than infants of 2 months of age.[1] During this period from 2 to 10 months of age infants become better learners. They begin to understand that some of the changes they experience around them depend on what is called 'contingency'.

In an experiment, 2-month-old infants learned to turn their heads to move a mobile above their cots. When their head turned so did the mobile. Infants in the experimental group were presented with a mobile that responded to movements in a predictable way, whilst another control group had a mobile which was activated but in a random way. After four 10 minute daily sessions of exposure to the moving shape above their head, and an average of approximately 200 responses, the babies in the experimental group detected the existence of a pattern of movement. They smiled, wriggled, changed colour and became more active. This we call a contingency!

Now get a robot that has what looks like a face but is not very human beyond that. Infants of 10 months sit in front of the robot and are either in or out of an experimental group. To those who are in, the robot responds to their behaviours, movements and noises. In the other group the robot is responsive but not to anything in front of it. The predictable robot creates learning after about after 3.5 minutes of exposure. Children learn that the robot is a 'contingent' social agent. It responds to their attention. They exhibit five times more noises than the others. Moreover, they followed the eyeline and direction of the robot when it rotated, showing evidence for shared attention.

While it takes 2-month-olds about 40 minutes to learn new contingencies, by 10 months it takes them less than 3.5 minutes. Explanations are possible in terms of changes in brain structures. New brain structures grow, in a genetically predetermined manner, which supports more efficient learning. An alternative hypothesis is that the increase in learning efficiency is itself the result of a learning process that operates on the timescale of months. Under this view, better learning is the consequence of learning itself. In other words we are programmed to learn to be learners. Either way, you cut your learning teeth!

What's the case for learning to learn?

Why should we bother developing learn to learn 'teeth'? Why not struggle on with our gums or accept the ill-fitting dentures we've already got? Learning to learn approaches provide more than the sum of their parts. For a student learning how to learn, properly done, soon becomes an accelerant to all round improvements.

Our observations of over a hundred lessons, visits to dozens of schools and conversations with students, teachers and school leaders have left us with an appreciation of the benefits of what we call the learning to learn approach. We use the term 'approach' advisedly. It's not a course, a set of study skills or thinking skills lessons, it's not a programme – no one will be programmed; it is a way of thinking about, relating to and supporting learners, hence the term 'approach'.

But why go this way? Why not revert to what we used to be good at, or what we convinced ourselves we were good at? To a traditional, subject based curriculum, to whole class transmission teaching methods, to summative testing, setting and early specialisation? Why do we need the 5R's we describe later when for years three – reading, writing and arithmetic – have done us proud?

Achievement

In the UK the gap between rich and poor has widened. Social mobility has stalled. We know that in countries where there is a big gap between the incomes of the rich and the poor the number of cases of mental illness, drug and alcohol abuse, obesity and teenage pregnancy are higher, as are the murder rates. Life expectancy in these countries is shorter and children's educational performance and literary scores are worse. It is not only the poor who suffer. Rates of mental illness are likely to be as much as five times higher in the population *as a whole* in the most unequal countries.[2] Where there are large and obvious disparities, tensions arise.

The lowest achieving groups in English schools are Afro-Caribbean boys on free school meals, followed by white working class boys on free school meals, followed by white working class girls on free school meals. There remains a performance gap, in this case a gap of 27%, and the better the school the poorer the child on free school meal does.[3]

Education can still emancipate. It can make a difference and offer a solution. Good teaching in well led schools can cut through this gap.

Good schools and good teachers make a difference. A really effective teacher can add significant value to a student's life chances. We want to put the tools to be really effective in the hands of as many teachers as possible.

Families

In the UK 'family' life has changed considerably since the 1950s. More and more children grow up in second families or in one parent families. There is no judgement intended in this observation; indeed it would be too easy to assume that this was indicative of demise.

According to the Future Foundation, 80% of the population believe that parents used to spend more time with their children than they do now. The reality is that time spent with children has actually started to go up, jumping from an average 34 minutes per day in 2000 to 45 minutes per day in 2005. Although this doesn't seem much, the Future Foundation argues that more mothers now work and are generally better remunerated than in previous generations, technologies have freed up time on household chores and greater gender equality within household responsibilities has freed time for both mothers and fathers. Many families try hard to sit down together regularly to spend time as a unit and catch each other's news; indeed, the average family eats just under four evening meals together a week according to the latest findings from the British Household Panel Survey (2008). According to the Future Foundation, in 2009 children feel satisfied with family life on the whole.[4]

We want to involve parents and carers. Research we cite in this book shows that effective links between schools and parents can help make a difference in raising student attainment. We believe in providing effective strategies for parents to learn about learning.

Communities

In the UK, 'community' life has also changed considerably since the 1950s. The opportunities for informal networking and social activity are changing. More variety and choice in leisure and recreation activity have come hand in hand with less 'mass' participation. Changes to the patterns of the typical working day, increasing numbers of people working in small to medium sized businesses, more home and portfolio working and increased geographical mobility has contributed to a more individualised and dislocated approach to recreation. The obvious example would be the decline in the traditional works' social clubs which provide sports and leisure facilities on site, cater for family events such as children's parties and do so as a focal point for the entire workforce.

With fewer and fewer formal outlets for social activity, decline in grassroots political and community activity, plummeting levels of trust – UK levels of trust are amongst the lowest in Europe – and an economy in recession, people have less scope for purposeful face-to-face interaction with others. In this scenario we see an emergence of 'networked individualism' – where huge numbers of individuals access social networks and develop virtual relationships. When children learn their emotional intelligence from the television and practise using it on a social networking site we may have the beginnings of a problem.

Social skills are a shortcut to success. The soft skills are increasingly important in a dramatically changing world. We believe in equipping young people with soft skills, especially resolve and self-efficacy.

Responsibility

According to Professor Jean Twenge young people in the West today are 50% more extrovert than people of the same age were in the 1960s.[5] She analysed every comparable study and concluded that by 2010 the typical Western teenager will be more extrovert than over 80% of the population were in the 1960s. Research on personal responsibility suggests that young people in Western societies are increasingly externalising locus of control. If this is true, what it means is that fewer and fewer are learning to assume responsibility for the consequences of their actions; and more and more are looking for some sort of justification or excuse that is external to themselves. So, if we put the two trends together, we could face a situation where more and more of the young people in our classrooms are extrovert in their behaviour at the same time as they run from the consequences of it. Suffice it to say, this becomes very difficult ground for a teacher.

It is now a truism to say that the pace of change in the world has exceeded our education system's ability to keep up. Whilst we may not all fall for what we see and hear on *Shift Happens*, we are savvy enough to know that informal and formal learning will increasingly overlap and mix like two tins of paint spilling. So too will the spaces in which learning takes place as we move from place-to-place connectivity (think red telephone boxes and underground cables laid across the floor of the Atlantic) to person-to-person connectivity (think people on the Atlantic communicating from their yachts by mobile phone).

We can already shift money, ideas and products instantly in cyberspace so even the concept of globalisation has become dated. *Around the World in Eighty Days* has become Around the World in Eighty Nanoseconds. The collapse of the sub-prime mortgage market brought this home to us and is our banking system's equivalent of the butterfly's wings flapping.

Informal and formal learning will continue to overlap and opportunities to learn will occur beyond classrooms. We want to endow young people with an understanding of the processes of learning and spaces in which to take responsibility.

Cyber relations

The existence of a digital environment means that learning will become less exclusively focused on institutions and a handful of prestigious universities. Learning will occur in informal networks and arise out of expediency or playfulness. The BBC began television broadcasting in earnest in 1936, with a charter that requires it 'to enrich people's lives with programmes and services that inform, educate and entertain'. Since then, we estimate, it has accumulated about a million hours of programming. That's a lot of programmes and a lot of influence. YouTube, a different creature and certainly not a quality broadcaster, has provided more in the last six months. Each day over 200,000 videos, typically of three minutes duration, are uploaded.[6] Some 88% of the content is new, most of it aimed at less than 100 people and only some of it of any interest.

One of the most jaw-dropping instances of how connected this community is lies in the story of 'Numa Numa' – a Moldavian pop song which was recorded in 2003 and became a hit in 2004. A young man in New Jersey picked up the song, recorded himself miming to it in front of his computer and uploaded the grainy video onto YouTube. Since then the video of Gary Brolsma dancing to the tune of 'Numa Numa' has had more than 700 million views, it has been replicated 58,000 times, there are animated versions, army and navy versions and even a version with several hundred prisoners dancing in the exercise yard of a Philippine prison.

In Chapter 9, we look in detail at the world of wikis, social networking, search engines, blogs, online simultaneous gaming, user generated organisation and distribution, virtual worlds, creative commons, open source software, YouTube, file sharing and all the communities that are sustained by these technologies. We refer to these new and ever present media types as 'emergent ubiquitous media'.

Our emergent ubiquitous media can be characterised by the 6P's. They are media like no other. We write 60 years after the publication of George Orwell's *1984*, but even the ailing author hammering away at his typewriter could not have imagined the degree to which the prevailing media would be so *persuasive, powerful, participative, pervasive, penetrative* and yet *playful*.

Emergent ubiquitous media:

- [ ] Persuasive
- [ ] Powerful
- [ ] Participative
- [ ] Pervasive
- [ ] Penetrative
- [ ] Playful

We want to ensure that our approach helps to produce young people who are confident in their use of appropriate media, capable of critical judgement and who can switch with ease between consumption and production.

Information fluency

In our view, formal education is floundering about and has yet to get a grip on some of these phenomena. At an international conference Alistair had the temerity to suggest that *The Simpsons* was the contemporary equivalent of Alexander Pope's *The Dunciad*, and was howled down by those who saw education's role as equivalent to inoculation against such mass media products.

So it is that a whole new set of skills – information fluencies – are required in order to become critical thinkers, producers and consumers of the new media. Consumption without gumption awaits and is the default should we fail to foster a grammar of understanding. In the midst of this we have in the UK a school curricula which has become so stuffed with content it's akin to a ghastly parody of Monty Python's exploding diner, Mr Creosote.[7]

This is particularly so in England where every now and then the National Curriculum is open season for some politician or interest group trying to squeeze some more content in – cookery classes, an additional language, Latin or Greek, money management – to the point of explosion. Lost in all of this is the space to develop responsibility so we have a vacuum right in the centre of our school offer. For many students, the school experience has led to boxed thinking where knowledge is assigned a value based on its relevance to a test.

We wish to encourage schools to design thematic challenges using time and space imaginatively to break out of 'boxed' thinking.

Outstanding schools – their view

In 2006 a group of 100 principals from 14 countries met in Beijing, China, to discuss the transformation of and innovation in the world's education systems.[8] These principals led schools which were regarded by others as outstanding. They came together believing that there should be a global sense of moral purpose in education and they represented many different school systems from around the world.

Recognising that education systems and their schools existed in different cultures with policies and practices which may be unique to their own contexts, the group nevertheless attempted to extract a common manifesto for moving forward. They identified 'an emerging global agenda for educational reform based on the personalisation of learning, the professionalisation of teaching, networking and collaboration and the intelligent and ethical use of data'. The group published a short résumé of its findings which it called the 'G100 Communique'. It's worth reading the recommendations to other principals in full.[9] They recommended:

1. All schools must provide high quality education to all students. The quality of schools and school systems should be judged by their ability to both raise the achievement and reduce the negative impact of social economical and other background factors on the learner.

2. All schools must take the responsibility to prepare learners through curriculum provision as global citizens who are capable of negotiating cultural and linguistic differences, respectful of others and aware of their interdependence.

3. All school leaders must embrace the personalisation of learning as a means of enabling every student to reach their potential, to learn how to learn and to share responsibility for their own education.

4. All schools must expand their definition of success to include more than student performance in academic subjects. Current measures of educational outcomes are limited in what they measure, but we still affirm the importance of basic skills in laying the foundations for a successful education.

5. All school leaders must recognise their moral obligation and powerful influence with their students and staff and thus act responsibly and energetically to develop a school culture that is outward looking in engaging with the wider community, as well as developing the school as a professional learning community.

6. All school leaders must become active members of global networks of educational transformation. Through these networks, they contribute to and benefit from an international repertoire of knowledge and expertise because their responsibilities are not only limited to the well-being of students in their own schools, but children in other schools and other nations.

The G100 principals did a great job of placing the need for more independent, responsible learners at the heart of a school's core purpose. We feel that the broad benefits of a learning to learn approach have been recognised and endorsed by a voice more powerful than our own but, at a more local level, here are what we consider to be the specific benefits.

The benefits of a learning to learn approach

Reposition student perceptions about learning

As students go through secondary schooling there is a slow but steady decline in engagement. This is put down to an excess of old fashioned teaching – often whole class and transmissive, a perceived lack of relevance to their world, lack of challenge, patchy access to and use of technologies and lack of consultation. However, on numerous occasions students have reported to us that they have enjoyed and been challenged by the learning to learn experience. For many, though certainly not all, it has positioned learning in a fresher and more positive light. As a consequence of teachers having to teach in a different way, relationships can be more open, positive, mutual and honest.

Develop transferable skills

What do we want our young people to leave with? What should they be able to do? What should they know of themselves and others? How do we want them to think? How would we wish them to cope? The school curriculum can be, and often is, stuffed with content so that this very content, and the need to cover it, drives out the spaces for learning. As Howard Gardner and others have said, 'coverage is the enemy of learning'. The next enemy is the urge to parcel up the curriculum in neatly tied and labelled subject boxes. Too much of what young people consider to be learning has come to them pre-packaged in a subject 'box' with an attendant way of positioning that box. For example, a Year 5 group was asked the following question during a maths lesson (or maths 'box'): 'There are 15 cats and 3 dogs on a big ship, what's the name of the Captain?' Just over a half of the group came back with the answer – '18'. Thinking has taken place within, and not outside, the box – which, in this case, happens to be a maths box. If we had asked the same question in another box (say, English, drama or history) then we would have got other answers! Maybe we need more skills and less stuff?

Provide significantly higher levels of student self-awareness and a vocabulary for learning

In a very short space of time – within weeks – students begin to exhibit an improved awareness of what's going on as and when they learn. This heightened awareness of the processes that underpin learning allows scope for many more formal and informal conversations about learning. Students will 'second-position' as though their process soul temporarily leaves their learning body and they can observe themselves in action.

Foster student independence

There are lots of ways to learn to swim. Experimentation can be dangerous, lessons can be helpful, so can buoyancy aids, but being towed up and down through the water is not the best way. Too many teachers have constructed study tools to help tow their students through the water. They do all the work whilst the student has an effortless swimming experience and so remains inept. One simple rule would be: 'Never work harder than your students!' By improving their ability to study independently, manage themselves, persist in the face of difficulty and understand their responsibilities in making themselves better, we create independent learners.

Integrate meaningfully with emerging technologies

A learning to learn approach must recognise and engage with the prevailing technologies which are portable, powerful, persuasive, penetrative, participatory and pervasive. Properly developed, a learning to learn approach will encourage the use of social networking tools, personalised profiling and goal setting opportunities, research, information sharing and portfolio building.

Improve morale amongst teachers and practitioners

Study after study has shown that the individual teachers that students have from year to year have a greater effect on their learning outcomes than the schools they attend.[10] This means that there is more variation in student performance among classrooms within schools than among schools. If you get a bad teacher you are in trouble. Despite the best of intentions, some teachers have lost their way. A vibrant learning to learn approach can refresh the parts …

Generate more reflective teachers and school communities

The introduction of a learning to learn approach will provide opportunities for an unremitting and highly compelling professional dialogue around teaching and learning. This does not happen often enough or with sufficient depth within many, maybe most, of our secondary schools.

Guarantee more engaging learning experiences

By its very nature, a learning to learn approach asks questions of teaching methods, provides skills and attributes that transfer beyond school, is structured through challenges, delivered through technologies and necessitates deeper engagement.

Restore and affirm ownership of a school's core purpose

How a school sees its core purpose shapes its everyday preoccupations, directs staff behaviour and guides thinking. Some schools have circumstance or outside agencies determine their core purpose for them, for example when inspectors deem the school to be inadequate or 'failing'. Others *allow* circumstance or outside agencies to shape their core purpose, such as national initiatives or Local Authority imperatives. Others are more expedient and select what they will do from what's on offer. The very best determine and own their core purpose for themselves.

We visit lots of schools and are often told that they are 'all about learning and learners' but this is not always reflected in the everyday preoccupations that we find there. Often they are about readiness for inspections, welfare of staff, student behaviour, budgets, meetings, data collection and coping, just. For us a key learning to learn insight has been for schools to avoid going into a tailspin by chasing other people's initiatives. This is especially so when the initiative does not align with the school's local context, its existing systems and structures and its talent pool.

When schools agree, share and focus – relentlessly – on core purpose it provides them with energy and direction. We would argue that helping young people become more independent by being better all round learners is the core purpose. Once schools are clear about this, every decision, every appointment, every purchase can be tested against it.

Pull together and simplify national strategies

Schools we have visited have, in the very worst scenarios, dissipated huge time and energy chasing too many agendas. Audits, checklists, frameworks, policies, protocols, procedures, evaluations, improvement plans and organisational plans can bury staff under a mountain of paper – and the typical secondary school goes through a pallet of paper a week. Arteries harden in a sclerosis of strategies: the English QCA Personal Learning and Thinking Skills framework, for example, is a positive step away from models of transmitting content knowledge, but there are 37 outcomes, differentiated to, say, three levels and that's 111 things to tick. This would be too much time ticking and not enough time teaching, in our view. A well thought through learning to learn approach can cut through some of this and, at the same time, provide an 'umbrella' to align and deliver chosen key national strategies such as Every Child Matters (ECM), Assessment for Learning (AFL), Social and Emotional Aspects of Learning (SEAL) and Personal Learning and Thinking Skills (PLTS).

Dramatically enhance student feedback and reporting

Powerful student feedback permeates the best learning to learn models. However, many teachers believe that they are engaging students through feedback when what actually happens resembles the performance management interview in which the employee tells the manager all the things *they* think they are not so good at, then the manager tells them which ones they've missed! Feedback needs to go beyond copying outcomes off the board, discussing drafts with your study buddies, three stars with a wish and a plenary review. That's not to say that these things are all bad but in a properly considered learning to learn approach what matters is that, in a learning environment where it is safe to take social, emotional and cognitive risks, there are rich exchanges around improvement. The skills that underpin this rich exchange have to be explicitly taught but, having taught them and positioned them in a considered system, they will lever up engagement.

Provide a mechanism to involve parents and carers more meaningfully

As a parent you may have enjoyed reading that your son or daughter has been given 4 out of 5 for effort and 3 out of 5 for behaviour. It may have exceeded your wildest dreams! But what, as a parent, could you have done about it? Through the mechanism of the 5R's, learning to learn offers a clear opportunity to replace effort and behaviour grades with something more engaging, motivational and suited to the 21st century.[11] Let's take a well aimed shot at this Victorian anachronism, the shadow of which darkens so many children's lives, and bring it down. That's just the start. Imagine online reporting where at any time of the day you can check up on your child's progress across a range of dimensions. For each of the 5R's there is not only a set of activities for parent and child, there are some observations based on a profiler completed by the student, an overview chart and some parent and student guidance. Shift what we ask schools to report on and you shift the educational outcomes.

Can and should be locally owned

The food from your allotment will taste better, you will enjoy the reward of seeing it grow from seed and you will have chosen what it was you wanted to grow. Home-grown initiatives are usually the most powerful but they do require foresight, resolve, patience and time. We may have to content ourselves with beetroots and radishes when what we really wanted was avocadoes. Our learning to learn approach assumes that people ultimately want to grow their own but that they will have to start with what they've got. Schools are mixed motivation and mixed ability organisations; that mix will either inhibit or drive any change. It is an important part of our learning to learn approach to provide a variety of different delivery models where possible.

Give impetus to creative thinking about the curriculum

Learning to learn approaches will provide opportunities to freshen up thinking around the use of curriculum time and space. By asking questions about the nature of the school day, its duration and segmentation, what is done in that day (including both the formal and informal curriculum offered) and who the players are in the day we come upon solutions which are within our grasp.

Improve exam results

We are often asked, 'Can we do this and improve our exam results?' It would be foolish to attempt to push schools down a route which threatened their public exam outcomes or which was based on some unproven theory. This book attempts to provide a compelling case for an approach that will improve the all round learning capacities of your students. Get better at learning and the chances are you will get better at performing. This will be evidenced by more mindful learning behaviours in all learning experiences including classroom lessons and the addition of more absorbing learning led by more informed teachers with less content and less content fever across the school.

Amongst the schools we have worked with closely we have had no instances of year-on-year drops in student performance following the introduction of a learning to learn approach. So that's the first thing: we've no evidence it will make you worse. Next, in many schools we have had successive year-on-year improvements, so it *could* contribute to making you better. In a few, we have had significant year-on-year improvements, so it *could* contribute to making you a lot better. It has not been possible for us to completely disentangle the role of a learning to learn approach in contributing to all of this. However, we don't have any evidence – which is not the same as there is no evidence – of a school making an *informed* commitment to this approach and then abandoning it. In the course of the book we will provide the case studies and the data for you to reach your own conclusions.

Enhance employability

In the world of employment and opportunity beyond school the so called 'soft' skills are in increasing demand.[12] Our inventory of outcomes itemised in Chapter 3 works like a checklist for the soft skills, particularly when a school has augmented them to accommodate the local context.

What do we think schools could begin to do better to prepare learners for the challenges of the 21st century?

One of the most impressive longitudinal studies into resilience gives hope. It was conducted by Emmy Werner and Ruth Smith and looked at all those born on the island of Kauai, Hawaii, from shortly before their birth until they were in their thirties.[13] Even though many had been born into poverty, experienced the break-up of their family or watched a family member die, they were able to overcome these problems and became competent and caring adults. These people succeeded because they were resilient. On the other hand, some who had no adversity in their lives gave up easily when faced with problems. Werner and Smith found identifiable factors which build resilience. Each can be developed, but the process is best begun early. These factors are:

- Making connections and being mentored. Resilient people remember one or two adults who made a difference in their lives. Being emotionally connected with adults and people in communities is a significant part of what allows nearly 70% of young people in even the worst conditions to thrive.

- Responsibility. Looking out for the welfare of others builds resilience. Children who are engaged in 'required helpfulness' are more resilient.

- Core skills. Resilient children learn to read early. Werner found that having 'effective reading skills by the age of eight was one of the most potent predictors of successful adult adaptation'.

- Problem solving and information fluency. When faced with adversity, resilient children know how to find and use information to solve problems.

- Social skills. The chief determinant of a youngster's popularity during adolescence is his or her social skills. Popular children have more friends and are more confident. Unpopular children are more likely to be low achievers in school, drop out of secondary school, have learning disabilities, show higher rates of delinquent behaviour and suffer from emotional and mental health problems as adults.

- Engaging interests. Children who participate in hobbies and activities feel more confident, competent and positive about themselves. Hobbies and activities bring children into contact with more people and can provide solace during times of stress and turmoil.

- Aspirations and goals. Resilient children have hope and the capacity to set personal goals and behave in ways to secure them.

Our schools could do very well by looking at this list and challenging themselves, as we did, to try to create an approach which will go some way to delivering rounded and resilient learners. For this to happen, learning should not be built around developing knowledge alone. Arcane arguments about content – What classic literature texts should all 16-year-olds have read? – miss the point and lead us into a cul-de-sac. We need to go beyond knowing by developing a combination of knowledge about the process of learning itself, the skills needed to transfer that knowledge and the accompanying personal attributes. Maybe we should also be thinking about guaranteeing experiences. Doing this will help us to deliver core purpose and help learners to reclaim their own lives.

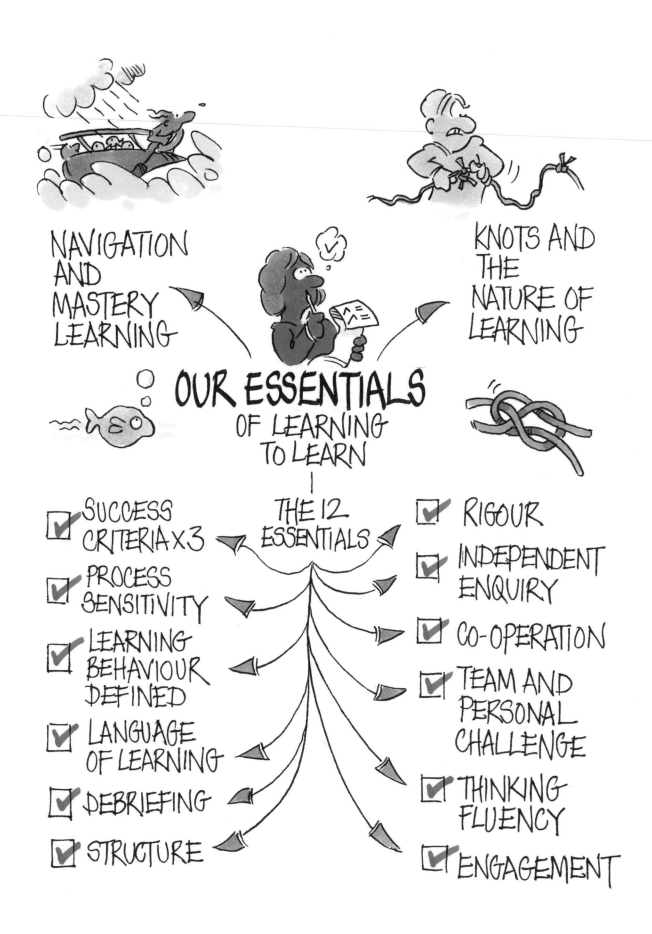

KNOTS Mastery Experience Activities Essentials Students Teachers
Schools Begin Explore Great Learning Three Dimensional Success Criteria
Process Sensitivity Behaviours Language
Debriefing and Reporting Structure Engagement Thinking Challenge
Theory of Self
Co-operation Independent Enquiry Rigour

1. Our essentials of learning to learn

In this chapter we:

▨ Learn about navigation and mastery learning

▨ Use knots to experience the nature of learning

▨ Summarise our 12 essentials

▨ Explain what each essential means for students, teachers and schools.

And ask the following questions:

▨ Do we really know what great learning looks like?

▨ Is there a difference between great learning activities and great learning?

▨ What can an individual do to extend an understanding of learning?

▨ Is there anything different about learning to learn?

Navigation and mastery learning

Fishermen in the remote Pacific have for centuries used intricate string nets as maps. Navigating the trade winds and sea currents, fishermen of the Marshall Islands would use nets of rope, sticks and shells. The shells represented islands and atolls and the sticks the currents and winds. A thousand years ago Polynesian islanders could navigate across the Pacific Ocean. The best sailors felt their way across the seas using these maps as prompts. They didn't look at the sails – they felt the wind on their cheeks, judged the latitude by the sun, their course by the stars and remembered the movements by rhythmic chants.

Mastery learning involves seeing not only the bigger picture but the patterns and shapes that are connected together to make that bigger picture. The intricate string nets are maps. Understanding the position of the shells depends on knowing their position in relation to other shells. The ropes stretched apart then knotted together as a net form the basic gridlines of the map to help do this. Finding the atoll or island represented by the shell may depend on knowing the currents and winds – represented here by the sticks twisted into the grid of ropes. The net maps would be shared amongst the community, discussed before and after voyages, added to and repaired, passed down from father to son. Mastery learning involves recognising meaningful patterns of information, whilst simultaneously and at lightning speed being able to see the bigger picture and know how the component parts fit into that picture. The fishermen had learned to learn.

How knots helped us examine the nature of learning

God created the knots, all else in topology is the work of mortals.

Leopold Kronecker

Imagine you are in an organisation that wants to change the way it works. The organisation is very large – with over 50,000 delivering its core product. It's also an organisation with a long history, saturated with traditions, some of which are resistant to change. To complicate matters, it also has a parent organisation to which it must pay some heed and which lays down the broad operational guidelines.

This is the Football Association, the world's oldest. With a core product – coaching the national game – overseen by full time professionals but delivered by enthusiastic amateurs. The task is to enliven the way that football is coached. This is why we have got out the ropes and will learn by tying some knots.

The exercise, which takes place in a lecture theatre with 64 leading football coaches, is designed to extend our appreciation of the complexities of learning and to contribute to a two day Football Association 'think tank' on the future of football coaching. The group has been charged with making the coaching of the national game more player-friendly, less dependent on the coach's wisdom and charisma and more dependent on the players' capacity to solve problems. A challenge you might say. To introduce this possibility each of the coaches holds a one metre length of rope in their hand.

The task is first to learn a knot so that you have sufficient confidence to teach it. There are eight possible knots which progress in their complexity. The knots are reef, bowline, half hitch, sheepshank, running knot, rolling hitch, round turn and two half hitches and the figure of eight knot. You have to learn one, then teach it to others. To help you learn to tie this first knot, you are put in a group. The group provides support and, if there are any sailors, scout leaders or outward bound types amongst the group, a possible 'expert'. Once you have learnt to tie the knot, the challenge is to teach someone else.

Groups will each be teaching the members of other groups. Except that they will have to do so with conditions imposed. With eight knots we have eight groups. Each of these eight groups has a different knot to learn first then teach. The knots vary in complexity. As the knots become more complex, the teaching 'conditions' become less constraining. This is to get participants to think about their own teaching or coaching and to think about which methods are best. The teaching constraints are:

- verbal instruction only

- instruction and showing the picture of the knot

- instruction, showing the picture and demonstration

- instruction, showing the picture, demonstration and intervention

- in a pair, find a solution for a given knot

- in a pair to find a solution for a chosen knot.

So one group can only teach by talking, another by talking and showing, another talk, show, demonstrate and so on.

If you should ever be charged with initiating lasting debate around the learning experience – try this. For a start, the energy levels soar. Then there is a moment when individuals revert to type. Some become childlike and limiting beliefs about their knot tying abilities emerge, others become 'teacherish' and take over, others go into quiet contemplation, some ask questions and others want someone to discuss it with.

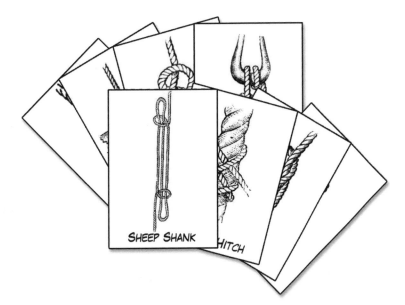

Figure 1. Eight different and increasingly difficult knots

What the coaches discover is that the learner's 'theory of self' emerges as the most crucial component in engaging and succeeding with the challenge. It's as if a large label has been attached by each person to their forehead. Each label has different glue. Some labels resist removal; they are superglued to the forehead and say things like 'I'm not very practical' or 'I've never been any good at knots'. Others are stuck on with classroom glue; they could be removed but Gloy hardens over time so 'What's the point in this?' soon becomes 'There's no point in this'. Some glues have been applied by others – 'I was never any good at knots when I was in the Brownies' and so, later in life, may be peeled off with care. Some glues are manufactured so that they are not really sticky at all – 'I'll give this knot a go anyway' – like sticky notes. Finally some labels never have any glue so need rewriting each time – 'I'll give this knot a go, it looks fun. I enjoy a challenge and it might be useful'. Everyone in the room adopts a label. The nature of the learning experience depends upon the coming together of the labels!

If we raise the stakes for getting the learning right by suggesting that the knot you will now teach will be used to save someone who is, unfortunately, 'hanging over a cliff', then motivation shifts up. Explain that 'it's your child who is hanging over the cliff' and it goes up again!

If you ever wanted an argument for differentiation, personalisation and clear examples of why no one way of learning is inevitably superior to others, then this is it. For some, direct instruction was what was needed, for others co-construction worked best.

All the things that knots told us about learning

What sorts of experiences did our 'knot-ers' have and what did those experiences tell us about learning?

1. Understanding the place of the activity and its **purpose** in helping them learn was important.

2. A sense of what **success** might look and feel like was motivational.

3. It was clear that the participants knew and were using a **diversity** of strategies.

4. Motivation went up after some small successes had been achieved or when the participant increased their **engagement** with the task.

5. Many participants brought a **theory of self** which significantly shaped their progress.

6. A high proportion of time was spent in attempting **pattern recognition**.

7. There were **different styles** of approaching the task – socially, emotionally and cognitively.

8. In some pairings the **feedback** was constant and mutual; in others it was teacher or student initiated.

9. In many cases participants talked themselves through the experience in an attempt at **surface thinking** and to record their progress.

10. There was a constant referral to existing knots, others' knots in progress and a visual search for reassurance in an attempt to **measure progress**.

11. Many participants took part in successive **rehearsals** until confident.

12. With more complex challenges the need for **basic knowledge** and some **expertise** surfaced and so direct instruction was useful.

13. In some instances the **mental model** was represented as a metaphor or storyline such as 'a rabbit climbing out of a hole and behind a tree ...'

14. Every participant found it constraining to be limited to one way of instructing and so sought **multi-dimensional instructional materials**.

15. We saw evidence of what could be labelled **social constructivism** – the involvement of another who asks questions, provides summaries, encourages reflective thinking and sometimes helped to learn.

In a group of 64 there was one individual who on his iPhone had an application called 'Knot Time' which took you through animations of all the knots!

Our 12 essentials to develop independent learners

As to methods, there may be a million and then some, but principles are few. The man who grasps principles can successfully select his own methods. The man who tries methods, ignoring principles, is sure to have trouble.

Ralph Waldo Emerson

Alistair observed a lesson with modelling clay. Under competitive conditions, groups had to replicate what they saw projected onto the screen. They then assessed their 'finished' model and scored it out of 5. Buzz Lightyear, a medieval fort and a helicopter gunship later left each of the five groups in the class excited, engaged and appreciative of the complexities of any group challenge. The activity had been one he had devised himself around problem solving and collaboration. This teacher had developed it further and Alistair admitted to feeling a mix of admiration for his initiative and frustration at an opportunity lost. It had been an experience in problem solving and collaboration but it had not been a lesson in learning. It had been so close.

Any learning activity has within it the beginnings of an opportunity to learn about learning. In this case, an emphasis shift away from scoring the quality of the product and towards scoring the quality of the process behind its development would have been enough.

The first and essential point about any learning to learn approach is that it is largely about process and not about content. The real challenge is to sensitise learners to the processes of learning and, in doing so, give them simple representations of those processes and a language through which they can describe them. Once this point is recognised, any content can be used to drive the experience. So this simple lesson could have been 'converted' by doing three things: providing different outcomes, actively debriefing the process and developing a vocabulary with which to describe group performance.

So now the lesson looks like this. The teacher starts with a simple, short connecting activity as the students arrive consisting of a picture of huskies pulling a sled through deep snow. Underneath is the question: 'Is this a team?' The students discuss their answers. Ideas are exchanged.

'Yes, it is a team because there's more than one dog.'

'No, it's not a team because they are not in a competition.'

'It's not a team because they are just doing what they are told.'

'The dogs at the front do all the work.'

All the responses have value. The teacher now explains the outcomes of the lesson in terms of what they will learn, how they will learn and why they are learning: content, process, benefits. Again, some explanation and discussion follows.

The learning is activated by each group of six having to agree and record five features of a successful team. The teacher explains that she is considering entering their best team for the next Olympics so their lists had better be good. Each group writes up its five features as bullet points on large sheet of paper. So now we have independent criteria for a successful team and, as a result, a mechanism for each group to evaluate their own success. At this point, out comes the modelling clay and up goes Buzz Lightyear. Before you know it, the teams are immersed in a timed challenge and the chaos only ends when they are asked to score each of their five 'effective team' features out of 5. The question is: 'As a team how well did you do?' This is where the learning takes place.

Figure 2. Using the picture to identify as many different ways in which you can learn independently

Learning to learn necessitates 'foregrounding' the processes of learning. That is, talking about how pupils are learning, the skills that they are using and developing. The more the teacher can sensitise learners to the processes they undergo when learning, the sooner those learners will become self-directing. The teacher may use the content and process 'hats' – sometimes called split-screen thinking – with process and content outcomes defined separately. In addition, any content can be used to help this process. It could be a practical 'connecting' activity such as showing a simple picture at the beginning of the lesson and asking pairs of students to identify, discuss, then rank the different independent learning activities they can find (see Figure 2). Alternatively, it could be a more structured debrief, involving close scrutiny of the learning processes used.

The 12 essentials

All learning to learn interventions make a difference, though some do so more immediately and some with greater impact. Here is our list of essentials for any learning to learn approach:

1. Three dimensional success criteria
2. Process sensitivity
3. Learner behaviours that are well defined
4. Language of learning
5. Systematic debriefing and reporting
6. Coherent structure to learning
7. Engaging experiences
8. Thinking fluency
9. Team and personal challenge
10. Co-operation skills
11. Independent enquiry
12. System rigour.

Plus use of the most up-to-date technologies

Within and across each of these essentials, we embrace the prevailing technologies of the age. Learning to learn approaches that are entirely paper based have scant appeal and limited shelf life in an electronic age. To underpin and enrich each of our 12 essentials we need to be able to move with some comfort between different learning technologies.

1. Three dimensional success criteria

Our learning outcomes are always expressed in terms of content, process and benefits. The content describes what will be learned, the process describes how it will be learned and the benefits describe why we learn it. These outcomes can be revisited at any time by teacher or student. There is a tendency to neglect process and benefit in favour of content and coverage. Content is the false god whilst coverage is the enemy of learning.

Fifteen years ago Alistair used to try to persuade educators about the imperative of sharing content and process by wearing two hats – the fez, worn by the intelligentsia represented content and knowing, whilst the Panama was woven with leaves and represented a deeper understanding of process. Some commentators now talk about split-screen thinking: content and process held in shot simultaneously. We have added a third dimension – purpose. Three dimensions are better because purpose gives motivation to the learner. (Think back to the knot tie-ers who were saving their children from falling off a cliff.) Three dimensions are better because we have to draw attention to purpose and to benefits.

2. Process sensitivity

This is what Ellen Langer calls 'mindfulness'. She contrasts an outcome orientation which is about results and a fixation with completion, with a process orientation which is about solutions and steps along the way. This is really about heightened self-awareness. In this case, the awareness is about the processes of learning. In order to promote it in classrooms we take care of the labels we assign to experiences and to behaviours. We get more of what we deliberately reinforce so we talk up effort, practice, trial and error, drafting, and we do so by deploying our 'process investigators' and our 'process promoters'.

Process investigators use the tools of the detective. They are students who take their turn in observing the processes of learning as they unfold in front of them. We pull them aside, give them a digital camera and ask them to look for evidence of a process being used. It may be great teamwork, or reflection, or the use of a thinking tool, or good use of questions. The evidence is recorded, shared and examined. Process promoters engage in advocacy and agitprop for their specialised learning method. They may be the class expert on memory mapping or Kipling Questions or Anderson's revised taxonomy or on search engines. They are encouraged to develop and share their expertise as and when required.

3. Learner behaviours that are well defined

Start with the outcomes in mind. Ask 'What is it that we want our learners to leave with?' We define our outcomes in terms of a body of knowledge about learning, five core attributes or personal qualities – which we call the 5R's of resilience, resourcefulness, responsibility, reasoning and reflection – and a set of personal learner skills which can be transferred into different contexts.

4. Language of learning

Those of you who have ever taken part in a consultation with a student around learning targets will have quickly become aware of the constraints of their language.

Without a vocabulary to describe the processes of learning and their experience of those processes, a learner is disenfranchised. We teach and use an extended vocabulary of learning. A 12-year-old child is expected to understand and use words such as these from the various Key Stage 3 subject disciplines: *perception, artefact, polemic, multi-modal, interdependence, sustainability, causation, chronology, genre, notation, polynomial, loci, dissipated, doctrine, secular, pluralism* and *interfaith*.

And yet we cannot find time to introduce and use a vocabulary of learning. Without a vocabulary it is more difficult to make and describe connections. It is the capacity to find and secure these connections between what would otherwise be discrete units of information that accelerates learning. Researchers Newmann and Wehlage talk of the importance of 'substantive conversations' which comprise considerable interaction with the ideas of a topic, consequently building a collective understanding of the topic and sharing it.[14] We have developed bronze, silver and gold vocabulary banks from which students can develop their ability to describe their own learning and have these substantive conversations. You will find these in Appendix IV.

5. Systematic debriefing and reporting

There are two dimensions to this process. The first is to build into the everyday learning experience opportunities to give and receive purposeful feedback. This we do by developing coaching and assessment skills at individual, pair and group level. This can be achieved by a combination of direct teaching with support resources such as Profilers, Success Mats, Electronic Portfolios and Electronic Assessment Tools of the type we discuss later in the book.

The second, and equally significant dimension, is in whole school reporting. We strongly advocate reporting to parents against the 5R's. Doing so removes at a stroke the cul-de-sac of effort and behaviour grades and provides a genuine mechanism for student voice, target setting and focusing on core purpose.

6. Coherent structure to learning

We organise our learning experiences around an informed pedagogy. We choose the 4 stage accelerated learning cycle of Connect–Activate–Demonstrate–Consolidate described in detail on pages 100–102. This provides the school community with a mechanism for sharing understanding about the component processes of learning.

The latest research affirms the common sense view that rote, rehearsal and regurgitation – sometimes fed by the need for 'coverage' and the desire to have 'pace' – are of little or no value for true learning.[15]

7. Engaging experiences

Quality learning to learn experiences should provoke curiosity whilst being relevant, extend whilst being accessible and scaffold challenge. We know that children recognise and choose different strategies to remember, speculate, hypothesise and solve problems and we want them to apply their choices in very different situations. Learning to learn whether it takes the form of lessons or challenges – where they are experiences extending over time or opportunities – or where they arise in the debriefing of subjects, should be exciting, refreshing and equivalent to 'the best party in town'. A worthy approach saturated with teacher checklists, paper based activities and occasional balloon games will not do this.

8. Thinking fluency

Developing the ability to think independently is more than the ability to use a given thinking tool. It requires the learner to become more adept at analysing a problem, generating alternative solutions and using appropriate modes of thinking – which could be supported by a 'tool' – to work though to a relevant conclusion that can be evaluated and adjusted for improvement. This should happen to such a degree that the learner becomes fluent in problem solving and thus capable of transferring this set of skills into every context.

9. Team and personal challenge

In our approach, challenge is more than pace and rigour in a lesson. It's more than differentiation by task, duration, method or outcome. It is about individuals – and teams comprising those individuals – habitually setting and being set extending tasks and being given space to evaluate the factors contributing to their success. A 'challenge' could, for example, comprise a student or group of students undertaking some new learning in or out of school and then using our 5R's framework of competencies to detail what factors contributed to progress. Most of our learning to learn lessons are set up around 'challenges'. All modules require authentic presentations.

10. Co-operation skills

Participation in any group requires a high level of process skill. We deliberately identify, share and develop the skills of learning in a pair, in a small group and in a class. We work on the premise that 'you get more of what you reinforce' and so we would draw attention to examples of good group work, reinforcing the underpinning behaviours whilst building the language so that learners have a vocabulary of co-operation.

11. Independent enquiry

The capacity to conduct independent research is the equivalent of a 'learner superhighway' lending momentum to the skills of finding, sorting, judging and presenting information.

12. System rigour

Learning to learn approaches can be easily marginalised in the life of a school. Schools differ in their vision of what it can offer and bring different degrees of enthusiasm, but without commitment the whole enterprise will perish. To have an impact, our approach needs clear leadership, status, resources, talent and a high degree of scrutiny. Simple things give off powerful messages: no reporting, no home learning, no accreditation can equal no worth in the eyes of students and the wider school community.

It is entirely possible for these approaches to occur within one solitary 'pioneer' classroom or across a school community as a whole. The latter is more desirable and obviously so; the former is more likely to be the starting point.

The 12 essentials	Benefit for students	Benefit for classrooms	Benefit for schools	Benefit for parents
Three dimensional success criteria	Better motivation and engagement	Clarity over what is to be learned, how it will be learned and why	More consistency in briefing and debriefing	Easier to understand the point of lessons
Process sensitivity	Increases a sense of responsibility for their own learning	Demystifies all the 'processes' of learning	Ensures teachers regularly question their practice	Opportunity to talk with children about methods
Learner behaviours that are well defined	Know what it means to be a 'great' learner	Constant focus on the most important learning behaviours to develop them	Core purpose is built around what we seek to do for our learners	More easy to understand what the school is trying to achieve
Language of learning	Better able to describe progress in their learning	Groups of learners who can talk about learning	More sophisticated learning conversations	More meaningful conversations
Systematic debriefing and reporting	Involved in identifying the steps to become better at their all round learning	Better structure to each learning experience	Changed emphasis on what is reported and how	Easier to measure all round progress and be involved in helping improve
Coherent structure to learning	Structure of lessons is understood	Easier to design and deliver learning experiences	Planning, delivery, evaluation and improvement of learning is easier	Easier to understand lesson plans
Engaging experiences	Remain excited about learning	Teachers can promote the joy of learning	Improved morale	Fewer behaviour problems at home
Thinking fluency	Transfer into life beyond school	Fewer passive learning experiences	Improved depth of engagement	More mature approach to problems

cont.

The 12 essentials	Benefit for students	Benefit for classrooms	Benefit for schools	Benefit for parents
Team and personal challenge	Creates positive bonds	Brings energy and pace	More opportunity for different abilities to shine	Creates a focus for family discussion
Co-operation skills	Improves understanding and acceptance of others	Good learning behaviours	Transfers into all lessons and learning experiences	Can be shared at home
Independent enquiry	Provides opportunities to practise learning skills	Allows for differentiation	More independence in learning	Can be continued at home
System rigour	Students can see that learning to learn matters	Assessed formally in classrooms	Given status across the whole school	Reported on to parents

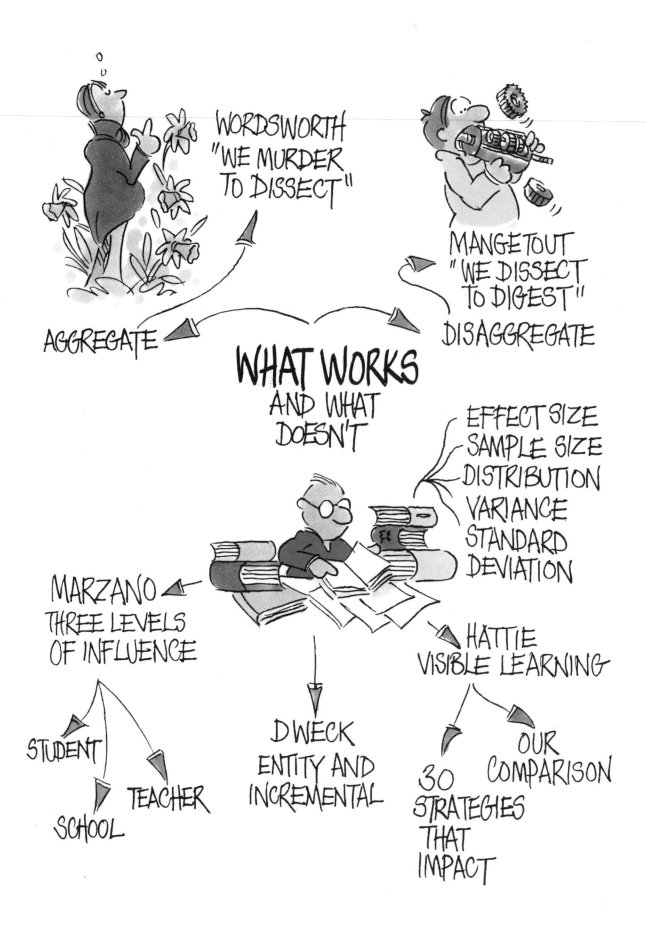

WORDSWORTH "WE MURDER TO DISSECT"

AGGREGATE

MANGETOUT "WE DISSECT TO DIGEST"

DISAGGREGATE

WHAT WORKS AND WHAT DOESN'T

EFFECT SIZE
SAMPLE SIZE
DISTRIBUTION
VARIANCE
STANDARD
DEVIATION

MARZANO THREE LEVELS OF INFLUENCE

STUDENT

TEACHER

SCHOOL

DWECK ENTITY AND INCREMENTAL

HATTIE VISIBLE LEARNING

30 STRATEGIES THAT IMPACT

OUR COMPARISON

Research Marzano
Journey Mangetout **Hattie** Caution Consensus Guidance
aggregate *effect size* disaggregate **Dweck**
Attribution Wordsworth

2. What works and what doesn't

In this chapter we:

- Explain what international research says about learning

- Explain what our research says works

- Describe how to adapt attribution theory.

And ask the following questions:

- Where should I begin?

- Whose guidance should I listen to?

- What's worth doing?

What international research says about learning

Monsieur Mangetout was a French entertainer whose act consisted of living up to his stage name – 'Mister Eat Everything'. That's what he did. He ate everything or, more precisely, anything. Quite what the Romantic poet, Wordsworth, would have made of the man who, when invited to open a new garden centre in the United States, began by eating some of the lawn on which the ceremony took place, we can only guess.

Mangetout, whose real name was Lotito, ate large items – such as a bicycle, televisions, a car and, on one occasion, a Cessna 150 light aircraft – by breaking them up, reducing them to their smallest parts and taking his time to eat them. The Cessna took two years to be 'eaten' (from 1978 to 1980). Lotito didn't get ill very often, even if in a career lasting nearly 40 years he consumed around nine tons of metal. He consumed around a kilogramme of 'stuff' daily, preceding it with some mineral oil and lots and lots of water during the 'meal'. Bananas and hard-boiled eggs left an aftertaste and made him sick so he avoided them!

The poet William Wordsworth was a radical in his early life. In an age when civilised people would rather close the carriage curtains than look out upon the landscape, Wordsworth wanted the readers of his poetry to learn from the whole of nature. In his 1798 poem, 'The Tables Turned', he wanted the learned sages to close their books, trust their natural instincts and open their eyes to what was in front of them. He warned:

> Sweet is the lore which Nature brings;
> Our meddling intellect
> Mis-shapes the beauteous forms of things:
> We murder to dissect.

In looking at what research tells us about learning we lurch between Mangetout and Wordsworth. The Mangetout method is to take the whole and break it down into edible chunks. By finding out more and more about lots and lots of these little chunks we can lose sight of the bigger entity it once was. Sometimes when we think we have a really small chunk we discover when we try to digest it that it's not quite small enough and on it goes. At this end of the research spectrum there is a tendency to know more and more about less and less.

The Wordsworth method involves aggregating up so as not to lose sight of the whole entity. So now we have meta-studies, which are studies of studies. Often done through elaborate computer driven searches, these desktop analyses take us further and further away from the original subject of the study and into the world of effect sizes, sample sizes, distributions, variance and standard deviations. At times, the explanation of the methodology takes up more space than the findings. Occasionally, the authors fall victim to their mathematical modelling and common sense departs. At this end of the research spectrum there is a tendency to know less and less about more and more.

So with this in mind we would like to draw upon two academic researchers whom we think manage to negotiate a carefully chosen route between Mangetout and Wordsworth, before looking at another whom we recommend for her pragmatism.

Robert Marzano

Robert Marzano is based in the United States and has been researching in this field for over 35 years. His attempt to translate international research on what works in schools identified three levels or factors of influence: student, teacher and school. We draw on two of his publications for the following summary and hope that we do him justice.[16]

Student-level factors

Home environment
Parental encouragement through frequent and systematic discussion with their children about learning; encouraging interest and helping with school tasks including home learning are highly correlated to academic achievement. Marzano suggests parenting sessions where parents can, amongst other things, learn how to 'enhance their communication with their children about school'.

Learned intelligence and background knowledge
Marzano talks of two types of intelligence, crystallised and fluid, and describes direct and indirect ways of developing both. They include: increasing the number and quality of life experiences that students have outside of school through schemes like mentoring, placements, after-school clubs, work experience and similar; improving reading abilities to enhance vocabulary development; and providing direct instruction in relevant subject-specific vocabulary. In our learning to learn approach we argue for extended challenges which interface with the community, such as 'Personal Challenge Week'. We also show how and when to build a vocabulary of learning.

Student motivation
Achievement goes up when the student is motivated to learn. That's the easy bit. Marzano addresses different theories – drive theory, attribution theory, self-worth theory, emotions and self-system – and recommends four action steps to enhance motivation: (1) focus on individual growth not comparative gain – provide feedback which allows this; (2) make the activities and tasks engaging by ensuring that they are achievable, arouse curiosity and foster unfettered creativity; (3) provide opportunities for students to experience 'flow' by working on long-term projects of their own design; and (4) teach students about motivation and motivation theories, especially attribution and self-worth.

School-level factors

A guaranteed and viable curriculum
Marzano identified that there was insufficient time to deliver a curriculum that was laden with content. He commended schools to consider what the essential content is, and ask how it could best be sequenced and organised so that teachers can focus on it. A criticism of this would be that it assumes a transmission model in which teachers deliver units of learning and students follow them through in a given order. With enhanced learning to learn skills, improved technologies and a different approach to how time is used, we would expect a more effective coverage of content with more responsibility on the part of the students.

▓ *Challenging goals and effective feedback*

High expectations of students supported by an assessment system which gives specific and timely performance feedback is very high on Marzano's summary of what works in schools. He says that goals should be set at an individual level with the active involvement of the student and that they should be reviewed regularly and utilised in lessons.

▓ *Parent and community involvement*

Marzano reports that schools that involve parents and communities in their day-to-day operations have reported lower absenteeism, truancy and dropout rates with a possible 'spill over effect' into the home. Again the messages for us are a little more complex. The picture changes as students get older with a pattern of less involvement as they go through secondary education. Parental engagement issues vary considerably according to the socio-economic profile of the community, its ethnic mix, the differing expectations of the school and its role and, of course, parental access to the language. In other words, it is too simple to say more necessarily means better. That's why there is a job to be done in helping schools create local solutions.

▓ *Safe and orderly environment*

There is a great deal of research this topic. Based on his interpretation of the research, Marzano argues for ecological interventions – in other words, solutions that fit the local environmental challenges posed by the school (narrow corridors, confined play space, split sites, adjacent attractions and the like). He also affirms common sense procedures such as clear rules and procedures consistently applied, appropriate chain of consequences, programmes to promote responsibility and self-reliance and early detection of students at risk.

▓ *Collegiality and professionalism*

Schools that are most effective have a collegiate culture defined by the manner of social and professional interactions between all staff. Marzano cites Fullan and Hargreaves, who say that professional norms include 'openly sharing failures and mistakes, demonstrating respect for each other and constructively analysing and criticising practices and procedures'.

Teacher-level factors

▓ *Instructional strategies*

The more effective the teacher, the more effective strategies they use and have at their disposal. Marzano categorised strategies which had a large positive effect on student achievement and recommended that teachers become familiar with using them.

Marzano category	Average effect-size - D*	Our learning to learn examples
Identifying similarity and differences	1.61	Use of selected thinking tools
Summarising and note-taking	1.00	Feedback protocols

Marzano category	Average effect-size - D*	Our learning to learn examples
Reinforcing effort and providing recognition	0.80	Positive learning environments
Home learning and practice	0.77	Extended research projects
Non-linguistic representations	0.75	Use of Success Mats and teaching of visual tools such as memory mapping
Co-operative learning	0.73	Paired and group work, team challenges, peer and group assessment
Setting objectives and providing feedback	0.61	Three dimensional success criteria, goal setting
Generating and testing hypotheses	0.61	Prediction exercises, use of debriefing during and after learning
Questions, cues and advance organisers	0.59	Connecting activities, teaching of success criteria and how to benefit from using it

(Effect Size is a measure of the significance of the intervention, the higher the effect size the more significant the intervention. An effect size of D=1.0 indicates an increase of 1 standard deviation of the outcome.)

■ *Classroom management*

Classroom management is mentioned in virtually every study of student achievement. The definition is not so simple, but Marzano talks of the importance of four areas: establishing and enforcing rules and procedures; carrying out disciplinary actions that balance positive reinforcement with sanction; establishing purposeful and professional relationships with students; maintaining an appropriate 'mental set which involves "withitness" ' – the ability to identify issues quickly and deal with them – and emotional objectivity.

■ *Classroom curriculum design*

Marzano believes that many breakdowns in student learning can be a consequence of poor classroom curriculum design. He shares three principles which arise from a need to dispel confusions around constructivist and brain based models of learning. His three principles should inform curriculum design: (1) learning is enhanced when a teacher identifies specific types of knowledge that are the focus of a unit or lesson; (2) learning requires engagement in tasks that are structured or are sufficiently similar to allow for effective transfer of knowledge; and (3) learning requires multiple exposure to and complex interactions with knowledge. In our learning to learn approach each of our recommended teacher strategies and all 180 hours of lessons emerge from a set of principles around learning. We have tried to be pragmatic and so operate on a continuum between transmission and constructivist models. Obviously, we also benefit from Alistair's work on brain based learning, particularly his 2002 book on what science could tell us about learning.[17]

Having done a Monsieur Mangetout on Marzano's work it is only right to try to go Wordsworthian and say what we think the bigger picture looks like for our learning to learn approach. It is clear that to impact on achievement we need to do more than give teachers lesson content. We need to provide a whole school strategy, informed by a philosophy of learning, which the entire school community, parents and carers can support and engage with. This strategy needs to permeate down and through the school, and at each level be supported by impactful tools and techniques.

Marzano's research does not explore the impact of ICT. However, we do need to embrace the prevailing technologies as part of our approach. This way, we can continue to focus on the holistic, 21st century needs of the learner. Paper and pencil programmes bolstered by worksheets have a limited future.

We will also assume that motivation is as important for the teacher, as well as the students, in our approach. Feedback needs to be timely, task focused and capable of being acted upon by both sides. Teachers need to be clear about the content they teach and why it is taught. In curriculum design, we try to be pragmatic and draw from a balance of direct transmission and constructivist tradition. Schools won't be able to design quality learning experiences without better use of time. This may mean taking more time or using technologies and independent learning skills; it may mean making better use of the time we've got. Finally Marzano asks teachers to be flexible in the instruction strategies they deploy.

John Hattie

Professor John Hattie is based in Auckland, New Zealand. He studied over 800 meta-analyses that included over 52,000 education research papers to look at what 'actually works' in schools to improve learning. Hattie asks why it is that we can have so many published papers on teaching, so many new initiatives and so many academic careers spent producing books, yet our classrooms are not much different than they were 200 years ago. Whilst some publish their books and papers, the teachers get on with teaching. The research has had variable impact. Some of it has pointed in the wrong direction.

> *There have been hundreds of studies on reducing class size, for instance. It is the wrong point of comparison. The right point of comparison lies in other areas such as the curriculum, teachers and most importantly, what kids bring to the classroom. The power of peers is also a force – teachers avoid this factor at their peril.[18]*

Hattie is concerned with effect sizes and what he lays out are analyses of the impact of strategies used by students in classrooms, across schools and at home. He wants to get under the skin of what really contributes to good learning, and in this correlates are not to be confused with causes; there may be a correlation between the uses of, for example, advance organisers and student engagement but that doesn't mean it's a cause of good teaching or of good learning.

Hattie's model of 'visible learning' is premised on the idea that what works best is when the learning is highly visible to the teacher and to the students. He summarised his philosophy of effective learning as teachers seeing learning through the eyes of their students and students seeing themselves as teachers.

The remarkable feature of the evidence is that the biggest effects on student learning occur when teachers become learners of their own teaching and when students become their own teachers. When students become their own teachers they develop the self-regulatory attributes that seem most desirable for learners (self-monitoring, self-evaluation, self-assessment, self-teaching).[19]

From his extensive analyses Professor Hattie has identified that excellent teachers:

- Are aware of the learning intentions and know when a student is successful in attaining those intentions.
- Teach in active, calculated and meaningful ways.
- Know enough about the content to provide meaningful and challenging experiences in some sort of progressive development.
- Teach learning strategies for surface and deep learning that lead to students constructing learning.

Professor Hattie believes that feedback rates are highly in effective learning:

Studies have shown that a student receives on average three to five seconds of feedback per day. Most teachers think when they give feedback to the class they are giving it to individuals. This is not how students see it.[20]

Provided below is an outline of the top 30 of the 138 strategies which Hattie researched. We have added our interpretation of what each means. Lists such as these can be useful but they are a bit like those Russian dolls which only ever reveal themselves on closer inspection. Beneath each of these strategies there is much more to uncover, argue over and put to the test.

Rank	Domain	Influence	Average effect-size - D*	Description (our description)
1	Student	Self-report grades	1.44	Students' estimation of their own performance. Living up or down to one's own estimate of what can be achieved. Self-theory is very important
2	Student	Piagetian programmes	1.28	Teachers must devise challenges which are appropriate to developmental stage not age
3	Teaching	Providing formative evaluation	0.90	Iterative changes by the teacher to teaching methods based on regular feedback from students
4	Teacher	Micro teaching	0.88	Student teachers improve by teaching mini-lessons in a 'goldfish bowl' and receiving feedback from others

Rank	Domain	Influence	Average effect-size - D*	Description (our description)
5	School	Acceleration	0.88	Fast tracking through the curriculum *cont.*
6	School	Classroom behavioural	0.80	Positive, secure and ordered classroom climate
7	Teaching	Comprehensive interventions for learning disabled students	0.77	Well thought through interventions add considerable value and contribute to remediating learning disabilities
8	Teacher	Teacher clarity	0.75	Excellent communication skills
9	Teaching	Reciprocal teaching	0.74	Students taking turns to be the teacher having been taught cognitive strategies
10	Teaching	Feedback	0.73	One of the most powerful influences on achievement and at its most powerful when it's from student *to* teacher. Feedback is different to reward because it contains task information
11	Teacher	Teacher–student relationships	0.72	High regard for and interest in the achievement and well-being of the individual student
12	Teaching	Spaced vs. mass practice	0.71	Spaced rehearsal with multiple opportunities to apply new learning and transfer. Three to four exposures – often over several days
13	Teaching	Meta-cognitive strategies	0.69	Thinking about thinking – particularly error-spotting and self-questioning
14	Student	Prior achievement	0.67	The 'Matthew effect' – the 'advantaged' become more so as they progress through school
15	Curricula	Vocabulary programmes	0.67	Vocabulary instruction and knowledge of word meanings
16	Curricula	Repeated reading programmes	0.67	Reading and rereading a short passage until fluency is attained

Rank	Domain	Influence	Average effect-size - D*	Description (our description)
17	Curricula	Creativity programmes	0.65	Programmes based on developing thinking, though it is easier to improve fluency than originality
18	Teaching	Self-verbalisation/ self-questioning	0.64	Questions asked of oneself before and after learning improve performance, as do questions where we return to learning and where they are modelled by the teacher
19	Teacher	Professional development	0.62	Difficult to compute as the outcomes are about teachers not about students
20	Teaching	Problem solving teaching	0.61	Using a step-by-step approach to solving a given set of problems
21	Teacher	Not labelling students	0.61	Labels can help attract funding but do not of themselves improve performance
22	Curricula	Phonics instruction	0.60	Powerful in the process of learning to read
23	Teaching	Teaching strategies	0.60	Clear instructional goals which align to cognitive, meta-cognitive and affective domains
24	Teaching	Co-operative vs. individualistic learning	0.59	Both co-operative and competitive learning are more effective than individualistic methods
25	Teaching	Study skills	0.59	Combining study skills with a variety of contexts in which to apply them: not taught as a one-off or out of context
26	Teaching	Direct instruction	0.59	Not didacticism – but structured interventions
27	Curricula	Tactile stimulation programmes	0.58	Work with infants and young children to avoid developmental delay

cont.

Rank	Domain	Influence	Average effect-size - D*	Description (our description)
28	Curricula	Comprehension programmes	0.58	Reading intervention
29	Teaching	Mastery learning	0.58	Lots of feedback loops based on well-defined tasks with clear outcomes which can be easily tested
30	Teaching	Worked examples	0.57	Modelling what success 'looks like' and the steps needed to get there

(Effect Size is a measure of the significance of the intervention, the higher the effect size the more significant the intervention. An effect size of D=1.0 indicates an increase of 1 standard deviation of the outcome.)

What guidance can we derive from Hattie's meta-analysis for our learning to learn approach? There's an old joke about schools being places where students go to watch teachers work. In Hattie's view it's what learners do, not what teachers say, that matters. Classrooms need to be active places but it's the learners who need to be most active. The high resonance teaching approaches include the following:

Hattie's visible learning approach	Our learning to learn approach
Deliberate attention to learning intentions and success criteria	Deliberate attention to learning intentions and three dimensional success criteria
Exposure of learning processes	Process sensitivity
Active engagement	Learning 'challenges' throughout
Feedback which provides task information and is easily understood	Self and peer evaluation alongside debriefing against the success criteria
Multiple opportunities for deliberative practice	Consolidation phase within each cycle and blocks of time for extended enquiry
Students construct and then reconstruct knowledge and ideas	Cognition, meta-cognition and affective engagement form part of the reflection process
Critical role of teaching appropriate learning strategies	Programme built around appropriate learning strategies
Constant monitoring of progress based on student feedback to teacher	Teacher is one of a number of individuals involved in estimating progress
Recognise the range of contributions: student, home, school, teacher, curriculum offer, teaching methods	Our approach is structured to impact at student, classroom, school and community levels

Adapting attribution theory

'Why not give it a go? You might find you like it!' The teacher can sometimes resort to pleading in order to secure student involvement in their topic. Attribution theory explores the process an individual student would be going through as he or she makes their decision about the teacher and the topic. Attribution theory asks: To what do they attribute failure or success? Weiner[21] suggests it measures such decisions on three dimensions: locus, stability and controllability. The way the individual habitually assigns failure or success to internal or external factors will shape their willingness to get involved.

Other researchers in this field talk up the importance of 'pre-decisional' and 'post-decisional' phases.[22] By this they mean that students will use the pre-decisional phase to weigh up the value of a topic before committing effort to it. The post-decisional phase is about 'having got involved how do I now feel about it – Is it worth persisting with? Will it help me towards my goals?'

Have you ever taught a group where you found that some students were driven by a strong desire to look smart, especially in front of you, the teacher, whilst some of the others were more driven by a desire to become smart and didn't care who noticed? According to Carol Dweck[23] learners can hold one of two very different implicit beliefs related to learning – 'entity' or 'incremental'. These beliefs impact very differently on how and when individual students commit to the challenge of learning.

Entity View of Self	Incremental View of Self
Believes ability is related to gifts	Believes ability is related to effort
Sees intelligence as fixed	Sees intelligence as malleable
Explains failure in terms of lack of ability	Explains failure in terms of lack of effort
Is attracted to affirming tasks	Is attracted to extending tasks
Evades challenges	Embraces challenges
Receives ego-related praise	Receives task-related praise
Favours comparison feedback	Favours improvement feedback
Feels threatened by the success of others	Is curious about the success of others
Is more likely to cheat in tests	Is unlikely to cheat in tests

In a learning to learn classroom how we give feedback and what we give it for will make a considerable difference to the way students perceive themselves as learners and how they make sense of success and failure. Choh and Quay suggest that entity theorists are 'more likely to react helplessly in the face of failure and show negative feelings'. On the other hand, 'incremental theorists' 'focus more on behavioural factors as the causes of failure and they view intelligence as something that can be cultivated through effort. Setbacks motivate them to continue to work toward mastery of the tasks.'[24]

Learner motivation is affected differently by success and failure, depending on the theory of intellect held, shaping both attitudes to achievement and the rationale for progress.[25] An incremental theorist may be highly motivated by failure because they are more likely to believe that, if they simply try harder, the task can be achieved. The implication is therefore that, despite inherent dispositions towards particular aspects and ways of learning, learners are not born with particular beliefs about intelligence or learning. These beliefs are formed through their experiences of, and interaction with, the environment in which they find themselves. If it is the case that these theories of self are created, then teachers can influence positively the beliefs that learners hold.

So there we have it – attribution theory, self-theories, pre-decisional and post-decisional phases, entity and incremental learners. It should be simple enough to hold this in your head when you are working with a group of 28 14-year-olds! If not, remember that the true worth in this is that it can take you to a place where the students will work harder for you because you have worked smarter for them.

> *There is another alternative, one that addresses students' achievement and their self-esteem: teaching students to value hard work, learning, and challenges; teaching them how to cope with disappointing performance by planning for new strategies and more effort; and providing them with the study skills that will put them more in charge of their own learning. In this way, educators can be highly demanding of students but not run the risk that large numbers of students will be labelled as failures.*
>
> Carol Dweck[26]

As a teacher you can help your students become more incremental. Focus on students' efforts and not on their abilities. When students succeed, praise their efforts or their strategies, not their intelligence. When students fail, give feedback about effort or strategies – what the student did wrong and what he or she could do now. Avoid doing easy tasks for the sake of it. They are a waste of time. Capture, draw attention to and reinforce resilience: praise for persistence, for problem solving, for positivity. Teach your students that intelligence is not fixed but is malleable and that with effort, practising techniques and thinking about their thinking, it can be developed. Researcher Joshua Aronson of the University of Texas demonstrated that college students' grade point averages go up when they are taught that intelligence can be developed.[27]

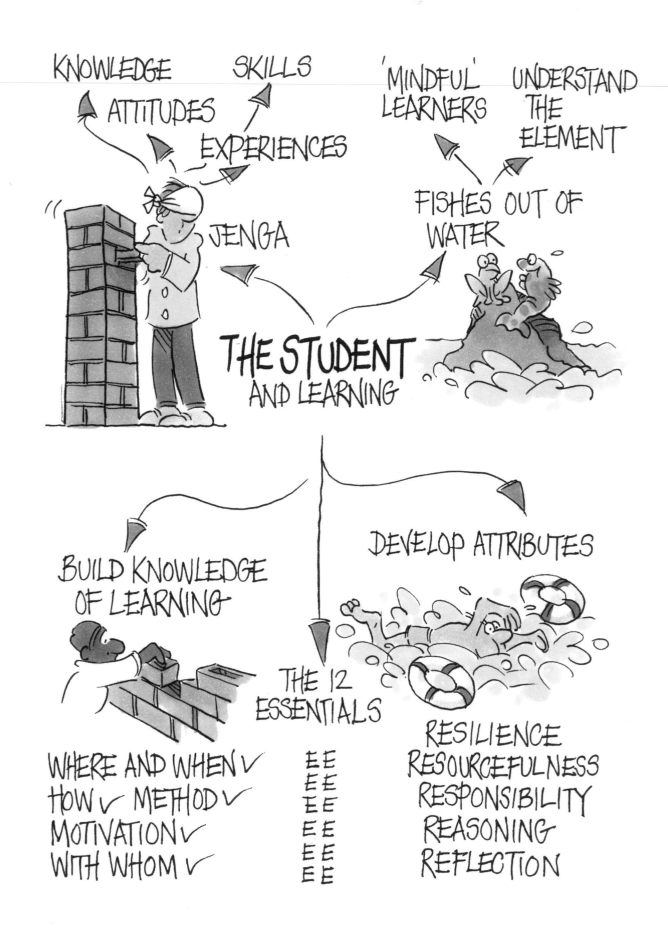

KNOWLEDGE SKILLS
ATTITUDES
EXPERIENCES

'MINDFUL' LEARNERS
UNDERSTAND THE ELEMENT

JENGA

FISHES OUT OF WATER

THE STUDENT
AND LEARNING

BUILD KNOWLEDGE
OF LEARNING

DEVELOP ATTRIBUTES

THE 12
ESSENTIALS

WHERE AND WHEN ✓
HOW ✓ METHOD ✓
MOTIVATION ✓
WITH WHOM ✓

E E
E E
E E
E E
E E
E E

RESILIENCE
RESOURCEFULNESS
RESPONSIBILITY
REASONING
REFLECTION

Students Jenga Knowledge **Sacred Orb** Fish
Peer Skills Dependence Attributes Curiosity Experience Assessment
Independence Superheroes Myself **Billy Blunder**
Learning Preference Top Trumps

3. The student and learning

In this chapter we:

- Discover what a great learner might look like

- Use Jenga to revisit the knowledge, attributes and skills of a great learner

- Find out how to build student knowledge of learning

- Show how we help students develop positive learning attributes

- Examine the student experience of the 12 essentials

- Track student engagement in the learning to learn classroom.

And ask the following questions:

- What are the signature characteristics of a great learner?

- How do I develop positive learner behaviours?

- How does a student benefit from the 12 essentials?

- How do I get better learning behaviours in my classroom?

- What do students actually do in the learning to learn classroom?

Fishes out of water: what does a great learner look like?

Fish is curious about what it's like to be on land. Fish has only ever known water. Fish befriends another fish who, funnily enough, begins to grow legs and turns out not to be a fish but a tadpole. Time goes on and Fish grows into a larger fish and the tadpole into a frog. Finally, the frog is able to leave the pond, but eventually he returns to tell his old friend about the world and what he has seen there. The frog describes cows, birds and people and, of course, Fish imagines them all to be variations of fish just like himself. The cows are hairy fish with horns and udders, the birds are fish with wings and the people walk on their tailfins and are hairy upright fish. Fish can't wait to see these things and so he jumps out of the water only to find that he needs to be in his own element to survive.

Leo Lionni's book *Fish is Fish* from the 1970s is a great metaphor for teachers and students trying to understand each other's perspective on learning.

Whilst at school, learning is the 'element' in which young people are asked to exist. However, unlike Fish, they may be quite content when they are out of their element and they may even prefer it there. Fish may have been sad to discover that he lived in water. The saying goes, 'fish are the last to recognise water'. Sadly, too many 'students are the last to recognise learning'. We can change that.

A great learner would have a balance of knowledge, attributes and skills each of which would be susceptible to development. Exposure to the right sorts of experiences, with those experiences filtered through carefully selected tools, will create a more 'mindful' learner. A mindful learner is one who understands the processes that shape their learning, has an awareness of themselves and others being part of those processes and is ready to become dramatically more independent as a consequence.

Part of what we do in developing independent learners through a learning to learn approach is to turn students into mindful learners who are equivalent to 'scientists' of learning. They use scientific objectivity; they detach themselves and become informed observers like the best scientists; they share their findings and present their conclusions. Thus, every classroom becomes a laboratory where students are taught 'investigative strategies', construct hypotheses about their learning, think about their thinking in context, review their experience and are aware of their own and others' feelings of self-efficacy – self-efficacy being a strong sense of being in control of one's life – as each 'experiment' unfolds. In order to create a community of mindful learners operating with scientific scrutiny we need to have a view on what a great learner knows, behaves like and can do. That's when we need Jenga.

Using Jenga to discover what a great learner might look like

Schools and teachers (and researchers) may need to be more explicit that learning dispositions should be key performance indicators of the outcomes of schooling.

John Hattie[28]

We are about to discover the qualities of the great Jenga player. For those who may not know, Jenga is a popular game requiring players to carefully remove wooden bricks from a tower. The tower gradually becomes unstable as successive bricks are removed. The winning team is the one left when the tower collapses. The losing team is the one that knocks over the tower. In our version, we have three teams, each consisting of a coach and a player. One student in each of the three teams is blindfolded. This player is the only one who can touch the tower. The coach guides and instructs but cannot touch the tower or his player. The audience have to observe carefully and identify the knowledge, attributes and skills needed to be great at Jenga.

Each team takes its time during round one but thereafter the referee – in this case the class teacher – insists on a time penalty. In round two, as the bricks are removed, the tower becomes increasingly unstable. Eventually the tower collapses.

It is at this point, having been prompted beforehand, that the class considers what it takes to be great at Jenga when playing as part of a team. We start with what a Jenga player would have to know and very quickly the ideas begin to tumble out.

'She would have to know right from left.'

'She would have to know up from down.'

'Yes, that's it – basic instructions about what to do. You need to understand them.'

Eventually we agree on our top five:

Knowledge

 Have a shared language

 Know what success means

 Have/give basic instructions

 Know about the structure of the tower

 Know the rules of the game.

So that's the knowledge base need to excel in Jenga. What sort of personal qualities would the great Jenga player display? In those high pressure moments when the tower is rocking slightly and everyone around is holding their breath, what attributes are needed for success?

'You need to be able to concentrate.'

'It helps if you can think clearly.'

'You've got to have the bottle to pull the brick out.'

Again, we agree on our top five:

Attributes

 Patience

 Trust

 Remain positive throughout

 Calmness under pressure

 Ability to adapt.

If a great Jenga player has to know about Jenga and have the personal qualities to be good at playing it, are there skills that are specific to this game? What things would he need to be really good at doing if he were to be world class at Jenga?

'It helps if your hand doesn't shake!'

'When you pull the block out you need to do it slowly and gently.'

'Someone tells you what to do but because you're blindfold you have to see it in your head.'

Finally, we agree on our top five:

Skills

▨ Manual dexterity

▨ Ability to interpret instructions

▨ Ability to anticipate consequences of movements

▨ Recognition of the feel of the blocks

▨ Balance.

So, for the international superstar Jenga player we have an identifiable body of core knowledge, some personal qualities or attributes and a set of relevant skills. This same thing could be done for a great scientist, linguist or mathematician. It can also be done for a great learner and, as you would expect, here's one we did earlier:

Knowledge	**Attributes**	**Skills**	**Experiences**
▨ where and when I learn	▨ resilience	▨ how I know	▨ authentic challenge
▨ my learning methods	▨ resourcefulness	▨ how I organise	▨ live performance
▨ who I learn with	▨ responsibility	▨ how I judge	▨ community visits
▨ my motivation to learn	▨ reasoning	▨ how I transfer	▨ extended research
▨ how I learn	▨ reflection	▨ how I innovate	▨ prevailing technologies

This is the foundation upon which our learning to learn approach rests. The list, left to right is not in any priority order. The construct is intended to be easy to understand, easy to use and easy to develop further. This inevitably means shortcuts have been taken, particularly when we try to express it in simple terms for students.

Our thinking is that knowledge, attributes, skills, experiences (KASE) can be used in any learning or development environment. KASE is not ours; it appears in various guises in education, training and development. Here's a little more of the thinking behind it.

There is a body of knowledge to do with learning. This is not always obvious. For those of us adults who are professional educators we exist within this body of knowledge like a fish exists in water. Our questions about learning are sophisticated and driven by a desire to understand so that we can talk sensibly and with purpose. For young people they may go through their entire school lives and never ask, or be asked, any questions about how they learn. This is absurd. Equally absurd is the expectation that when on the few occasions a student is required to talk about their own learning – consultation evenings, progress interviews, target setting – they should be able suddenly to shift up a gear and talk with insight and some fluency about their experiences of learning. It doesn't happen and it's no fault of the student.

There are a set of attributes of a great learner. An attribute is different to an attitude, which is temporary, and also different to a disposition, which is a leaning or tendency towards behaving in a given way. An attribute is, we feel, more solid and a personal characteristic, which is shaped in a similar way to one's personality. It would be a mix of inherited factors, early experience and subsequent strategy learning. Whether or not we can educate someone into being, for example, more resilient is open to debate. We can certainly develop awareness of the attribute, its worth in society and show what people who have lots of it do that is different and indeed admirable. We can create a taxonomy of resilient learning behaviours. We can then locate, reinforce and reward those behaviours in our classrooms and schools. We can generate curiosity and maybe even desire in students to know more resilience and be more resilient. We can show parents and carers how important it is for their children to have these attributes. But ultimately we must have confidence that the set of attributes upon which we focus are those which are most important for our young people.

There are skills which are to do with learning. We have drawn ours from a narrower domain, those more closely associated with thinking. We have created a basic hierarchy which starts from remembering and knowing information, moves through organising and categorising, to judging or estimating the integrity of the information, to transferring it into different contexts and finally using information for creative purposes and for innovation. Within each 'rung' of our hierarchy we have identified a number of tools which could be used to develop thinking. We describe them in more detail later. Some are well known tools and some we developed ourselves. Students are given opportunities to practise and so build familiarity with the tools in a variety of practical situations. By carefully debriefing the use of the tool we unpack the nature of the thinking that lies behind it.

There are experiences which are necessary to authenticate and deepen learning. Ours include authentic challenge, live performance, community visits, extended research and the use of prevailing technologies. By authentic challenge we mean the opportunity to contribute to solving a real problem. The closer the problem is to home, the less it is school focused, and the more obvious and immediate the impact the better. For example, students working together with a budget and access to a designer to improve an outdoors social space to encourage vertical tutor groups to meet together.

Live performance is important because with it comes an adrenalin rush that seldom features in formal schooling. For example, the students who as part of their personal challenge were tutored in the skills of stand-up comedy and who had to perform 'live' in front of 450 pupils in a partner middle school.

Learning to Learn in Practice

Parochialism is endemic in many of our communities. Many of us will have taught in schools where students have never left the confines of their own inward regarding community. In a global economy this is an anachronism. Schools can and ought to do something about it. Learning to learn offers an opportunity. For example, a trio of primary schools in Burnley partnered with a company called The Life Channel and installed television screens in covered areas in playgrounds to show programmes made by pupils from each of the three schools. A partnership was then formed with schools in South Africa and the process was repeated.

Without an opportunity for extended research students never have an opportunity to test out their independent learning skills. Students need time to deploy their newly acquired research skills. For example, students in one London school are helped to identify their life goal and career choice. This may include the expected (e.g. model, footballer, singer, actress, doctor, pilot) but also the less expected (e.g. benefit claimant, accountant, teacher, solicitor, games designer, stallholder, property developer, nanny, street vendor, soldier or entrepreneur). Students then have to create a timeline of what is needed to take them from where they are to where they want to be. Part of this is regression planning. So, for example, should they wish to be a footballer they need to have 'banked' about 10,000 hours of practice before they are 18 years of age. Have they done this? If not, what time commitment is now required? Is it realistic to be able to do this? At the end of a six week research period – which must involve interviews with 'role models' which they arrange and conduct, evidence about how to get into the career, what personal attributes, commitment and qualifications are needed – each student makes a formal presentation of their findings including the timeline and their action plan.

Finally, learning to learn programmes which are exclusively paper based are a contradiction in terms. Balance is needed; 21st century students develop information fluency in and out of school, engaging with very sophisticated technologies as they do so. Imaginative teachers exploit this transition. For example, a very simple software tool such as Wordle allows students to create clouds. Clouds are summary lists. Wordle generates 'word clouds' from texts that students provide. The clouds give greater prominence to words that appear more frequently in the source text. You can tweak your clouds with different fonts, layouts and colour schemes. These are great for debriefing, for consolidation activities and for summarising the content of a topic (we use them at the beginning of each chapter). We could do a paper version or use the software tool or do both.

For our learning to learn programme, having identified what we think we want our learners to leave with, we set about constructing an architecture to deliver it for us. This comprises parental involvement, whole school systems and classroom interventions along with formal and informal opportunities or 'experiences' to develop the agreed knowledge, attributes and skills. We then include a guarantee of experiences so that our learners leave having stretched themselves in a wide variety of contexts.

52

How to build student knowledge of learning

The first outcome we sought was for students to have a bigger knowledge base about learning and to be more knowledgeable about themselves as learners. If we accept that this is worth doing we can then explore the most effective way of getting there. For us the process entailed long discussions about the building blocks of learning and how we could simplify and categorise them in such a way as to be easily accessible to any learner without rendering the content naive. The building blocks had to be of use to teachers and also to schools. We created five categories:

1. Where and when I learn

2. My learning methods

3. Who I learn with

4. My motivation to learn

5. How I learn.

These categories were designed to raise the awareness of students, and staff, that learning is a dynamic, active process which is worth reflecting upon. The first category, the simplest, looks at the circumstances in which learning occurs and is used to alert students to simple everyday choices that can affect their learning. The second category, *learning methods*, is about the particular approach to learning to which the student naturally defaults – Do they do things at a gallop or do they break tasks down? Do they waste time? Do they start straight away? By now students will have begun to realise that they have choices! The third category, *Who I learn with*, helps students realise that skills are needed when learning on your own, in a pair or small group and in a class. The fourth category, *My motivation to learn,* is a great way to start talking about and sharing experiences of motivation and de-motivation. The final category, *How I learn*, is a more detailed breakdown of the stages in formal learning. This helps the students better understand what's going on in class.

Each category is broken down further into sections and then again into a focus area. For example, in the category *Where and when I learn*, we have readiness, lifestyle choice, food and drink, surroundings and timing. Under *readiness* we would ask students to consider seating, materials and distractions. For each there would be a choice of statements from which they would decide which was 'most like me'. The whole structure of category and section looks like this:

1. **Where and when I learn**

   - Readiness

   - Lifestyle choice

   - Food and drink

   - Surroundings

   - Timing.

2. **My learning methods**

   - Intensity

   - Formality

- Information processing

- Steps

- Pathways.

3. Who I learn with

- Individual

- Pair

- Group

- Class.

4. My motivation to learn

- Reward

- Approval

- Targets

- Satisfaction.

5. How I learn

- Linking to what is known

- Finding out what will make you successful

- Practical or thoughtful

- Problem solving

- Random or sequential

- Feedback

- Transfer

- Review.

Each focus area has a set of accompanying statements which are very easy to understand and practical to manage. We have designed a complete set of illustrated cards so that students can get involved in activities (these cards are provided on the CD which accompanies this book).

The cards are colour coded by category. This allows a student to slowly build up an understanding of themselves and others category by category. Our aim is to help students to have greater understanding of the processes of learning and this is an opportunity for them to begin to appreciate, perhaps for the first time, that learning is best when it's not done to them but when they are actively involved, and that needs some basic building blocks and vocabulary.

There are a total of 70 Learning Preference Cards. This is far too large a number to use in any one activity, but because they are in five categories there are different opportunities to use the cards.

We can, for example, use them in individual reflection activities, for paired discussion around perceived similarity and difference, for group activity, to raise teacher awareness of each learner, to build vocabulary, to share and so respect difference and for discovering something that has been in front of us for so long yet we knew nothing about!

Typically we would use the cards before students take part in the electronic profiling version. We use the cards with staff when we undertake public training events. Over the years, teachers have come up with lots of suggestions for their use in awareness-raising. Here's a selection of activities.

Activities using the Learning Preference Cards

1. Explain the card to someone else.

2. Explain the card to a Martian or a 5-year-old or a person who doesn't speak your language.

3. Explain the picture without reference to the words.

4. Sort the cards – a lot like me or not like me.

5. Compare your cards with someone else's.

6. Design a learning space for yourself or someone else based on the cards.

7. Use the content on the cards as the basis for target setting.

8. Use the cards to help with consultation meetings; the cards can be organised on the table and you get to talk about them and what it means for your learning in different subjects and with different teachers.

9. Make some changes at home to help you learn even better – sort my bedroom!

10. Play *Blind Date* – who is this person?

11. Go speed dating – you have 90 seconds in which to introduce yourself.

12. Play *Mastermind* – one student sits in the chair and others ask questions about their learning.

13. Devise some strategies to be better at those you aren't so good at.

14. Role play or mime the learning behaviour – broken down by category to make it easier.

15. Draw a cartoon of 'Me and my learning' using some of the statements on the cards.

16. Problem solving teams – helping each other be better at some of their weaker areas.

17. Lay out a continuity line with 'strongly agree' at one end and 'strongly disagree' at the other. Read a selection of statements and students take up their position on the line.

18. Sit in mixed groups with each group member's card profile on the table; a group member stands with others in a line; a preference is drawn and if someone from within the team learns in that way the representative takes a pace forward; if not he or she steps back. See who is first across the room.

19. Play Learner Bingo based on your card profile and pre-designed 'learner bingo' cards.

20. Create a real or mock up of your social networking profile (LearnSpace) to let others know about you, your interests and your learning.

How to help students develop positive learning attributes

We don't just want to talk about attributes. The work we do to develop student understanding of attributes is powerful. By being able to understand what shapes behaviours generally and learning behaviours specifically, students become more insightful.

Students can start by profiling themselves. As part of our own learning to learn approach we go beyond bits of papers, lists and worksheets to three interactive Electronic Profilers: one for knowledge, one for attributes and one for skills. Each comprises questions or statements to which the students respond and the tool then creates a profile of the student with accompanying guidance. The format of the guidance varies by profiler. With knowledge, it comes in the form of written bullet points, for attributes it is in written bullet points and graphics and for skills it's a recommended thinking tool. Each profiler also has a vocabulary builder, a goal setter, an integrity rating and a folder to store evidence.

We want students to understand the purpose of, and background to, the profilers so we would do a KAS exercise to get them to recognise the knowledge, attributes and skills needed for different roles: for example, gymnast, historian, dancer, lighthouse keeper, baggage handler, dental receptionist, scientist, cat owner and perhaps even some cartoon characters.

This is all part of the first stage of becoming more aware of themselves not just as learners but as sentient human beings who interact with others, have personal drivers, make choices in their lives and have autonomy. So we start with Myself.

Myself	Imaginary Superheroes	Real Superheroes	My New Self

Helping students to become aware of their own personal combination of knowledge, attributes and skills can be a dispiriting task for a teacher if it's poorly thought through. We try to get around issues of self-consciousness by taking the discussion away from the students. This frees us up to talk about human qualities. To do this we have devised a series of chained activities built around the concept of imaginary superheroes. As part of this we created a set of Top Trumps-type cards we call Imaginary Superheroes (these cards are provided on the CD which accompanies this book).

The versatility of the cards allows us to fashion a whole range of activities which will, in turn, lead us to being able to better understand the lives of real individuals in our Real Super-heroes inventory.

So our method is to move from the student to the human qualities as epitomised by the Imaginary Superheroes, to the effect on lives as epitomised by the Real Superheroes and to the possibilities for them in My New Self.

There are 12 cards. Each card is colour coded, is slightly larger than playing card size and is laminated.

Superhero status is earned by being able to make a difference in the lives of others: Atavius, below, is an activist.

The Superhero characters are male, female and uncertain gender. They derive from the superheroes found in action comics and real life heroes.

Each Superhero has a special power which is used in pursuit of his, her or its role. In this case it is Independence.

Each card has a set of power words and a catch phrase which are associated with the Superhero's special power.

Like many other superheroes, and all of the rest of us, each has a flaw. The flaw, often an unusual one, threatens to undermine their ability to fulfil a mission. Atavius's flaw is queuing.

Each card has separate percentage scores based on each of the 5R's. This allows students to quickly compare Superhero attributes. It also allows the teacher to work with percentages.

The bottom third of the card is colour coded to help students move quickly into home groups.

In the bottom right hand corner there is a magic number. This allows the teacher to work with numbers. These can be short ice-breakers. For example, 'In your group of three, work out the shortest way to get to a total of 36 ...'

In the bottom left hand corner there is a shape. There are three shapes – a square, circle and triangle. This allows students to quickly organise themselves into groups.

Within the shape there is a symbol. There are six different symbols. This provides another way of organising groups or can be seen as a supplementary tool to help the Superhero.

Activities for Superheroes

1. **Top Trumps** – Use cards as regular Top Trumps. In Top Trumps players each have a hand of cards on which there are numerical values for attributes. We have percentage scores on ours against each of the 5R's. Students get to know the cards and the Superheroes by choosing an attribute and seeing which card has the highest percentage for that attribute. If you happen to choose responsibility and your score is 85% but you opponent has 86%, she gets your card. Whoever has the most cards at the end wins.

2. **Shape Teams** – All cards have been allocated a shape (triangle, square, circle) The teacher can then use these to formulate teams (e.g. 'All the triangles now get together to complete a team challenge'). The shape helps the teacher to quickly organise teams.

3. **Teamwork** – Every time a new team gets together to complete a task they have to discuss what their individual strengths are, how these will help them to complete the task and how they think they will work best together as a team. This can be done in role or out of role as themselves.

4. **Superhero Me** – Students create their own Superhero card based on themselves.

5. **Meaty Challenges** – Groups have an allocation of Superheroes and the teacher starts the challenge by posing a problem to which the groups propose a solution using their Superheroes. Typically, they would be things like: end bullying forever, provide clean water for everyone in the world, prevent all wars. These are all meaty challenges and for each one the students describe why their team would have the best balance of attributes.

6. **Go Local** – Lighten up the challenge by going local. For example, get groups to put together a team of Superheroes to fix Mr Lovatt's shed roof or to improve school lunches or to give Mr Turner a sense of humour!

7. **Find Your Team** – Students are given descriptors of the Superheroes in their team. By asking questions of all the other Superheroes in the room they have to identify and collect all their team members. This can be done as a communication activity on its own or as a precursor to that team completing a challenge once they have found each other.

8. **Who am I?** – All students create a hat band for their Superhero card. You stick a card on your forehead or in your hat band and have to guess what it is. All cards are then given out at random and the students, in fours, have to ask questions of their fellow team members to establish which Superhero they are. This should only be played once the students have had plenty of time to get to know the cards and the Superheroes. The first team to identify all four Superheroes wins.

9. **Fantastic Four** – Having spent time with the cards and on understanding the Superheroes and their abilities, students are given a scenario for which they have to choose the three, four or five Superheroes they think would best be able to achieve this mission. They have to be able to justify their choice and explain what will make them so successful. This could be completed by way of a poster, PowerPoint presentation, movie maker, storyboard or spoken presentation using the cards.

Search for the hero inside

Having spent time with imaginary heroes to make it acceptable to talk about flaws, we can now turn to real life heroes. This is still safe and should be free from discomfort, as there is still some distance from talking about the students themselves. We give students a research task around the concept of Real Superheroes like this: 'You will be asked to research the lives of three different people to find out what lies behind their success. Choose three "heroes". Each must be from a different category.'

The categories are:

Campaigners – who devote their life to one cause

Community activists – who work for a better world

Politicians – who help us make good decisions

Business people – who create wealth and employment

Scientists and doctors – who discover what makes our world tick

People with creative talent – who entertain and intrigue

Explorers and adventurers – who find out what's out there

Sportsmen and women – who excite us with their skill

Personalities – who entertain and annoy

Musicians – who create sound for pleasure

Actors – who help us to understand human behaviour

Writers and artists – who make us think about everyday life.

RealSuperheroes

martinlutherkingjr.

Campaigner

Someone who devotes their life to one cause

Campaigner

born **1929**
died **1968**

Martin Luther King Jr was an African-American Baptist minister who fought peacefully for the rights of black people. He was well educated and having considered how black people were unfairly treated in his country, decided to devote his life to doing something to change the situation. For his efforts, he was arrested more than 20 times and assaulted on at least four occasions. He was the youngest man to have been awarded the Nobel Peace Prize in 1964, but was murdered four years later.

Because we start the process off by insisting that there are three different people and that those people must come from three different categories we avoid the rush to get to the same pop star, celebrity chef or Britain's Got Talent winner. We can also strive for gender balance and representation from a variety of ethnic groups.

If necessary, we can further separate the searches by insisting on three people from three different clusters. Our categories above are clustered to help with this process. Students using our L2 approach get a preliminary overview such as the one above on Martin Luther King by going to our catalogue or its web based equivalent and from there they can click on a further source. Under campaigners they might also find a less well-known 'hero' such as Muhammad Yunus; or under sportsmen and women, Bethany Hamilton; under writers and artists, Damien Hirst; or under scientists and doctors, Stephen Hawking. Our L2 programme has all the information in an easily accessible language and format plus links to other websites.

It may take you longer to organise it, but this activity can also be done directly from the web so please take the approach and work it through.

Muhammad Yunus (born 1940)

www.muhammadyunus.org

Mohammad Yunus has received 75 international awards and 29 honorary degrees from around the world for his work as a banker to the poor. He created 'micro-loans', which are small amounts of money lent to the poorest people so that they can work to get themselves and their families out of poverty.

He believes that poverty is the greatest challenge in today's world and that is why he set up the Grameen Bank over 30 years ago. Mohammad saw a problem and did something about it – he was Resourceful to find a solution and is Responsible because his work helps others. Over 100 million families have been helped by his banking system but his work continues because he can see that poverty, hunger and inequality are still problems today.

The student then sets off on a more thorough and independent research but benefits from having been given a link to the 5R's – in this case resourceful and responsible. The teacher knows that the class research community activity will have a structure and balance built into it (and so will avoid arguments over who gets Justin Timberlake). The summary research sheet prompts questions about the 5R's and about sources of information.

Example one

Name of the hero you researched ....

Which of the 5R's did the hero use in their life?   What did they do?

Resilience	....	....
Resourcefulness	....	....
Responsibility	....	....
Reasoning	....	....
Reflection	....	....

Sources of information   Is the source reliable?   How do you know you can rely on this source?

Website	yes/no/maybe	....
Magazine article	yes/no/maybe	....
Newspaper article	yes/no/maybe	....
TV or radio programme	yes/no/maybe	....
Book	yes/no/maybe	....
Gossip	yes/no/maybe	....

Bethany Hamilton (born 1990)

www.bethanyhamilton.com

Bethany Hamilton was born in Hawaii into a family of surfers. By the time she was 13 she was a talented surfer herself when she was attacked by a shark which tore off her left arm.

It is believed that her positive attitude helped her overcome her injury and she has since committed her life to spreading a positive and Christian message and to fulfilling her dream of being a professional surfer.

We may ask the student to think of a moment in life when they had a setback. How did they deal with it? How would Bethany have dealt with it?

Damien Hirst (born 1965)

www.damienhirst.com

Artist Damien Hirst was born in Bristol in 1965. His career took off when he organised an art exhibition whilst he was still at university. He is possibly best known for displaying dead animals preserved in glass cases, which not many other people have done with success before in the world of art! Death is a central theme in his work. He won the Turner Prize in 1992.

We may ask the student to think of a breakthrough moment when they took responsibility and did something for themselves? What impact did it have?

Stephen Hawking (born 1942)

www.hawking.org.uk

Stephen Hawking is a theoretical physicist known for his research into black holes. He was 21 when he was told that he had Motor Neuron Disease and no one knew how long he would live. However, he showed great Resilience to his diagnosis and continued to study and work and is now married with three children and a grandchild. Despite being unable to speak or to move from the neck downwards he has written many books and research papers.

We may ask the student who else do they know who has shown great resilience to overcome a difficulty? What have they learned from them?

The student experience of the 12 essentials

Teacher talking to a 6-year-old drawing a picture of a daffodil:

'What is this flower called?'

'I think it's called Betty.'

Quoted by Robert Fisher in *Teaching Children to Learn*

L2L Essential 1: Three dimensional success criteria

In some school situations the starter activity at the beginning of a lesson is deliberately mundane in order to 'settle' the class. This is a disappointing state of affairs. For the student, those crucial moments at the initiation of any learning experience – the pre-decisional phase – mark the point when the individual locks on to a level of commitment which will then influence what they give and get from the lesson. It's worth a teacher being creative around those moments. If one of the aims is to create a settled and purposeful start then that doesn't need to be done through the mundane. An activity which requires focused attention, which links to prior knowledge and hints at what is to come is the ideal. Producing something short, arresting and attainable is well within the design ability of any teacher. For example:

- **Number:** 305 – how does this number link to our lesson?

- **Word:** 'Learnosaurus' – what does this word tell you about learning?

- **Phrase:** 'Measure twice, cut once' – explain why this is good advice for learners

- **View:** Video of extreme wheelchair from YouTube – what can he teach us?

- **Listen:** 'I have a dream' – what's the worth in dreaming?

- **Artefact:** How might this item (a fishbowl, for example) link to our lesson?

- **Activity:** Using the three items on your table explain how they link to our topic.

- **Observe:** What is the teacher doing (eating an orange) and what does it suggest to you about our lesson?

Ian Gilbert's *The Little Book of Thunks®* is a great resource for connecting questions. It's full of mind-bending propositions which children love and which provoke thinking – or thunking. The connecting experiences should precede any exploration of success criteria in a formal lesson but it is also possible to roll the two together. For example, we use illustrations of different flowers, including one drawn by a child, another by a botanist, one by an impressionist painter, one which is coloured by numbers and another by a professional artist. We ask which is the best? Most students plump for the professional painting as it's the most attractive and striking. The lesson is built around success criteria and why it's important to ask good questions around success criteria. So then we might ask why is it the best? What makes a good illustration of a flower? Discussion follows before we ask the same question again but this time we specify the purpose of the illustration. We ask which is best for:

- Sticking on the fridge at home to cheer us up in the morning

- A cover of a scientific book about botany

- A birthday card for your grandmother

- A CD cover for a heavy metal band

- A poster for a doctor's surgery about hay fever.

Quite clearly the point is made that the criteria for success is dependent on how the illustration will be used. From here we can discuss being clear about what success will look and feel like based upon what it is we set out to achieve. Again in the learning to learn approach we can help students better understand success criteria by getting them to be precise about the characteristics of success. We can ask them to define success criteria for the sorts of activities they know and understand:

- What makes a good pop video?

- What makes a good skateboard move?

- What makes a good joke?

- What makes a good song for an assembly?

- What makes a good lunch for someone on a diet?

- What makes good party for a 5-year-old?

- What makes a good YouTube video?

If we are going to benefit from using three dimensional success criteria students need to be able to understand more about success criteria in general. In one lesson we observed a very skilled teacher introduce the success criteria for completing a product and write it up on a flip chart. Two girls who were constructing a three dimensional model of the brain approached the teacher to ask if what they had done was any good. He did no more than nod his head in the direction of the success criteria. They walked over and checked it out. They read there that the model, which was intended for use in a school for partially sighted schoolchildren to help them understand more about the brain, had to be strong enough to feel without it breaking, have simple labels that were easy to understand and see, and be colour coded in primary colours. As they read the criteria the girls compared them to what they had done and quickly realised that their labels were too small. They didn't need the teacher.

L2L Essential 2: Process sensitivity

What are the essential learning processes we want children to know about and feel confident about using? One way to beguile students into being more aware of such processes is to talk to them about their brain: what's good for it and what's not so good. As we are not neuroscientists it works better when we simplify it down. For an 11-year-old there is something compelling about finding out for example, that:

- You could hold your brain in the palm of your hand. It has wrinkles and folds. If it were unfolded it would cover a kitchen table.

- Your brain represents about 2% of your total body weight but uses nearly 20% of your total energy intake.

- Our brain is made up of about 100 billion cells each of which can connect with any other. This means that it has up to a thousand million million connections. Awesome!

- Your brain floats in fluid inside your skull. If you bash your head, your brain can 'bounce' off the inside of your skull and be bruised.

- The two halves of the brain are called hemispheres. They are joined together by over 250 million tiny connections like an old fashioned telephone exchange.

- Our moods are related to the chemicals which are present in our brain. Drugs alter the chemical balance in our brain. We can become addicted to the changes.

- Thinking is about connections. Your brain cells make new connections every time you think. If you get stuck, think of it as being exercise for your brain!

When these 11-year-olds find out that there are ways to learn which are brain-friendly and ways which are unfriendly then we can layer in our processes. For the 11-year-olds these brain-friendly processes might include:

- **Three Up** – Thinking about what we will learn, how we will learn and how we will benefit before starting

- **Busy Brains** – Learning with lots of brains connected together

- **See, Hear and Do** – Learning in different ways

- **Nibbling** – Doing a little bit at a time and coming back

- **Spacing** – Practising again and again

- **Talk it Up** – Explaining things in our own words to someone else or to ourselves

- **Tries** – Trying things out to see if they work

- **Connectors** – Making and explaining connections

- **WAND** – Wide And Narrow Deliberate thinking

■ **Double Think** – Thinking about how we think

■ **Candu** – Staying positive with a 'can do' attitude.

As students get older we may replace some of the terms for these 'processes' with some which look and feel more mature and are more tightly defined. For example: success criteria replaces Three Up; self and peer assessment replaces Busy Brains; learning preference replaces See, Hear and Do.

Having labelled the processes, we can then use our different strategies to draw attention to and encourage awareness of the processes. Freeze the moment – how are you learning at this exact point in time? Tell your friend. Pole-bridging – talk yourself through what you are doing as you do it. Process Investigators and Success Sleuths – who both use the tools of the learning detectives – the PI's look at how people are learning and capture the evidence maybe with a digital camera and the SS's find the success stories.

L2L Essential 3: Learner behaviours that are well defined

Where our learner outcomes work best is when students are encouraged and helped to translate these for themselves as personal goals. The more the teacher designs the student learning outcomes, and the narrower the definition that is used, the less space the student has for taking responsibility for achieving it.

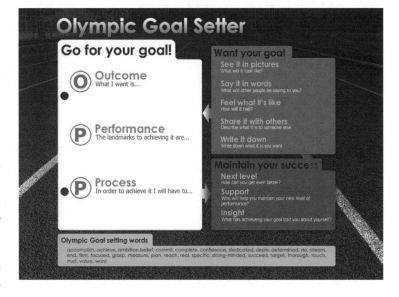

Where possible students should be shown how to set learning goals and do so by using a method which brings together outcome, performance and process. Outcome is what is wanted when the experience is complete; performance is what methods are used along the way to secure the outcome; process is what behaviours have changed or been given up along the way to achieve the outcome. Amongst the tools it is possible to use are Learner Passports and Success Mats.

Learner Passports can be paper or electronic or both. Simple paper versions are carried by the student between lessons and completed by any combination of student, peer, teacher or parent. They provide evidence of when an attribute has been displayed, a thinking tool used or a record of an insight into a learning process. The content of the passport should form the basis of a regular review activity.

Success Mats are A2 or A3 laminated mats which contain guidance on how to complete a given learning process. The mat also provides guidance on behaviours, phrases or words to look out for and use, and some essential vocabulary. Typically Success Mats would be used for skills such as self and peer assessment, questioning skills, listening skills, presentation skills, thinking skills, independent enquiry, coaching and goal setting.

When a goal is too narrow or does not embrace learning then experiences that occur around the edges do not always get attended to. Unintended outcomes are often the spaces in which some real learning occurs. Equipping students with the skills and tools to reinterpret and personalise the broader outcomes helps them get more from the whole experience.

Another one of the simplest ways to reinforce learner outcomes is through the use of Learner Passports. A paper Learner Passport might contain each of the 5R's with a grid to record instances of success, some or all of the thinking tools, diary pages for reflection on learning, goal setting pages and some simple review tools such as WWW (What Went Well) and EBI (Even Better If). Key learning words with definitions can be placed at the back.

L2L Essential 4: Language of learning

Develop the learning vocabulary of your students so that they have a basic grammar and can use it on a day-to-day, moment-by-moment basis. You would do this for maths, for geography, for physical education so do at least this much for learning. Fluency in learning, what others call 'learnese', requires a vocabulary.

As part of our electronic profiling we identified 60 banks of words for each of learner knowledge, learner attributes and learner skills. We categorised these words as bronze, silver or gold and students were able to 'tick off' a medal icon when they were confident about using the word. By creating the banks of words, we now had 180 key vocabulary items in three categories. This allowed us to create activities around the words.

The bronze vocabulary for learner attributes comprised:

achieve, adapt, aspire, barriers, compare, confidence, consequence, desire, determination, dream, goal, honesty, judge, listen, plan, practice, risk, target, task, team

The silver vocabulary for learner attributes comprised:

assess, attitude, considerate, co-ordinate, develop, emotions, empathy, endurance, experience, flexibility, growth, habit, obstacle, opinion, organise, outcome, ownership, participate, persistence, role

The gold vocabulary for learner attributes comprised:

altruism, attribute, coach, context, disposition, initiative, intuition, mentor, model, morals, preference, process, reasoning, reflection, resilient, resourceful, responsible, self-belief, solution, stereotype

We deliberately included each of the 5R's in our gold list to give every learner a head start and a little morale boost to make them think they were already capable of working with this sort of gold vocabulary. In addition we created electronic dictionaries which the teacher could minimise and have on screen to call up any word at any given time.

Many of the schools we work with put these and the equivalent banks for knowledge and skills in their student planners.

L2L Essential 5: Systematic debriefing and reporting

It is important to teach students how to give and receive feedback and then create real 'space' for them to do so – that is, to actually give and receive feedback. If they are not good at it at first (and why should they be?), let them have time to improve. Don't abandon it. The strategies include process awareness strategies – How do we get better at getting better? – and assessment awareness strategies.

Process awareness strategies include some of the following;

- **Peer Challenge** – Can you work together to improve your answer?

- **Peer Points** – In pairs discuss what are they key points? Can you reduce them to the absolute minimum? Try them on another pair. How did they compare?

- **Peer Guidance** – Each member of a pair prepares a solution to a separate question then, having developed 'expertise', swaps the question but not the solution. After a period that is not quite long enough to work out a full response, the partners guide each other through their solutions.

- **Peer Drafting** – Students work in a small group and are asked to bullet point an answer with only a pre-determined number of points, say five. They write them on a card. The cards are then passed around, swapped and discussed. Alternatively, they are stuck to a wall or a convenient surface and are then compared. Another alternative is that students are responsible for one part of the answer which they then present to the others who ask clarification questions.

- **Peer Questions and Answers** – In pairs, students write likely exam questions and then bullet point the answers; questions and answers can then be swapped around the larger group.

- **Peer Testing** – Students test each other, formally and informally.

Assessment awareness strategies include some of the following:

- **Dodgy Assessment** – Students working in pairs annotate two or more pieces of work including one which looks bad but is quite good, and one which looks good but is quite bad. They have to explain their thinking to another pair. You oversee the process and draw out essential points.

- **Self Assessment** – Students annotate their own work first and do so against a rubric or against the success criteria. They then swap with a partner and see if they agree or disagree with the comments they find there.

- **Peer Assessment** – Written answers are photocopied, the names obscured and then in a small group they are passed around. Each member of the group is allocated a separate focus for assessment and they add their comments either to sticky notes or to an accompanying sheet. This way the original remains intact.

Peer coaching and peer assessment are powerful learning processes but the teacher must be patient in teaching the techniques, the para-methods – productive words and phrases, body language, pacing, when to listen and when to speak, eye contact and so on – and putting up with lots of false starts along the way. Whole class debriefing is also important. Teacher Katy Argent, an experienced user of L2, provides these 10 generic ideas for whole class debriefing:

1. **Sticky Note Board** – At the beginning or an early point in the lesson, all students write a question or something they don't understand on their sticky notes. These all go up on the board. At the end of the lesson ask random students to collect their notes and see if they can now answer their questions. Alternatively, get all students to collect

their notes and to complete the activity by writing the answer on their sticky note. These can then be stuck up again for the teacher to see.

2. **Three Up** – Ask students to write down three things they have learnt that lesson and to tell them to their partner.

3. **WWW and EBI** – Ask students to evaluate their performance that lesson by reflecting and writing down three ideas of What Went Well (WWW) and one Even Better If (EBI).

4. **Graphic Summary** – Use a graphic organiser to get students to write down their learning and their thoughts in an organised way.

5. **Teacher Led Review** – At the end of the lesson, use the learning aims that were set to promote a class discussion on what the students think they did in the lesson to meet each aim.

6. **Make a Connection** – Give a statement or picture that relates to the learning that lesson and display this at the end of the lesson. In pairs or small groups, students have to discuss what they have learned in reference to the statement/picture and then feedback as a class.

7. **Circle Time** – If the lesson has been discussion based, bring the class together as a circle and then ask each student for their thoughts or reactions to the discussion and the ideas that have been generated that lesson.

8. **Student Led Review** – Ask the students to lead the debrief – each student/pair/group has to generate three questions based on the learning aims and the activities that lesson to test the learning of the other students in the class.

9. **Puzzle Away** – Use puzzles and quizzes to test the learning of new words, key terms, knowledge and understanding. For example: crosswords, jumbled words/anagrams, definitions, Blockbusters, Battleships, Connect 4, Who Wants to be a Millionaire?, University Challenge and missing words

10. **KAS List** – Ask every student to tell you something they have learned today for knowledge, attributes or skills before they leave the classroom.

Those schools that choose to replace the traditional effort and behaviour 'grades' with a skills or competencies profile take a big leap forward in shifting the culture. We have chosen to base our approach on reporting the 5R's and later in the book we provide a case study on how we did so.

If a teacher is required to identify how well a student is demonstrating, let's say, 'reflection' then student, teacher and school need to share a view on what reflection may look and feel like across each of the subjects.

L2L Essential 6: Coherent structure to learning

By using a simple learning model that is easily recognised, students and staff can understand the structure of the learning experience. A generic model, which can accommodate different dimensions such as more open ended challenges, can also be used as a template for lesson planning.

Many of the schools we work with use the simplified accelerated learning model. It is used to plan class lessons and is shared with students and staff. Because of its common 'architecture', lessons can be placed on the school's virtual learning environment. The true value of a coherent structure is that students better appreciate that learning is a series of unfolding processes with an underpinning logic rather than an arbitrary collection of events to which they must submit.

To extend the students' understanding of how lessons are structured we use a variety of activities including one in which we ask them to review their formal classroom based learning over the previous week and identify where and when they have been asked to do the following activities:

1. Anticipate what is to come

2. Ask questions

3. Copy something down

4. Demonstrate a solution

5. Do an activity on the board

6. Get new information

7. Go over your outcomes

8. Listen to each other

9. Listen to the teacher

10. Make a presentation

11. Make changes

12. Make suggestions

13. Mark someone else's work

14. Mark your own work

15. Plan how you will learn

16. Remember what you did last time

17. Research

18. Say what you already know

19. Summarise what you learned

20. Think about how you will benefit

21. Think about how you will use what you learned

22. Think about what you will do

23. Use a search engine

24. Use the library

25. Watch a short video

26. Work in groups

27. Work on a problem

28. Work out a quick puzzle

29. Write down homework

30. Write out answers

This list forms the basis of some discussion over a number of lessons. We have to break it down and expand on what each might mean and therefore which classroom experiences they may have experienced. Our aim is to help students appreciate the thinking behind lesson design, to have some awareness of how activities should link coherently and be able to identify stages in their own learning. We share what we do with the other teachers because, inevitably, some positive and some less than positive patterns emerge.

We have an electronic version of this checklist. It allows students to collaborate in pairs and check any activity they recognise. The tool then re-organises the linear checklist into the 4 stage learning cycle with which they are becoming familiar, and which is designed like this:

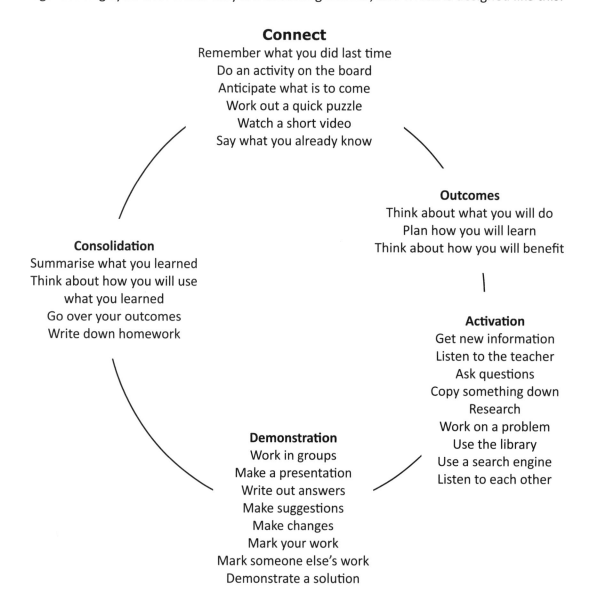

Connect
Remember what you did last time
Do an activity on the board
Anticipate what is to come
Work out a quick puzzle
Watch a short video
Say what you already know

Outcomes
Think about what you will do
Plan how you will learn
Think about how you will benefit

Activation
Get new information
Listen to the teacher
Ask questions
Copy something down
Research
Work on a problem
Use the library
Use a search engine
Listen to each other

Consolidation
Summarise what you learned
Think about how you will use
what you learned
Go over your outcomes
Write down homework

Demonstration
Work in groups
Make a presentation
Write out answers
Make suggestions
Make changes
Mark your work
Mark someone else's work
Demonstrate a solution

L2L Essential 7: Engaging experiences

Students on our learning to learn programme are shown a short presentation comprising photographs of different learning activities and are asked about the 'what' and the 'how' of the learning they see there. Great learning activities such as those listed below do not in themselves constitute great learning but they do give a leg up to student engagement.

building   display   writing   singing   learning games
working it out   experimenting   making a model
sequencing   trying something new   learning outdoors
making mistakes   having a go   solving a problem
matching up   discussing   practising   reading
calculating   thinking   memory mapping   sleeping
planning   predicting   using computers
thinking   reflecting   learning alone   asking questions
researching   discussing   predicting   learning in pairs
learning in groups   teaching someone else

In the book *Accelerated Learning: A User's Guide*, which Mark and Alistair were both involved in writing, they set out their principles of learning. They said that learning:

- is about thinking through, seeking and securing connections – it's connected

- evolves through exploration, mimicry and rehearsal – it evolves

- occurs when we scaffold high cognitive challenge and negotiate risk – it's negotiated

- requires optimism about realisable learner goals – it's realisable

- occurs through the senses – it's sensory

- is socially constructed with language as its medium – it's constructed

- thrives on immediate performance feedback and space for reflection – it's reflective

- benefits from a view that intelligence is neither fixed nor inherited but complex, modifiable and multiple – it's complex and messy

- involves the active engagement of different memory systems – it's active

- requires rehearsal in a variety of situations – it's rehearsed

- can be transferred into a variety of contexts – it sustains.

We would stand by these principles and add that a great teacher can construct learning experiences which by their very nature are engaging for the learners. It does not require the teacher to be the main act but it does require the teacher to be composer, conductor and orchestra. It's a real skill to be able to design engaging learning experiences and, having done so, to step back and not do all the work for the learner.

L2L Essential 8: Thinking fluency

The first maxim of questioning is this: the best questions are those the learners ask for themselves, with the best learners asking the best questions. To ask the best questions you need to want to do so, feel safe to do so and know how to do so. Overcoming these potential obstacles is part of what great teachers do. Here are some scenarios and how they might be dealt with.

High levels of anxiety inhibit a student's ability to take risks and all meaningful learning involves negotiating a degree of risk. The more anxious the student, the more likely the exhibition of what have been called survival behaviours – fight, flight, freeze and flock. In these circumstances attention will be limited in duration, unfocused and fitful. More tellingly the preoccupation will be about emotional and physical safety and in this state higher order thinking is secondary to coping with the immediacy of the moment. A great teacher will create a secure and orderly environment where students feel uninhibited.

Where a student is uncertain of the benefits of fully committing to a lesson the decision point is deferred. This 'pre-decisional phase' to which we referred earlier is a bit like riding the clutch on car. The full power of the engine is never felt until the pedal is released. When a student is uncertain of the nature of a question, why they are being asked and what will come about as a result of their response they may choose to offer, then it's tempting for them to 'ride the clutch' a little longer. Sharing the thinking behind the question as part of the ritual of asking the question, doing so in accessible language and making it a habit can go a long way to motivate students.

Think about the questions you ask and how you ask them. Inexperienced teachers can too easily ask:

- questions to which they don't get answers or attempted answers

- questions to which they don't wait for an answer

- questions to which only they know the answer

- questions within questions which confuse through over use of clause and sub-clause

- too many closed questions

- questions which invite understanding or description rather than higher order thinking

- questions intended to shut someone up or catch them out

- questions to fill the space with noise.

Whilst at the same time being:

- rushed

- intent on a pre-determined answer

- too dismissive of 'incorrect' answers

- arbitrary in their choice of questions

- over-reliant on 'hands up'.

Here are some ideas for asking great questions and avoiding some of the above pitfalls:

- ask fewer but better questions

- build upon the answers you are given

- insist on paired discussion before accepting an answer

- insist on students writing down or describing three possible answers before offering one

- pre-process students' thinking by giving notice of a question which is to come later

- allow wait time for the students to hear the question, compare the question to others from their experience, formulate a response and surface the response in an appropriate way

- share a taxonomy which explains the sorts of questions we can ask

- ask 'what would be a good question to ask?'

- think aloud and as you do so ask yourself questions and provide a chain of thought which includes some alternative solutions

- use question games such as 10 questions, buy the question or mantle of the expert

- use question templates to help students plan what sort of questions to ask.

Good questioning habits can be further developed through the use of visual reinforcers such as the Success Mat.

This example (which is provided on the CD which accompanies this book) shows the before, during and after of a questioning process. It has a hiererarchy printed down the centre. On the left are four things the student can work on as they begin to ask the question and four follow-up considerations once they have heard an answer. Along the bottom are the typical words used by schools and examining bodies and which, over time, students will have to become familiar with. By using the Success Mat to guide the process of thinking about, asking and responding to questions it becomes a productive habit.

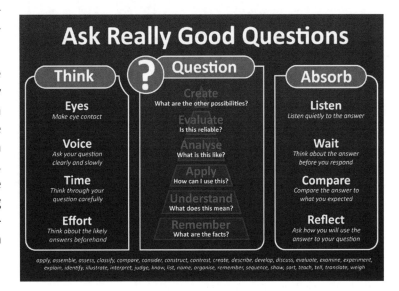

Other tools, such as the cartoon cards we call Billy Blunder – he's no exam wonder (and which are provided on the CD which accompanies this book), can be used to stimulate different types of thinking through discussion and debate. Examples are given below.

Billy Blunder – he's no exam wonder: Using cartoons to ask questions about learning habits

A diamond nine prioritising exercise completed in pairs then in groups.

Put them in sequence. Which are more catastrophic?

Discuss each cartoon in turn. What exactly is he doing wrong? What's the likely consequence?

Exam clinic – give Billy some advice as the exam doctor.

Create a set of do's and don'ts.

Create a set of cartoons for your group's positive and negative learning habits.

Honesty session – do you do any of this?

L2L Essential 9: Team and personal challenge

Team and personal challenges can be exhilarating for teacher and student. The example of the Sacred Orb requires several lessons, a lot of resources and good preparation. The purpose is to get teams to understand the importance of careful planning.

THE SACRED ORB

The Sacred Orb began life as a plain old golf ball.

It was dropped from the dry toilet of a passing airliner in the 1950s and had lain on the floor of the Amazon Jungle for four years before it was discovered by an Indian tribesman. The tribesman was amazed by its perfect shape, its clean white colour, the little markings and tiny recesses on its surface. He took it back to the village.

Great excitement greeted its arrival. Word had gone ahead that something special had been found. In the village, only the leader and his immediate circle of elders were allowed to see it. It was placed in the centre of the floor of their hut. As the rains fell outside, they stared at it for days and days. They waited for it to do something. Nothing happened. Arguments raged as to what it might be or who it might be from.

'It is an egg from the gods of sky and seasons,' said one.

'No, it is a talisman with healing powers for those who hold it,' said another.

'It is a charm made of a special stone which is stronger than any other in the jungle,' argued an elder.

Finally, the leader said that it must be incubated for 30 days to allow it to hatch and display its secrets.

So it happened that the golf ball, which by this time was called the Sacred Orb, lay in the centre of the hut on a small platform covered in cloth, dry twigs and feathers for the next 30 days. Meanwhile word of this 'great spirit' that 'glowed and spat fire' upon anyone who came near it had spread throughout the village. Rumours grew. It was said 'It had taken three men to lift it.' Villagers brought sick children and elderly relatives to be near the hut where it lay. Everyday life in the village stopped: no one went hunting, no one fished, clothes lay unwashed, apathy spread. Hungry crowds came from far away to be near the orb.

After 30 days the leader and the elders gathered to uncover the Sacred Orb and ask it to reveal its secrets. Great care was taken. Songs in praise of the orb were sung, a special dance was rehearsed and ceremonial fires were burned.

The moment came and the orb was slowly uncovered. It lay there unchanged, perfectly still, with no signs of any cracks. The leaders and the elders retreated. They were disappointed that the orb had not revealed its secrets, but convinced that they had not been worthy and must renew their efforts. Long discussions followed. What must they do?

After a long night of argument, it was decided to re-unite the Sacred Orb with the god of sky and seasons. Only by doing this could they be given an answer. They must build a platform ...

THE SACRED ORB

BID AND BUILD

Teams bid for materials to build a structure. The structure must be capable of holding a golf ball independently. It is to be built within 30 minutes. The highest structure measured to the top of the golf ball wins. Teams are allocated a total of £100 and must submit sealed bids in advance for the items they feel they will need. The items and costs are below:

YOUR BID

Tabloid newspaper (£15 each)

Broadsheet newspaper (£20 each)

Magazine (£10 each)

Eggcup (£25 each)

Scissors hire (£5 for 20 minutes)

Sellotape hire (£5 for 20 minutes)

String (£5 per metre)

Card (£5 per piece)

Lucky dip (£10 a go)

<u>Total</u>

The challenge is a well used one dressed up in a bit of melodrama about a sacred orb. It works very well when the teacher dims the lights and reads out the story. Teams then have to plan how they will raise the golf ball the optimal distance off the floor and that's about it!

Except, of course, it is really about process investigation, about planning and preparation, about roles and responsibilities and finally about reinforcing the importance of the learning that arises from the experience and not the excitement of the experience itself. The teacher needs to give time to the process. For example: introduction and planning (one lesson); building the tower (one lesson); debriefing – using all the evidence, photographs and eye witnesses (one, maybe two lessons). Novice teachers don't allow enough time for what's important thus creating an expectation that it's all about being busy.

L2L Essential 10: Co-operation skills

The skills of co-operation need to be taught. We use a number of ways of doing this but our most successful is to reinforce good co-operative and team behaviours through Success Mats. Typically a mat would provide some guidelines, like these on team problem solving;

Team problem solving – Follow these steps to success:

- Step 1: Agree the outcome
  Decide what you are being asked to do
  Decide what success will be like

- Step 2: Decide how to proceed
  Sort all the information you need
  Sort the task into small steps
  Sort who is doing what

- Step 3: Begin
  Go over your plan
  Get started

- Step 4: Stay on task
  Check you are doing what was agreed
  Check you are on time

- Step 5: Review for improvement
  Ask if you were successful
  Ask what you would do differently next time

The mat might also have guidance about team roles such as these:

Team roles – Give out these jobs:

- Co-ordinator – Gets everyone involved and makes sure they understand the task

- Charter – Takes notes and writes down decisions

- Creator – Comes up with lots of useful ideas and keeps the team positive

- Clarifier – Asks useful questions and makes sure the group carries out its plan

- Communicator – Talks to other groups and presents back.

It would provide guidelines for behaving in a supportive way:

Team rules – Try to be a good team member:

- Positive enquiry – Your team makes progress when it takes on a challenge. When you ask a question try to make it a helpful one

- Accept others – No team is perfect. Build on each other's strengths rather than focus on weaknesses

- Support your team – Do your bit. In order for the team to progress you need to play your part

- Stick at it – At the very beginning agree what a good outcome would look like and who is going to do what. Once you get started, stay involved.

It would provide prompt words, phrases and questions to be asking:

Team questions –
Ask these questions as you go:

- What is it we are being asked to do?
- What will success be like?
- How can I help?
- What else do we need?
- What are our alternatives?
- Let's build on that idea
- How can we improve?
- Am I contributing?
- Is there a better way of doing this?
- Is everyone involved?
- What's the solution?
- Are we progressing?

Team words –
Use these words and phrases:

- Well done
- Good idea
- Connect
- Build upon
- Explain
- Let's think
- Take your time
- Progress
- Excellent
- Try again
- I'm responsible
- Stick at it
- Show me
- Thank you

By reinforcing the sorts of team behaviours we seek, and doing so across the school, we build capacity to be team workers working in supportive and co-operative ways. In a letter written by a Year 7 pupil, from Blessed Edward Oldcorne School, Worcester, the boy said: 'Mostly Learn 2 has taught me the importance of working in a group with other people that you don't really know, that way everyone has ideas.'[29]

We think that teachers who identify the co-operative skills they wish to develop, then create resources such as simple tools, Success Mats, visual reinforcers for classroom display and student handbooks, accelerate the likelihood of those skills being used in situ and being seen as worth using.

L2L Essential 11: Independent enquiry

To develop the skills of independent enquiry the very first step is to make it the norm to be curious and want to find out. That is closely followed by being very good at asking questions as we explored earlier. Here is a simple exercise which has multiple applications. It can be used for team building and group and inter-group co-operation; it can be used as a starter for looking at what makes a team or it can be used to develop different sorts of questioning and interviewing. When designing learning activities do not start with the resource; start with what it is you want students to learn and be able to do differently as a result of their learning. Our levels of enquiry are:

- Finding: do you know where to find the information you need?

- Sorting: can you organise the information you need?

- Judging: can you trust the information? How reliable is it?

- Applying: can you use the information in different ways?

- Innovating: can you originate new ideas or products using the information?

We want our students to be able to move through these levels asking the right sorts of questions as they go. Our next stage is to construct engaging, realistic challenges based on simple enquiry skills. Here's an example we call Find the Team.

The teacher explains that there are five hidden teams and each team has six members but does not say what those teams might be or what the members of the teams do as a job. The challenge is to find out what the five teams are, then to find out what the jobs within each team are and then to find out to which team they belong.

The class sits in five home groups and before any cards are given out the challenge is explained. The teacher explains that there will be a finding out phase, a sorting phase and a judging phase. Before each phase they meet as a home group and agree what questions they will go off and ask and what they will do with the information at each phase when they come back. Planning questions is important.

The teacher has 30 cards each of which contains a job description. The cards are mixed up. Each student gets a card with a job description and sits in a home group which will have a mix of job descriptions from the five teams listed below. The 'hidden' teams are:

- Intensive treatment unit (ITU) team

- Television news team

- Flock of geese

- Formula 1 Racing team

- House builders.

As part of the finding out phase each home group must sit down for 10 minutes and agree the questions each member will ask of the others in the class. They will also have to agree how they will go about asking these questions, who will ask who and then plan so that they will get as much useful information to bring back as possible. Then there is a 5 minute asking session with everyone up carrying their job description asking and being asked questions. Once time is called they sit back in home groups and begin the sorting phase.

In the sorting phase each student shares what they have found out. Now there is a lot of information to be managed so it has to be recorded in some way. The teacher has provided tools such as sticky notes, flip chart, pens and paper. The students have a 10 to 15 minute period to sort the information and to identify any gaps or further questions which need to be asked. Then there is another 5 minute asking session with everyone up carrying their job description asking and being asked further and more detailed questions. Once time is called they sit back in home groups and begin the judging phase.

In the judging phase they have to weigh the evidence, decide what the teams actually are and what the jobs in each team are. Each home group will then have to post its solution on a flip chart at the end of the 10 minute judging period.

What follows is an opportunity for each home group to take turns to explain their conclusions and how they were reached.

The teams and jobs are below. Remember the individual roles are cut up separately, laminated and then given out one at a time.

Intensive treatment unit (ITU) from a large hospital

Consultant, anaesthetist, theatre nurse, porter, ambulance driver, surgeon

- I am in charge of a team of medical specialists. We have years of experience and training behind us. We deal with emergencies of the worst kind.

- I know about biology, physics and chemistry. A surgeon could not operate without me being present. I put people to sleep.

- I work as part of a team. I am highly skilled and support a specialist. I have to concentrate for hours at a time. I see victims of accidents and have to help them.

- Without me the hospital wouldn't function. I move the patients around.

- I'm a driver with a difference. I see the victims first. You need to be positive in my job.

- I have to have skilled and steady hands. The slightest slip could result in someone's death. I've trained for years.

Television news team

Presenter, camera operator, researcher, runner, engineer, sound engineer

- You'll recognise my face. I talk to the camera but do more besides.

- I have to know a lot about light. Sometimes I go to dangerous places and you can see my work in the comfort of your own home.

- I work behind the scenes. It's important that I get all the details. Others rely on me. I am an information worker.

- I'm the go-for! If there's something needs fetching I go for it. I'm part of the crew.

- I make sure that our satellite points in the right direction and is properly wired up. Anything electrical is my responsibility.

- I wear the headphones. Background noise makes my job impossible.

Flock of geese flying in formation

Point of the V, immediately behind point, rotate from the back, assisting stragglers, honker, flyer

- I'm the leader. We take it in turns to be at the front. It's hardest when you have no one to follow.

- There are two of us and we both support the one who leads. Now and again we rotate and take a spell at leading. I benefit a great deal from the direction my leader gives.

- Because we share things out sometimes I have to get myself prepared for a sudden change. Usually I support everyone else but when it's my turn I don't hesitate in coming forward.

- If someone falls behind it's my job to help them. Sometimes it's difficult when you know they can't keep up and you have to leave them. We give everyone a chance.

- I make the most noise in the team. I'm very positive and lend my vocal support.

- I'm one of the ones in the middle. You may not notice me but I'm working very hard.

Formula 1 Racing team

Wheel nut person, mechanic, driver, car designer, race strategist, refueller

- The wheels would fall off without me. I'm busy in the wet and when it's dry.

- I like my work to be fine-tuned. The faster the better for me.

- My job is all about seeing ahead. I need lightning fast reactions and I'm in constant contact with my boss.

- I work out how my product will work beforehand. We then trial it again and again in order to improve. The slightest change makes a big difference.

- I put the plan into action. I get all the information and radio through my decisions. I have to think on my feet.

- I'm part of a team within a team. To do my job well I have to be fast. I wear protective clothing because I work with high octane fuel.

House builders

Bricklayer, plasterer, plumber, roofer, electrician, painter and decorator

- I'm one of the first on the job. I use my hands and I'm physically fit. I need to have an eye for a straight line and be able to estimate.

- Walls are my speciality. That's covering them, not building them.

- Pipes, drains, joints and taps. Sometimes it's smelly and messy but you can't move in without me.

- A head for heights and a good set of ladders are what I need.

- I need to be very careful. I provide the power that brings the house to life.

- I'm one of the last on the job. I use my hands and I'm physically fit. I have pride in the appearance of my work. This is important as you'll be looking at it for a long time.

An alternative enquiry sequence might be as follows. The teacher may or may not introduce the five types of team. Obviously, it's easier to guess if you know you are in one of five so it is maybe best to delay that information until some questions have been asked.

Individual:

- Start by answering the question – who or what am I?

- Look at your role – what would be the best three questions to ask to find out what your actual job might be?

- What would be three good questions to ask to find out what your team might be?

- What are the clues in your role description that help you guess your job?

Pair:

- Compare roles with your partner – what are the similarities and dissimilarities?

- If you were both in the same team what sort of team could it be?

- Find another pair, now repeat the same questions – what are the similarities and dissimilarities and what sort of teams could you all belong to?

Team:

- Meet another pair; you should now be in a group of six. Each person explains their role, everyone else takes turns to ask questions to help them understand what their real job might be and what sort of teams they might be in. No guessing allowed!

- If you were all in the same team what sort of team could it be? What's your evidence for agreeing this team?

- What questions would you like to put to other groups to find out about all the different sorts of teams that might be in the room?

Class:

▨ There are only five different teams. In your group work out what these five teams are most likely to be. Explain your thinking.

▨ In your group work the best way to get everyone into the right team.

▨ Finally the teacher can tell the class the five teams and allow the class to sort themselves out. Once together, the team has to work out who does what and what makes them a team.

Now the teacher can move the learning on into team roles and responsibilities: What makes a team? What other examples of teams are there? What makes a good team player?

L2L Essential 12: System rigour

From the student point of view when a school subject has no home learning, examination, reporting or accreditation it has a very different status in their eyes. This could create opportunities, but it can also create issues. Small scale research completed at St John the Baptist School, in Woking, confirmed that within a cohort of Year 7 undertaking a learn to learn course timetabled for an hour weekly, a very high percentage reported that they enjoyed the lessons but a significantly lower percentage said that they were of high value to them. When these outcomes were explored further, it began to emerge that the programme was seen as dislocated from the 'real' work of the school which resided in subjects for which there were exams and qualifications further up the school. Some of these issues will be overcome when a school has a whole school approach to learning to learn but if we take each in turn we can offer small scale solutions.

With home learning it should be easy for a teacher to ask for students to undertake preparatory, bridging or follow-up work of a type which is relevant, encourages transfer but is not onerous or detached from the spirit of the learning to learn approach. For example:

▨ Complete your learner journal by choosing a lesson and reviewing it.

▨ Choose one of our thinking tools and use it to help with a decision at home.

▨ Create a design for your bedroom which would help improve your learning.

▨ Find one television character from a programme you watch and explain how they might score on the 5R's.

▨ At home, practise using the memory tool SPECS and beat your personal best for items remembered. SPECS stands for See it, Personalise it, Exaggerate it, Connect it and Share it. The SPECS are tools to improve your memory.

▨ Take three processes you have used in learning to learn and say how you might also use them out of school.

We don't advocate learning to learn examinations, but we do advocate real opportunities for personal or team challenge where the skills learnt need to be applied. Each of our L2 modules concludes with presentational challenges which are intended to pull the learning together and inject a little more adrenalin.

If it is not part of your whole school strategy to report on any aspects of the learning to learn approach that does not mean that you cannot do so in your own teaching. This may be informal feedback from you to your students or it could be feedback from them to each other.

It could be organised in different formats with various degrees of frivolity or seriousness. It could be an award ceremony like the Oscars; it could be in the form of a review filmed in front of a studio audience where highlights of the year are revisited and analysed; it could be a set of small group discussions prompted by your review questions.

If the school does not wish to pursue external accreditation it can set up its own internal accreditation. Again, this could be whole school and culminate in an awards event or it could be within your class. In our experience this is an opportunity to validate the efforts of some youngsters who will not get near a clutch of good exam passes. Even better, if you can, persuade a local celebrity to come in and make the awards.

The 12 essentials	Sample experience	Sample process	Sample resource	Student benefit
Three dimensional success criteria	Students as teachers	Students have to define what will be learned, how it will be learned and say how they will know if the other person has successfully learned	Learning Planning Sheet	Begin to better understand success criteria
Process sensitivity	Learning Detectives	Identify and record examples of good collaboration	Digital camera and notebook	Opportunity for the whole class to discuss learning methods
Learner behaviours that are well defined	Top Trumps Superheroes	Students learn about attributes whilst swapping cards	Superhero Cards	Beginnings of a language built around human qualities
Language of learning	Buddy Goal Setting	In pairs, students help each other set goals	Goal Setting Success Mat and Electronic Vocabulary Builder	Build learning vocabulary in a shared setting
Systematic debriefing and reporting	Reporting	Individual and small group review interviews	Learning Passport	All round support to develop attributes
Coherent structure to learning	4 Stage Cycle	Students asked to review a sample of lessons to identify the four stages	Electronic Lesson Planning and Review Tool	Easier to understand why teachers do what they do!
Engaging experiences	Content with Process	Card exchange activity based on 'what makes me happy'	Set of Happiness cards (as described on page 109)	Appreciate that we are all different; develop empathy

cont.

The 12 essentials	Sample experience	Sample process	Sample resource	Student benefit
Thinking fluency	Junior Apprentice	Choose a problem solving tool to decide which one of five toys to produce and market	Paper versions of a sample of the Electronic Thinking Tools	Overview of different problem solving tools
Team and personal challenge	Live Audience	Your team has three lessons to prepare and deliver a presentation on how to make the school more green	Team Problem Solving Success Mat, debriefing tools	Working to an authentic deadline allows students to experience 'pressure'
Co-operation skills	Great Groups	Group agrees and defines five behaviours of a great group and then is tested against each	Flip charts, pens	Will be replicated across the school
Independent enquiry	Art of Persuasion	From an agreed list you have three weeks to prepare a strong case to persuade someone to …	An Independent Enquiry Toolkit which guides students through research methods	Showcases independent learning skills
System rigour	Home Learning	Your learning to learn homework is to make three people 10% happier	Happiness Guidelines	Transferring experience beyond the classroom

SYSTEM ISSUES

TEACHER IMPACT

7 to 21%

10 QUALITIES

OUTSTANDING LEARN TO LEARN TEACHER

THE TEACHER AND LEARNING

7 × 7

THE 12 ESSENTIALS

RESOURCES ON CD

...HOW TO...

SEVEN TOPICS AND SEVEN TECHNIQUES
• HAPPINESS
• SUCCESS
• COURAGE
• THE BRAIN
• MEMORY
• DIFFERENCE
• FRIENDSHIPS

Thinking Words *System Issues*
Teacher **Classroom** Discrete Specialism Great Teacher
Dispersed 4 Stage Cycle Subject *ask really good questions*
Diffused Observation Elephant Effective Teaching
Laboratories of the curious

4. The teacher and learning

In this chapter we:

▣ Learn from elephants

▣ Describe what a great learning to learn teacher might look like

▣ Examine the classroom experience of the 12 essentials

▣ Provide seven starter suggestions for seven topics.

And ask the following questions:

▣ Can any teacher work this way?

▣ What is the core of a learning to learn classroom?

▣ What would a great lesson actually look like?

▣ How could I get started?

Question. What animal does the outstanding learning to learn teacher look like?

Answer. An elephant

The social networking site, Facebook, has a series of applications where you can take a simple quiz to find out more about yourself. For example, Which Beatles Song Are You? It could be 'Fool on the Hill', but for the purposes of this short introduction let's assume it had been 'Paperback Writer':

> *You are a professional and are ready to make some cash! You have great intuition and artistic sensibilities. You are interested in success and prestige. Don't fall prey to self-satisfaction or grandiose fantasies about yourself.*

Or we could go on with some more opportunities for grandiose Facebook fantasies about ourselves: Which Leading Lady Are You? Which Pokémon Are You? Which Mighty Woman Of The Bible Are You? Which Gemstone Are You? Which Shakespearian Character Are You? Which Animal Are You?

If we were to apply Which Animal Are You? to the teaching profession, we might come up with some interesting outcomes. In our quiz to find out which animal most closely resembles the learning to learn teacher our conclusion was – the elephant!

Both are nimble on their feet. The teacher needs to be capable of shifting strategy quickly. The elephant weighs three tons but can walk on tip toe. Elephants cannot run or jump; they have four forward facing knees, but they can walk silently at up to 15 miles an hour. The teacher is constantly being asked to adapt their practice to reflect changes in the outside world. We call this 'innovation'. We have a special unit which helps us to innovate. Two million years ago the elephant had spread all over the planet except Antarctica and Australasia. Elephants survived because they adapted.

The expert teacher and the elephant both see the big picture but don't get lost in the detail. By noticing recurring patterns and recognising individual and group behaviours, the teacher anticipates problems and intervenes to prevent them. An elephant is so large that bending down is a problem. If it lost awareness of the bigger picture, bending down to drink could be risky in the presence of a predator, but thankfully the elephant has developed a seven foot solution called a trunk with which it can suck up a gallon of water at a time. The trunk is the perfect problem solving tool. It allows the elephant to stay upright and be aware of what is going on around whilst it deals with any problem. As it walks, the elephant probes the ground with its trunk to avoid traps.

The teacher works in an environment which can be heated. The best teachers can maintain their cool in the most pressing situations. So do elephants. Elephants overheat easily and would boil if they didn't have giant ears. The ears are the size of a single bed sheet, with skin that is wafer thin. By flapping their ears elephants drop their blood temperature by 5%. Watch out for the teacher with the flappy ears!

Teachers spend their lives communicating. They are good at it; so are elephants. Elephants can use their feet to hear and can pick up low frequency calls from up to six miles away. Teachers' highly developed skills allow them to simultaneously talk at length about Brownian motion, shuffle some agitated molecules in front of the whiteboard, watch young Turner eat his little sister's packed lunch whilst thinking about the latest episode of their favourite sitcom. The elephant, also a multi-tasker, can smell a python up to a mile away. If it does so it can use its trunk to communicate. The trunk is faster than MSN Messenger. It will utilise a variety of instantly recognisable sounds – trumpet, hum, roar, pipe, purr or rumble. However, males and females don't understand each other's calls!

Elephants can walk underwater. Some teachers think they can walk on top of it. When an elephant swims underwater it uses its trunk as a snorkel. The trunk has 60,000 muscles and is so sensitive it can curl around a pencil, draw characters on letter sized paper, uncork a bottle or remove a thorn. Equally, it can pull down trees and build bridges. The mature elephant can hold a coffee cup so firmly that only another elephant can pull it away. Some teachers are so attached to their coffee cup that no other teacher can pull it away.

Great teachers are able to empathise with those in their care. Elephants, like some other large primates and dolphins, can recognise themselves in the mirror. An elephant will mourn and have elaborate rituals for visiting the remains of the dead. In the presence of their bones they will caress and nudge the bones.

Elephants do an apprenticeship. They spend 12 years as calves learning how, amongst other things, to use their trunk. Some academics say it takes eight years to become expert at teaching.

What the great learning to learn teacher looks like

Becoming a great learning to learn teacher may mean unlearning a large amount of what has been assimilated as best practice. Much of what has passed for effective teaching is a form of concerned parenting with the teacher having higher levels of anxiety about the outcomes than the students themselves. We want to move away from a situation where the teacher is the one doing all the work.

Teachers make a huge difference. Work in the US by Sanders and others showed the difference over a period of a year made by the most effective as opposed to the least effective teacher:[30]

Teacher quality	Student achievement gain in one year
Most effective teachers	53%
Typical gain	34%
Least effective teachers	14%

Another researcher, Kati Haycock extrapolated these results over three years and made the point that the differences are so huge that it's the difference between a remedial class and a gifted and talented class.[31] We can see from this that identifying the qualities of the effective teacher becomes a bit of a search for the Holy Grail. Being able to tie down what differentiates an effective from a less effective learning to learn teacher will move us on enormously.

Teacher quality	Student achievement gain in three years
Most effective teachers	83%
Least effective teachers	29%

Robert Marzano took the work a little further in 2000 when he looked at the combination of teacher and school.[32]

Marzano's effects on student achievement of school and teacher effectiveness with students entering school at the 50th percentile	
School and teacher scenario	Student achievement gain after two years
Average school and average teacher	50th
Most effective school and most effective teacher	96th
Most effective school and average teacher	78th
Least effective school and most effective teacher	63rd
Most effective school and a least effective teacher	37th
Least effective school and least effective teacher	3rd

John Hattie points out that, on the basis of 18 studies investigating the impact of teacher effects, somewhere between 7% and 21% of achievement could be attributed to the teacher and that these effects were more marked in schools with a higher percentage of free school meals.[33] The message from all of this is to make sure that you get quality in the classroom.

What would be fascinating would be for us to look at a further combination based on the learning to learn approach advocated in this book.

There are some system issues which we hope schools will anticipate, address and overcome in order to help their teachers become great learning to learn teachers:

▩ Many novice teachers arrive to teach their first class with no prior experience of anything but schooling.

▩ The assumptions a novice teacher has about the groups in front of him or her may derive from a very different set of life experiences to the students' and never be challenged. If those assumptions about who these students are and what they can do are limiting, then we have an artificial performance ceiling and a problem. Teacher behaviours will not shift unless the underlying beliefs and assumptions which shape them are challenged.

▩ Hattie and others have pointed out that, 'students know the extent to which each teacher treats them differentially and also know that this is a reflection of the teacher's beliefs about them'. More worrying is when these beliefs become institutionalised into what have been described as 'expectancy processes'.[34]

▩ We are wrong to assume that the longer the time spent in teacher education, the better the likely outcomes for students. The meta-analyses compiled by Hattie show that the impact of teacher education on subsequent student outcomes is negligible.

▩ The age profile of teaching staff will begin to matter as the prevailing pedagogy shifts away from knowledge and teacher centric models towards a more skills oriented approach. Inexperienced teachers may struggle in the more interactive environment.

■ It takes many years to become really effective as a teacher. Experience in teaching helps a great deal and this will apply more so with learning to learn.

■ Whilst inspection data shows in-school variation is currently higher than between-school variation, this research has been based on a more teacher centric, whole class, knowledge based model with summative assessment at its heart. With a shift to the sorts of learning approaches which characterise learning to learn it will not be possible to continue to teach in such little islands of quality remote from the main and we anticipate learning to learn as we describe it could play a part in reducing in-school variation.

■ The skilled teacher uses time more effectively: in our classrooms students need to be learning more than how to look busy. A considerable amount of time is lost forever waiting in class for activity to be initiated and moving between classes.[35] This time seepage will impact dramatically on attainment. Longer periods and fewer transitions can have disproportionate impact.

■ A great deal of what is taught is already known. The late Graham Nuthall, one of the world's most respected researchers, suggested as much as 50% of what is taught is already known. True or not, time is wasted when teachers feel the need to go over material 'just in case'.[36]

■ Subject matter knowledge is no longer as important when you move away from a transmission model towards the sort of teaching required in our learning to learn approach. There is little research study evidence that teacher subject knowledge has a powerful impact on student success. Some argue that subject knowledge takes the student to a point of basic competency but not beyond. However, there is a correlation between teachers' intellectual orientation and student outcomes.

The great learning to learn teacher:

1. Expects
A fundamental belief in the value of learning – ahead of knowing or even performing – directs and shapes teacher expectation of what's worth pursuing. Believing that being better at learning is, somehow, transformative and that aspiring to be better at learning is worth being passionate about should be what gets our learning to learn teacher out of bed each morning! Hand in hand with a belief in the value of learning is a willingness to be surprised by what students can achieve. You cannot see learning as transformative and then allow your own or others' limiting expectations to set the ceiling on what's possible.

2. Designs
They can be strategic in their thinking about learning. They design learning experiences to develop deeper understanding. To do so, they deploy techniques from a continuum which moves easily between direct transmission and constructivist models. The designer is not dogmatic. Learning opportunities are often drawn from real life contexts, use prevailing technologies and take students beyond the classroom.

3. Develops
One of the more successful methods of teacher training cited in Hattie's research is micro-teaching. Micro-teaching is like laboratory work. A student teacher teaches a group of students in a mini-lesson whilst other student teachers watch. Afterwards they sit together and

watch a video recording and then pull the performance apart. The great learning to learn teacher wants to scrutinise their own practice and, by poring over it, make micro-adjustments in search of further improvement. They would welcome others in their classroom and actively seek, rather than actively avoid, feedback. The willingness to have a look, to be open to new ideas, to consider alternatives and perhaps allow the possibility that they are a teacher of learning first and a subject specialist second are characteristics of an exploratory mindset.

4. Cares

The saying goes that 'students don't care how much you know until they know how much you care'. Nice – but maybe too fluffy! Caring comes in lots of guises and, as said before, adopting the role of fussy parent isn't what teaching is about. Great teachers care sufficiently to want to understand the lives of the children who enter their classroom. By caring about all their students the teacher will be better placed to engage them, challenge, be demanding and have high standards and expectations. You cannot personalise provision from a position of ignorance. It is a mistake to assume caring means being their friend.

5. Communicates

Great teachers have clarity. They can communicate in a way which is not only clear, concise and structured but is also engaging. Of course, robots can be clear, concise and structured, but they are rarely engaging – with the possible exceptions of Metal Mickey, Marvin the Paranoid Android, K-9 and R2-D2. Whereas the great learning to learn teacher uses verbal and non-verbal skills to complement the message.

6. Adapts

Student teachers who have been educated in an assess then test culture, who are taught to plan and prepare schemes of work against proscribed criteria, are encouraged to assimilate wider issues such as Social and Emotional Aspects of Learning and who know they will be inspected against a framework, might be forgiven for being wary of creativity. Ours is no longer a system which celebrates freedom of expression so why would we expect a generation of young teachers to seek out regular opportunities to innovate? Great teachers have the flexibility to adapt to and work with the changing picture in front of them. Should we happen to experience the fall of a major power, the demise of a notorious celebrity, the repeal of an unjust law, the occurrence of a freak of nature, the disappearance of a species, the discovery of a miracle cure, a once in a lifetime sporting triumph or an election of an iconic president, it's to our collective shame if we cannot respond to the moment because it's not on the syllabus or in our schemes of work. Adaptability ensures the long term survival of the teaching species.

7. Senses

Great teachers develop an intuition for the health of the classroom. They begin to know how it all fits together and they develop a feel for when things are in place and when something is wrong. This cannot be taught in the short term. It has to be experienced in the long term and some will be more intuitive than others. There is a difference between 25 years of experience and one year repeated 25 times. The fact that great teachers have fewer confrontations, less low level disruption and smoother transitions between learning moments is helped by an ability to foresee and forestall problems before they emerge. The inexperienced observer may not notice the steady trickle of skilful preventative interventions which remove the need for later and more drastic palliative care.

8. Asks

John observed a training activity where, for three minutes, participants were only allowed to converse in questions. No answers, only questions. It led to laughter for a few, frustration for others and anger for some at not being able to take anything from the experience. It's a human skill which is independent of one's education to be able to pose questions in a productive way. To elicit a considered answer whilst maintaining or even growing the relationship with the person being asked the question, and find something of worth in what is offered, is what builds human capital. Great teachers don't rest with the quick and the correct response; they are curious to develop the considered and the uncertain response.

9. Detaches

Great teachers may be advantaged on their death beds by being naturally adept at the 'out of body experience'. As part of their professional repertoire and, for many, part of their survival mechanism, they develop skills in detachment. They are able to dissociate from the emotional heat of a given situation and position themselves as a curious observer. The best use this opportunity to refocus their teaching strategy. They listen to what's being said, observe behaviour and read the situation from what's called a second position.

10. Robust

If you work as a professional in education then you know of individuals who have given a lifetime to teaching and who are as enthusiastic and positive at the end as they were at the beginning. These individuals have made an enduring difference in the lives of thousands. If you were to read the pages of websites such as Friends Reunited, the comments about teachers proliferate and are mainly positive; they focus on quirks and unusual moments but have a special respect for the teacher who endured. The teacher who welcomes your arrival and wishes you the best on your departure always gains respect. Great teachers invest the time to see the difference.

The classroom experience of the 12 essentials

L2L Essential 1: Three dimensional success criteria

A lesson would be dull if we started every time with a walk around the success criteria. Yet this is what many recommend!

In our classroom learning model we build in a connecting experience which is deliberately designed to create some energy around the beginning of the lesson. We might ask students to complete a quick two or three minute intense activity which attunes each and every one of them to the questions we might ask, the solutions we may seek, the energy level we expect and the commitment we require. In other words, don't start any learning experience with something that is dull, emotionally negative and doesn't demand anything from the student: stop copying outcomes off the board!

Having begun learning together we suggest teachers manage smooth transitions between stages: our connecting activity has been debriefed, we have shared solutions, invited contributions, collected what we know about the topic and anticipated what is to come. Sharing three dimensional success criteria becomes a succession of opportunities rather than a moment. The learning to learn teacher draws attention to the what, the how and the why of learning early on, revisits it and also encourages students to do so frequently and independently. Sharing success criteria is not a moment in time to be arrived at and departed from; it is a process through which deeper learning takes place.

The criteria are in three dimensions to emphasise a balance of content, process and benefit integral to any learning experience. We can brief and debrief against all three in any manner we choose. In an ideal world we would negotiate; in most classrooms we do well to describe. To remind us, the three dimensions of success criteria are:

1. What – what will we learn? (not do, the difference being important!)

2. How – how will we learn?

3. Why – why do we benefit?

Here then are 10 possible ways of introducing three dimensional success criteria:

1. Having written them up beforehand, talk them through with your students.

2. Having illustrated them beforehand, show them and ask for interpretations.

3. Walk them through using a timeline to represent the stages in the learning experience or points in your lesson, and position students on the timeline. Ask questions: At this point how will you be learning? When you get to here what will we have learned?

4. Put up your success criteria and have groups generate questions.

5. Put up your success criteria, have groups generate questions and reward the most helpful questions; discuss what would typify a good question to ask at this stage of learning.

6. Role play the outcomes in character.

7. Stay in character, say nothing at all about the outcomes but groups have to find out by asking questions of you.

8. Use a flip chart or side of the board to annotate with comments or questions about the criteria; encourage students to do the same by using sticky notes.

9. Ask the class what would make good criteria and work with their outcomes.*

10. Ask each individual what would make good criteria and work with their outcomes.*

*scary for many of us!

L2L Essential 2: Process sensitivity

Often what works best for students is what works best for teachers. Getting learners and their teachers to be more aware of the processes used whilst learning is our 'Trojan mouse' – small but with spectacular effects!

It is difficult for a teacher to be preoccupied with content delivery, covering the ground and reinforcing discipline, whilst at the same time asking students to be observant of the learning processes they are experiencing. Inviting students to comment on their authentic experience is hard to manage if they are on a programme of spoon feeding. So, asking students to be more process sensitive also requires teachers to be so at the same time and, as such, poses hard questions about the worth, frequency and monotony of some teaching interventions. This is a wonderful, if slightly devious, all round development opportunity for undermining dull, uninformed teaching.

The processes you may wish to draw attention to are those which are valued in developing autonomous learners. For example: asking good questions, setting clear goals, supporting someone else, working through a difficulty, using a thinking tool appropriately, finding a source of information, contributing positively to a group, drafting and redrafting.

To draw attention to these learning 'moments' you have three sorts of tools: you and your students, knowledge of what great learning looks like and some practical bits and pieces to help speed things along. You and your students can quickly move into process investigator mode. For example, you may ask three of your students to spend all or part of a lesson as 'process investigators' employed by the Number One Learning Detective Agency to find evidence of great engagement. To do so you agree as a class what great engagement is, why it's desirable and how you might recognise it during the course of a lesson. Your detectives report back at various times on what they have observed. The more we draw attention to it, the more we make it desirable.

Detectives employed by the Number One Learning Detective Agency could be:

- Success Sleuths – who capture what's behind learning success stories

- Process Investigators – who gather evidence of learning processes as they happen

- Thinking Tecs – who find the trail of deep thinking.

When starting this process have a narrow and specific focus. Don't just ask them to observe group work. Ask for a specific aspect of group work such as involvement. Over time you should be able to build up a broader profile of great learning processes from across the knowledge, attributes and skills.

L2L Essential 3: Learner behaviours that are well defined

Given the time taken to define what it is that we wish our learners to leave with and the effort which has gone into articulating it through our version of KASE, we need to ensure that our community works towards achieving those outcomes.

We use and recommend others use the 5R's as the basis for the learning behaviours we seek in and around the school. They are simple, well thought through and comprehensive. Schools and teachers who find value in them are welcome to use them. We have broken them down into three levels of bronze, silver and gold with descriptors for the sorts of behaviours we would expect to see at each level (see Appendix IV for these tables). This allows us to share them with students in formal and informal learning settings.

In a formal classroom situation where you may have to deliver a lesson in a period of 45 minutes you could make reference to which of the 5R's you may be focusing on that day. Then, as the lesson progresses you would be noticing instances of exemplary 'R' behaviour, drawing attention to them where it was useful to do so. You would have included the chosen R's in the outcomes session and make reference to the posters around the room. If we were working on resilience you could use the poster to prompt your comments in the following way.

'Gather round everyone. Alistair is stuck. What's our class mantra for getting unstuck?'

'Getting stuck is not a problem, staying stuck is; great learners practise getting unstuck, here's how ...'

'Can you remember to add your persistence strategies from today's lesson to the back of your learning to learn manual please?'

'Can you please go into the electronic portfolio and add your comments to your partners' work? Only practical advice to do with improvements please!'

'John, ask Mark to talk you through your target ...'

'As I'm listening I'm hearing lots of positive discussion ... thanks for that.'

'Well done ... I noticed that you gave yourself a break when it was becoming frustrating for you then went back to it.'

'Show the rest of your group each of the drafts you have gone through and ask if they can see evidence of your thinking ...'

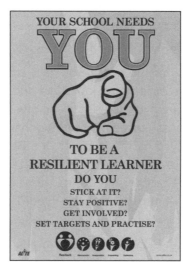

If we all know the learning behaviours we seek we can share responsibility for nurturing. The 5R's can also be used as the basis for target setting and, as we will show below, to replace effort and behaviour grades.

L2L Essential 4: Language of learning

Develop the learning vocabulary of your students so that they have a basic grammar and can use it on a day-to-day, moment-by-moment basis.

In an experiment with expert and novice teachers, Sabers showed a videotaped lesson on three screens.[37] On each of the left, right and centre screens simultaneous events occurred and novice and expert teachers were asked to comment in real time. Later they were asked questions. The experts noticed far more about the dynamics of the group as a whole and also the learning behaviours of individuals. They were better at holding the bigger picture and noticing its component parts. They had a flow of apposite words, phrases and descriptors ready to hand.

We discover things when we reveal patterns, and we create things when we impose patterns. Humans are habitual pattern seekers and pattern makers and the neural networks that are our brains are set up to make sure we remain so. What often inhibits our students in describing their patterns of thought and how they feel about and relate to their learning, is an impoverished vocabulary. When the expert teacher looks at a learning situation he or she is able to call on a simple descriptive vocabulary to explain what is happening. We want to provide a similar vocabulary for students.

Nagy and Herman estimate that, between starting school and finishing in the equivalent of our sixth form, students will encounter 85,000 different words in print.[38] Some of this grammar will be taught formally; most will be encountered in context. It is said that it takes at least six encounters before an able student begins to make connections and can use a word in context for themselves. However, the language of learning is unlikely to be encountered formally or informally. It's just not used except between teachers as they plan and review their teaching. We know a few things about developing technical vocabulary: direct instruction using the words works, learning the new words enhances students' ability to use those words in a variety of contexts, associating images and using graphic representations such as memory maps helps with learning the new words, and using the words aloud to explain to yourself or someone else dramatically increases their acquisition.

The strategies we use such as learning word lists, multiple exposure, on-screen dictionaries, passports, integration into Success Mats, direct instruction and rewarding usage through bronze, silver and gold medals is not gratuitous. We intend to create great learners.

L2L Essential 5: Systematic debriefing and reporting

Feedback, properly managed, is the single most powerful influencer on achievement. Given in appropriate 'dollops', feedback can increase performance by two and nearly three grades at GCSE.[39] Feedback needs to be given during or as near to the real experience as possible: you don't wait until the end of the month to find out how you are doing in your golf lesson. In general the longer the delay, the smaller the impact.

Feedback is not enough in itself. Feedback needs to be accurate and to be actionable. Research conducted by Nuthall in New Zealand showed that 80% of the feedback a student receives about his or her work is informal and from other students but 80% of that feedback is inaccurate.[40] In a classroom where we promote feedback but do not provide mechanisms for ensuring that it is appropriate, timely, accurate and actionable, we increase the likelihood for confusion.

Practising at the paired level will greatly enhance your students' capacity to give and receive feedback, to act on and to apply what they are told.

Students need to learn how to give and receive feedback. We use Success Mats for Smart Marking, Coaching and for Asking Really Good Questions to underpin the development of these skills. By using the Success Mats teachers can, once again, focus on the processes rather than the information provided.

Having three dimensional success criteria lends itself to 'dolloping' feedback. Pausing every now and again to ask pairs to evaluate their progress against what they set out to learn, how they are learning and how they think they will benefit is powerful and very time efficient.

The other dimension to systematic debriefing and reporting is how and when we provide information to parents. In our experience using the 5R's in classroom lessons, across the school and at home provides a window for being clear, consistent (even insistent) about the importance of personal attributes. The window for doing so with students will not stay open throughout their entire school career unless teachers and schools evolve a strategy for extending the thinking about and the use of the 5R's. Quite frankly, students get bored with paper checklists, reviews which are dislocated from their immediate experience and goal and target setting activities for their own sake. Progression needs to be planned.

L2L Essential 6: Coherent structure to learning

This is the 4 stage cycle we use broken down into the elements of the learning experience. This is a summary outline. It can be, and should be, tweaked and adjusted to suit. We provide you with a formal version on the left and a quick one on the right.

1. Connect

▨ Provide a stimulus which engages the curiosity of the learners and begins to direct them towards the topic.

▨ Lead into a short activity or dialogue through which students explore what they may know or would wish to know about the topic.

▨ Utilise their existing experience of, and knowledge about, the topic.

▨ Model learning behaviours and high expectations through your use of language, your interaction with individuals and groups and through references to the learning process.

▨ Explore the way in which the learning will link what has gone before with what is to come.

Outcomes

▨ Examine the learning outcomes in terms of content, process and benefits.

▨ Share what will be learned and any differentiation in outcome.

▨ Share how the topic will be, or could be, learned outlining the methods to be used.

▨ Share how individuals will benefit in the immediate and longer term.

▨ Where appropriate, refer to the learner skills and attributes which will be developed.

2. Activate

▨ Introduce the problem to be solved, or the issue to be explored, or the experience to be shared.

---

4 stage cycle shorthand version

1. Connect

▨ Use a short, engaging starter activity which is relevant.

▨ Discuss what they already know or want to know about the topic.

▨ Build on their thoughts.

▨ Be positive in what you do, what you say and how you say it.

▨ Connect it all up.

Outcomes

▨ Share content, process and benefits.

▨ Explain what we will learn.

▨ Explain how we will learn it.

▨ Explain why it's worth learning.

▨ Agree which of the 5R's we will focus on.

2. Activate

▨ Turn the information to be learned into a problem to be solved.

▨ Provide relevant and engaging learning activities.

▨ Provide any resources or information or advise where to get it.

▨ If required, encourage them into groups.

▨ Pause every now and again to draw attention to learning processes.

- Structure learning activities around the problem, issue or experience which relate to the learning outcomes.

- Provide any resources or additional sources of information.

- Guide students into appropriate groupings and provide support and challenge.

- Begin to draw attention to what's being learned and how it is being learned.

- Build a positive climate and maintain students' motivation, concentration and application.

3. Demonstrate

- Allow students to demonstrate their own solutions to, or observations about, the problem, issue or experience using a variety of formats and media.

- Allow students to evaluate and make improvements to their solutions.

- Facilitate teacher, peer and self assessment processes to inform improvements.

- Stay positive.

3. Demonstrate

- Ask them to work on their solutions.

- Allow them to present their solutions.

- Get them into pairs or groups so that they can help each other improve on their solutions.

- Invite really good questions.

- Be provocative and challenging.

4. Consolidate

- Review content, process and benefits.

- Ask them to explain how they used the 5R's.

- Talk with them about how they can use what they learned in other lessons.

- Preview what's coming next.

- Allow students to interrogate their solutions through the careful use of questions and thinking tools.

- Ask and encourage challenging questions.

4. Consolidate

- Take time to examine what has been learned, how it has been learned and how we will secure the benefits in the future.

- Where appropriate, refer to the learner skills and attributes that have been developed in the lesson.

- Highlight the transferability of learning skills used both to other lessons and experiences out of school.

- Preview and link work done in the lesson with future learning.

101

Coherent structure to learning

This is the 4 stage cycle set out as a cycle. In the previous chapter we described an activity which required students to identify stages of the cycle and activities that would go in each stage. This is the summary teacher version!

Connect
Use a short, engaging starter activity
which is relevant
Discuss what they already know or
want to know about the topic
Build on their thoughts
Be positive in what you do, what you
say and how you say it
Connect it all up

Outcomes
Share content, process and
benefits
Explain what we will learn
Explain how we will learn it
Explain why it's worth learning
Agree which of the 5R's we will
focus on

Consolidation
Review content, process and
benefits
Ask them to explain how they
used the 5R's
Talk with them about how they
can use what they learned in
other lessons
Preview what's coming next

Activation
Turn the information to be
learned into a problem to
be solved
Provide relevant and en-
gaging learning activities
Provide any resources
or information or advise
where to get it
If required, encourage
them into groups
Pause every now and
again to draw attention to
learning processes
Stay positive

Demonstration
Ask them to work on their
solutions
Allow them to present their
solutions
Get them into pairs or
groups so that they can
help each other improve on
their solutions
Invite really good questions
Be provocative and
challenging

L2L Essential 7: Engaging experiences

In 2009, the Chief Inspector of Schools in England suggested that too many lessons were insufficiently engaging. Ofsted's annual report, published the previous November, warned that secondary school pupils were too often set tasks that were not demanding enough and that teaching, particularly in primary schools, could be 'pedestrian'. Links were drawn between dull teaching and poor pupil behaviour. It is probably true that with a curriculum stuffed with content, in a culture of high stakes testing and in compartments of time comprising 45 minutes, it stretches the creative capacities of the best to turn out engaging learning experiences day after day. It's not impossible to do but it is difficult and it becomes considerably more difficult when we refuse to cede ground on curriculum content and design, use of time on the timetable, use of space and our status as subject specialists first and teachers second. Shift some of these and all sorts of possibilities emerge.

A starting question would be: Do you know, and do your staff know, what great learning looks like? Is this a live debate in your school? Do you and your colleagues spend time talking about learning or is that squeezed out by other concerns?

L2L Essential 8: Thinking fluency

Before you read any further try this exercise. Read each word below and try to link it to the next. Once you've done this we will take your thinking a little further.

learn planets idea space toy teach balance film category radio classify play compare sand contrast yacht decision talk different tie evidence partner fact sweet fair tree judge mum think know car memory elephant share opinion fish reason cards similar web prize solution lifebelt sort test plug sky plan mat

A simple exercise in free association for students can be used to help them begin to think about thinking. Here's one for them:

learn sand idea think photo study bulb connect song sort choose happy know space test climb organise cheese judge cloak transfer egg create run work

In our approach we developed a simple Electronic Thinking Toolkit comprising 48 tools organised in five categories. The categories are:

- How I know – find and remember information

- How I organise – make sense of the information

- How I judge – make decisions about the worth of information

- How I transfer – use information in a variety of different ways and contexts

- How I innovate – adapt information for a number of purposes.

We wish to encourage students to be able to use a range of thinking tools and then, over time, never use them again in their lives! Why? Dependency on any given thinking tool is not what we are after. Once you have fluency in a language you throw away your phrase book. The issue for us is not so much the use of a tool or a protocol but the quality of thinking which lies behind it. A student whose dialogue conveys an easy ability to classify, to compare and contrast, to weigh worth or to speculate about consequences is one who no longer needs to write it or type it onto one of our tools. To this end, we work hard to invite curiosity about information and its sources, about the domains of understanding, about the architecture of thinking. We have an aspiration that our classrooms are curiosity laboratories.

The laboratories of the curious:

1.   Train students to become scientists who do detailed studies of their own thinking. Encourage them to reflect on their cognitive, meta-cognitive and emotional processes – ask 'How did you think?' and 'How did you feel?'

2.   Create communities of learners by deploying home and away groups, envoys, speed sharing, instant reviews and activities which flow the information around the room.

3.   Use thinking roles such as Edward de Bono's Thinking Hats or, better still, devise your own to develop the sort of interventions you wish to encourage amongst your students.

4.   Make thinking visible by using graphic organisers, physical models and visual tools and ask students to explain the relationships within them.

5.   Share a taxonomy. Our 'categories' above can be easily replicated in a class poster and in the student planner; both student and teacher can then make regular reference to and use of the taxonomy.

6.   Give thinking space and processing time. When asking a question or posing a challenge allow 'wait' time. Students need to have time to try things out in their heads; this involves going up and down a few blind alleys.

7.   Practise using the shared language. Use the vocabulary of thinking we provide below. Make regular use of the words and encourage students to do the same.

8.   Connect it up. Fluent thinking is about pattern seeking and pattern making – work to explore the connections.

9.   Provide open ended challenges. Gradually work towards challenges that are more open ended.

10. Develop process awareness. Use the Learning Detective Agency staff – Process Investigators and Success Sleuths.

11. Ask questions about questions – like some of those we described in the previous chapter.

Gold thinking words	Silver thinking words	Bronze thinking words
Condition	Abstract	Balance
Conjecture	Assumption	Category
Corroborate	Belief	Classify
Data	Bias	Compare
Distort	Claim	Contrast
Empathise	Consequence	Decision
Exaggerate	Contradict	Different
Fallacy	Credibility	Evidence
Hypothesis	Criteria	Fact

Gold thinking words	Silver thinking words	Bronze thinking words
Implication	Estimate	Fairness
Inductive	Evaluate	Judge
Infer	Explanation	Know
Innovate	Interrogate	Memory
Interrogate	Locate	Opinion
Norm	Logic	Reason
Presume	Speculation	Similar
Supposition	Theory	Solution
Synthesis	Trial	Sort
System	Understand	Test
Viewpoint	Valid	Value

L2L Essential 9: Team and personal challenge

For a team or personal challenge to be effective it must be achievable. However, success should only be the reward of sustained individual or collective effort. Too easy and it's de-motivating; too hard and it's dispiriting. The individual working on his or her own may need more support; teams that have complementary talents can help each other. Short challenges which take place within formal lessons can be supported by regular short process review activities. There are also great opportunities around individuals being stuck: as we say, 'Getting stuck is not a problem, staying stuck is … great learners practise getting unstuck and here's how.' For more sustained challenges, progress meetings can be an opportunity to pull people back together and look at what is helping and what is hindering progress.

The best challenges are:

▨ Authentic: they have meaningful outcomes and are presented to real audiences

▨ Personal: they have some direct relevance to the student and require involvement

▨ Extended: they require preparation and commitment

▨ Challenging: they extend

▨ Reviewed: students derive added value from reflecting upon the experience.

L2L Essential 10: Co-operation skills

According to David and Roger Johnson, both recognised leaders in the field of co-operative learning there are five features of co-operative teams:[41]

1. Positive interdependence – they need each other to be successful

2. Face-to-face promotive interaction – they must support each other

3. Individual and group accountability – they are contributors to success

4. Interpersonal and small group skills – they need process tools

5. Group processing – they must be reflective.

We also know from Professor John Hattie that it is important to teach these features rather than to wait for them to emerge from the students themselves:

The effects of small group learning were significantly enhanced when students had group work experience or instruction, where specific co-operative learning strategies were employed, and when group size was small … simply placing students in small or more homogenous groups is not enough.[42]

We would encourage the use of group protocols such as home and away groups (home groups are friendship groups and away are non-friendship groups directed by the teacher), limitations on group size, a culture that expects groupings to form and re-form based on the nature of the task, and a clear understanding amongst teachers that group work is not expected to happen for every moment of every lesson. It's a method to be used appropriately not slavishly. Use team Success Mats to define roles, responsibilities, offer problem solving techniques and share a language of co-operation.

L2L Essential 11: Independent enquiry

In any enquiry project there is a continuum of direction. Students can be guided or directed towards a topic; they can select from a pre-packaged offer or they can elect a topic of their own.

The skills of independent enquiry relate to the stages of the enquiry. The more competent they are at handling a project, which may be open ended, the more autonomy they will be

Dummy Run	Real Thing
▦ High student competence in independent enquiry ▦ Low freedom of choice	▦ High student competence in independent enquiry ▦ Freedom of choice
Learning the Ropes	**Try it for Size**
▦ Low student competence in independent enquiry ▦ Low freedom of choice	▦ Low student competence in independent enquiry ▦ Freedom of choice

given. The table above sets out just how much direction a student may need.

Some schools will use the Thinking Actively in a Social Context (TASC) wheel developed by Belle Wallace as a means of helping their students set about their enquiry work. Her wheel has eight stages each with a set of prompt questions.[43]

L2L Essential 12: System rigour

As a teacher of learning to learn avoid giving out ambiguous messages about the status of what you are doing. Anything which diminishes the approach in the eyes of the students will come back and bite you. If the school resources learning to learn last, timetables it in the leftover slots, timetables staff who are unwilling conscripts, teaches it in rooms which are mostly corridor or cupboard; if it is never visited by senior leadership and no inspection

Sevens: seven starter suggestions for seven topics

As a guide to how easy it can be to begin a learning to learn approach we have included some suggested ways of teaching unusual topics with a rationale for doing so. The content of the topic is less important than what the experience tells young people about themselves – firstly as humans with a full life ahead of them and secondly as phenomenal learners, each of whom is capable of soaking up experience and using it to make positive life choices. We have provided seven sample topics which, by their nature, are of compelling interest to young people:

- Happiness
- Success
- Courage
- The brain
- Memory
- Difference
- Friends Test.

Each topic can be expanded into a longer and more demanding challenge. We have not included three dimensional success criteria, but in each case these would be shared after the connection activity.

The learning to learn dimension comes through the processes used. The topics are a wonderful opportunity for students to practise using just some of the following techniques:

- Authentic presentations
- Case studies
- Home and away groups
- Learning detectives
- Real contexts
- Using Success Mats including team roles and responsibilities, questioning, discussion and presentation
- Transferring experience into a different non-educational context.

Help Yourself to Happiness

Why?

1. Young people who invest heavily in the belief that wealth, fame, beauty or possessions will bring happiness are more vulnerable to depression later in life.

2. Much of what we are encouraged to believe about happiness is that it comes from outside the self; it's the reverse which is true.

How?

3. Start with the individual using a card swap exercise based on the different things that make people happy. Out of a total of 25 happiness cards, five swaps are allowed to get the best hand. Show your hand to a partner and see if you have anything in common.

4. Now, you will go into groups to share similarities and differences and see what you can find out about each other. Before doing so, number yourself one to six in each group. Later we will have some tasks by numbers!

    a. Number ones: explain one card you rejected.

    b. Number twos: tell your group one thing which makes you happy which was missing from the cards.

    c. Number threes: tell your group one thing you had in common with someone else.

    d. Number fours: explain what the cards with the yellow border might have in common.

    e. Number fives: explain your favourite card.

    f. Number sixes: tell us which was the most popular card in your group.

5. Now as a class let's look at a poll of our cards. What comes top and what comes bottom? What do we make of the results of this poll?

6. One of the ways to become happier is to focus on the happiness of others. In your home groups I want you to come up with seven ideas to make your school a happier place then, through envoying, I want you to visit all the other groups and add the best idea from each group to your list.

7. Your homework is to come back in a fortnight's time having carried out as many items on your list as possible: can you make your school a happier place?

Success Sorters

A COMPETITOR ON CELEBRITY BIG BROTHER
Bagz is now 40. When she was younger she was a well paid model. A period of her life she would rather forget left her with an addiction to drugs. Now she is clean again and hopes that appearing on this TV show will help her launch her career.

What would success be for Bagz?

Why?

1. Young people are bombarded with images of people who are 'successful' but these are more often or not stereotypes from a narrow range of human activity.

2. If we are to shift the view that success comes only to the beautiful, the popular, the rich and the winners then we must provide alternative models and starting points.

How?

3. Use a connecting activity such as 'success autograph hunters' to get students appreciating that success is a not an absolute. In the selection of 16 statements to which a student can sign an autograph, include some which are highly unlikely (e.g. owns a Ferrari), some which are likely (e.g. can ride a bike) and some which you can guarantee (e.g. owns a pair of shoes).

A STUDENT WHO IS BEING BULLIED
Cathy is 13 years of age and is bullied at school. Her family do not have money for designer clothes like some of the others in her class have. When she was younger Cathy had to have thirteen operations and now she walks with a slight limp. Some people call her names because of this.

What would success be for Cathy?

4. Alternatively, as a connecting activity, in groups quickly list as many *specific* examples of success from as many different walks of life as possible.

5. Now, in home groups, look at the seven case studies (we have illustrated three but a complete set is provided with the CD which accompanies this book) of success and decide what success for each person would be. Agree your decision. List three reasons in support of your decision. Your process investigator will be looking for evidence of listening skills.

6. Now put your case study cards in order of success with most successful at the top and least at the bottom. Before you do so as a group try it on your own.

7. How easy was it to order the success stories? What did the exercise help you understand about success?

A SHEPHERD WHO LIVES ON A REMOTE ISLAND
Gabriel decided to give up his job in London and become a shepherd on a remote Scottish island. He is in his second year. It is lambing time when he has to be there all night and all day to help. Last year thirty lambs were born and all but three survived. This year he is expecting forty lambs.

What would success be for Gabriel?

Crying Out for Courage

Why?

1. Courage takes many forms but is often conflated with expressions of physical strength, public acts of heroism or defiant gestures.

2. Shift the view of what constitutes courageous behaviour and you can radically change relationships within a class or school community. Often the small kid is the one who emerges as the true 'hero'.

How?

3. Use a paired share connecting activity in which students exchange stories of courageous behaviour.

Courage usually involves three or more of:

☐ Sustained over time

☐ Not done for show or reward

☐ Someone or something benefits

☐ It involves a decision

☐ Potentially dangerous

☐ There is a safer option

4. Now in a new group comprising three different pairings, exchange the stories again and this time see how many different types of courage you can come up with. See if you can find your own words to describe the different types of courage. Some people talk about moral courage and physical courage. Look at your list and see if you have examples of both.

5. In your original groups look at the examples and see if each of them can pass the three or more test. Who passes and who doesn't? What does this tell you about courage? Is courage something we should aspire to have or is it something that you are born with? Your Success Sleuth will be coming round looking for evidence of participation.

6. Using the Real Superheroes booklet let's look as a class at some life stories and ask ourselves if they pass the three or more test and what these life stories can tell us about our lives.

7. With copies of local and national newspapers find some stories about courageous behaviours. Sort them by moral and physical courage first then apply the three or more test. Do they pass?

Meet Your Brain

Why?

1.   Too many students assume that you are born clever. If we can demonstrate that the brain is phenomenally capable of adaptation, is malleable rather than fixed and builds like a muscle, then students invest in the view that science tells us we can all become smarter.

2.   There is so much potential in this topic for linking directly to students' perceptions of themselves as learners. We can easily do very engaging sessions on lifestyle, on thinking styles, on stress, on perception and on memory. It lends itself to simple and practical activities.

How?

3.   Our connecting activity is literally that. Using a ball of string we pass an end of it around the room, weaving across and through so that what we are left with is an interconnected if messy looking network. Everyone should be holding part of the string. Now ask the question, 'In what ways could this be like a brain?' Next, we tug the string and make the point that the brain is full of cells which are connected together and the more they are used the more connected they become. Thinking is about making connections and the more connections we make the better for the brain.

4.   Our next activity involves creating a large network of cells – a bit like a brain – in our class. Tell students: 'Each of you is a cell and each of you will be responsible for communicating some learning to other cells or groups of cells.' Each of you has a fact card. There are 36 cards and you are in six groups. Read your fact cards and in your group see if you can organise your selection.

     ▨ Brain Basics

     ▨ Brain Cells

     ▨ Bits of Your Brain

     ▨ How Your Brain Feels

     ▨ How Your Brain Thinks

     ▨ How Your Brain Copes

5.   Your cards are mixed up. So you have now to envoy with the other groups, listen to their facts and come back with a complete set. Read the new set. In a moment you will be presenting your findings to the other groups.

6.   Everyone must take part in the presentations which today must involve seeing, hearing and doing. A good idea to help get your message across effectively might be to act out your facts with a narrator and a sub-titler. Use the Team Roles Success Mat to help you with your decisions.

Memory

Why?

1. Students love the idea that they can improve their memory by using simple techniques.

2. One instance of being able to remember something which seemed impossible will be enough to hook them on to the idea that they have something special inside them!

How?

3. A PowerPoint slide on the screen shows various items and words which students have to remember on their own. After 60 seconds delay, they write and draw as many of the items as they can manage in 90 seconds. They then put their paper away. Students then get up and move to form a pairing. In pairs they talk through what they remember. Then, after two minutes, they each try to record as much as possible again but without looking at their original papers. The teacher leads a discussion on any differences.

4. To demonstrate the effect of 'chunking' information students are shown a set of slides and have to remember the information on each slide. The teacher shows a slide for six seconds then goes to black, waits ten seconds, then asks the students to write down the combination of numbers and letters. This is repeated until all the slides are used. At some point most students will start to make errors. The teacher leads a discussion on why this occurs and makes the case for using memory techniques.

5. The teacher shows the class the SPECS posters which summarise memory techniques and then students practise the techniques in pairs in a carousel activity around five 'islands', one for each poster.

6. Pairs are organised in larger groups – say six – in order to demonstrate their memory 'successes' learned from the posters used in the islands exercise.

7. The class is presented with the original PowerPoint slide. This time they are challenged to use their memory techniques to help them remember the slide. The slide remains up for 60 seconds as students apply techniques. Results can be written, drawn or described.

8. The teacher then takes contributions on what works and why – before putting up the slide summarising memory techniques.

Dealing with Difference

Why?

1. Understanding that we are all different is the beginning of mutual respect. Tolerant and fair societies are based on respecting difference.

2. Personal prejudices cloud our thinking and make dealing with difference a very difficult topic to access. By creating more objective and slightly absurd entities such as the Red and Green tribes we make it easier for students to talk about difference.

How?

3. Students watch a PowerPoint presentation on the stroop test. Guided by the teacher, they shout out the colours on slide one then do the same for slide two. Slide two colours do not match words. It is the colour and not the word that must be shouted out. Why is it more difficult? Because it's different and we are not used to it!

4. Students watch the on-screen information about the Red and the Green tribes. They are asked by a show of hands to say whether they are Greens or Reds. Students are now divided arbitrarily into being a Red or a Green. Whether you are Red or Green is kept secret. No one should know your identity. Now students watch the on-screen presentation that is a collection of images about the Reds and the Greens. In their Learner's Journals students will be asked to write three things they like about their tribe and three things they dislike about the other tribe.

5. Now everyone has to sit in their tribes. Reds sit on one side, Greens on the other. Reds and Greens share the things they like about their tribe and

The Red Tribe

- [ ] Live in the north
- [ ] Wear nothing but Red
- [ ] Make shuffles for a living
- [ ] Go to Red schools
- [ ] Eat Red meat, Red apples and cherries
- [ ] Live in square houses
- [ ] Worship the crimson
- [ ] Support the Red team and sing its songs

The Green Tribe

- [ ] Live in the south
- [ ] Wear nothing but Green
- [ ] Make wiffles for a living
- [ ] Go to Green schools
- [ ] Eat Green vegetables, Green apples and Green limes
- [ ] Live in round houses
- [ ] Worship the emerald
- [ ] Support the Green team and sing its songs

This is Life in Redland

- [ ] Every Green must move to a square house but Reds get first choice
- [ ] All Green items of clothing to be handed in; Red must be worn
- [ ] Green students don't go to school
- [ ] Green employees work longer hours for lower pay and have Reds as bosses
- [ ] Greens get the leftover food
- [ ] Greens cannot worship emerald, only crimson
- [ ] All Green football teams start two goals down

three things they dislike about the other tribe.

6. The 'This is Life in …' slides are shown, firstly on behalf of the Reds, then on behalf of the Greens. The questions are asked: How would your life change if you were a Red? How would your life change if you were a Green? How does all of this make you feel? What should be done to make sure Reds and Greens can live together?

Note

This is a deliberately provocative approach that needs handling carefully.

Students are initially invited to show a preference that will be based entirely on first impressions. Now you override these preferences by allocating Greens and Reds. This is best done so that no one else knows which tribe each person is in. This is done to build an atmosphere of unease.

Writing three things they like about their tribe and three things they dislike about the other tribe is done to show how easy prejudice can build around ephemeral loyalties. Sharing in tribes shows how quickly the process can occur.

When groups get together on the basis of some 'shared' similarity or interest they can encourage each other to exaggerate and distort those shared similarities.

This is what happens with Reds and Greens. When the 'This is Life in …' slides are shown students begin to unpack the consequences of living and behaving like a tribe.

This is Life in Greenland

- ☐ Every Red must move to a round house but Greens get first choice
- ☐ All Red items of clothing to be handed in; Green must be worn
- ☐ Red students don't go to school
- ☐ Red employees work longer hours for lower pay and have Greens as bosses
- ☐ Reds get the leftover food
- ☐ Reds cannot worship crimson, only emerald
- ☐ All Red football teams start two goals down

This is life in the Red classroom

- ☐ Greens must arrive on time, Reds can come late
- ☐ There are only enough books for Reds
- ☐ Only Reds get to ask questions
- ☐ Reds get spoken to by their given names; Greens are given a number
- ☐ Reds have the best toilets; Greens have to make do
- ☐ Reds have got their own play area; Greens have to stay inside
- ☐ Green students get half the time of Reds to sit exams
- ☐ Reds get longer holidays

Questions about life changes will cause unease and some confusion. We then ask how does all of this make you feel? Draw attention to how easy it is to fall into tribe behaviour even when we know it is unfair and wrong.

7. Students watch newspaper headlines on the screen. There is a mix of fact and fiction. Students are asked, 'What have we learned today about living with other people and about fairness?' and 'If there was one thing that you could change to make life fairer what might it be?'

Passing the Friends Test

Why?

1. For many teenagers, girls particularly, worries about staying within a friendship is all consuming. Time spent worrying about friendships can sap energy.

2. Knowing more about friendships and how to establish, manage and make sense of them safely is a potential life saving skill for a young person.

How?

3. A good start to this sort of learning experience is for the teacher to talk about his or her own friends and acquaintances saying a little more about the origin of the friendships and describing some which endured and others which did not. All the while the teacher is referring to the seven criteria from the Friends Test (opposite).

4. Next the teacher invites the class to offer some thoughts on combinations of characters who may or may not be matched up as friends. So we could have cartoon characters, historical figures, literary figures, soap stars, talent show panellists. Students then work on a pairing and see how they would rate on the Friends Test. Following this they can put themselves into the mix and see which, if any, character might match up or has the potential to match up.

5. In the demonstration phase we move across to the personal Friends Test. The criteria for the test can come from the class or from groups or you can use ours. Ideally the criteria come from the students themselves but often they omit some really important features such as forgoing or adversity, so may need prompting. The Friends Test needs to be done with discretion and some care, so be prepared to adapt our ideas. It may be that there are individuals for whom this is too raw and so a Plan B is needed!

Plan A would be for each student to take five people they know and 'put them to the test'. By going through the seven tests a judgement can be made about the durability of the friendship. Alternatively, Plan B would be to take some profiles of 'typical teenagers', write these up on case study cards and then provide opportunities for pairs of students to try combinations of these fictional characters.

The Friends Test

1. Shared background
   Do you have a lot in common?
   Score 1 – 5

2. Duration
   Have you known each other a long time?
   Score 1 – 5

3. Disclosure
   Are you able to confidently share secrets?
   Score 1 – 5

4. Adversity
   Have you faced and overcome a difficulty together?
   Score 1 – 5

5. Trust
   Could you trust this person to look after a valued personal possession?
   Score 1 – 5

6. Others
   In your absence, would this person speak positively about you to others?
   Score 1 – 5

7. Forgoing
   Would this person give up something of true worth to them on your behalf?
   Score 1 – 5

Different sorts of techniques can be taught to demonstrate patterns of friendship. One is a sociogram where the relations in a group are plotted, with people who are friends joined by solid lines and people who are acquaintances joined by dotted lines. Another comprises proximity circles with the student in the middle and the friend plotted at a distance from the centre which correlates to the strength of the relationship; the closer to the centre, the stronger the relationship. Concentric circles can be used to show the patterns. Another is a spider web based on an individual friend and each of the seven criteria. The criteria radiate in a line from the centre with scores on the line starting from one and going out to five. Each 'friend' would show a different pattern or web depending on their scores.

6. As a consolidation activity we can ask the question: Are you a good friend? Or as a Plan B, we could have advice for building friendships based on the criteria for the Friend Test.

7. As a home learning activity some of the written outcomes, scores or charts can be taken and shared with a parent or carer.

The 12 essentials	Sample classroom intervention	Adopted teacher role	Adopted teacher behaviours	Learning benefit
Three dimensional success criteria	Teacher takes the group to clarity about what is to be learned, how it will be learned and the benefits of learning	Can be anywhere on a continuum between directing and negotiating	Points up the importance of briefing and debriefing using the three dimensions. Creates time to do so	Enriches and emphasises 'quality' over 'quantity' of learning
Process sensitivity	Pauses class activity to focus on 'live' examples of specific learning behaviours	Intervening and guiding	Observing, noticing and focusing through good use of questions	Learners start to be more alert to ongoing processes
Learner behaviours that are well defined	Use of electronic student profilers to determine individual development	Organising students into pairs so they can coach each other	Modelling the use of the system and capturing the outcomes	Creates an opportunity for individual target setting
Language of learning	Adopting a vocabulary building opportunity such as Learner Bingo	Leading a whole class session	Structuring, nurturing and cheerleading!	Reinforce the use of learning vocabulary in a positive climate
Systematic debriefing and reporting	Subject reporting on students in each of the 5R's	Collating observations	Detailing structured feedback	Whole school clarity over progress
Coherent structure to learning	Preview and review of stages of the learning to come	Sharing information	Sequencing and walking through a process	Strong sense of beginning, middle and end

The 12 essentials	Sample classroom intervention	Adopted teacher role	Adopted teacher behaviours	Learning benefit
Engaging experiences	Teacher selects from a repertoire of possible learning opportunities	Challenging and scaffolding	Selecting, designing, adapting	Teacher knows, and responds to, needs of group
Thinking fluency	Teacher selects from a repertoire of available thinking tools	Orchestrating	Clarifying, reflecting, summarising, challenging, provoking	Deepens the level of engagement
Team and personal challenge	Scaffolded exposure to presentations	Directing, managing, guiding	Differentiating presentation challenges spaced over time	Students benefit from the 'pressure' of a live audience and a deadline
Co-operation skills	Class groups learn roles to adopt in a variety of groupings – irrespective of task	Leads the group learning at first, but steps back	Process investigation	Class quickly becomes effective group problem solvers
Independent enquiry	Teacher provides choice within topics – some being completely open ended and others carefully constrained	Facilitator and resource	On a continuum between directing and consulting	Independent learning skills need genuine space to be developed
System rigour	Teacher sets home and/ or out of class learning	Manager and guide	Making connections explicit, administrating where necessary	Learning to learn is given a significance consistent with other school experiences

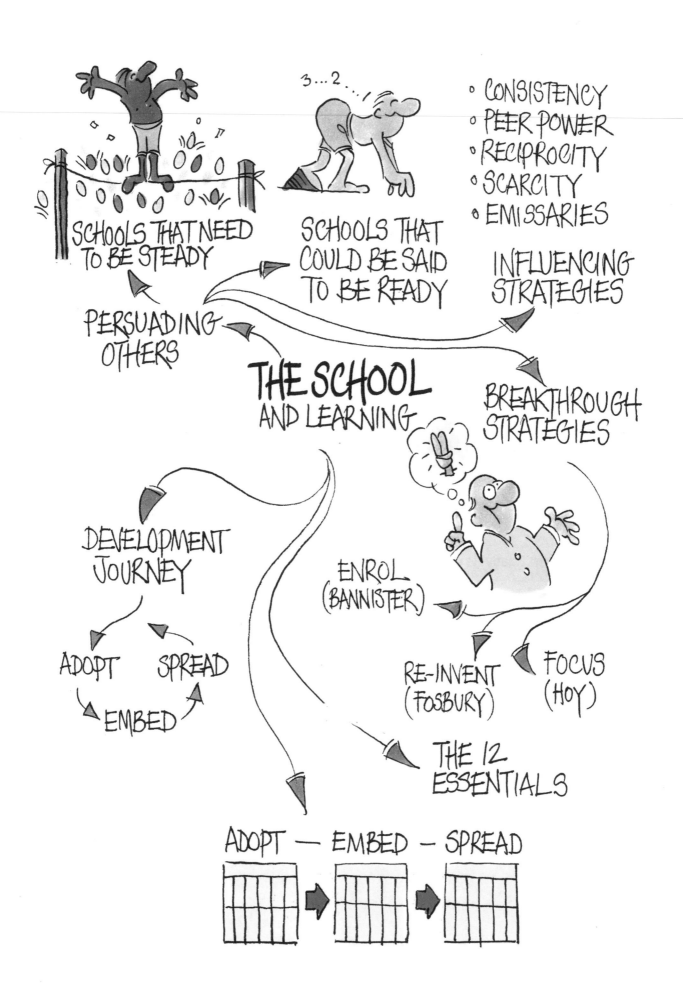

School Approach **Journey** Nudge Curriculum *Fosbury*
Assessment Creativity Effort **Interventions** Grades Feedback *Hoy*
Behaviour Peer **Group** Consistency Scam Compliance *Maven* Connector
Breakthrough Flow
Bannister Ready Influence Persuade Authority Trap Reciprocity
Steady
Adopt Embed Spread

5. The school and learning

In this chapter we:

- Explain how to persuade others to follow this route
- Describe influencing and breakthrough strategies
- Explain adopt, embed and spread
- Examine the school experience of the 12 essentials.

And ask the following questions:

- How do I overcome objections?
- What's a good way to plan for progression?
- What are the implications of a whole school approach?
- How do I introduce the 12 essentials across the school?

How to persuade others to undertake the learning to learn journey

The inventor of the system deserves to be ranked amongst the greatest beneficiaries to learning and science, if not the greatest beneficiaries to mankind.

This was Josiah F. Bumstead speaking about the 'invention' of the chalkboard in 1841.

Today's child is bewildered when he enters the 19th Century environment that still characterises the educational establishment where information is scarce but ordered and structured by fragmented classified patterns, subjects and schedules.

This was Marshall McLuhan speaking about the experience of classroom learning in 1967.

Some schools have changed, some are ready to change, some don't know how to change and some just don't see the point of change. How do you persuade others to take the 'risk' of going with you on the learning to learn journey or on a skills and competencies based approach if no one else is with you?

There may be as much risk in too easy an assumption that the sort of approach we commend is right as there is in it being dismissed out of hand. It is essential that schools go into anything which has this potential for change with their eyes open. Sadly we don't always walk though life with our eyes open.

In the typical secondary staffroom of a UK school at least six members of staff will have been a victim of a serious financial scam in this last year. The average loss will be about £1,000. You know the sort of thing I mean, someone sends an unsolicited e-mail – it used to be a fax, before then a letter – imploring you to take advantage of a one-off opportunity to invest. The institution looks legitimate, the font and letterhead is impressive, they seem to know that you have a little bit of experience in this field, and because it's such a high return you suspect it's not entirely ethical but nevertheless feel justified in exploiting a loophole within the law. Before you know it, you've sent your account details and 24 hours later your money is gone.

To find out more, researchers from Exeter University conducted in depth psychological interviews with victims and sent fake prize draw mailings to 10,000 people.[44] The profile of someone who is vulnerable includes:

■ having a good but not comprehensive background knowledge of the subject of the scam

■ being open to flattery

■ having poor impulse control

■ having a degree of isolation, for example living alone or not testing the decision by sharing it with others

■ having a history of already being scammed – 10–20% of the population are deemed vulnerable

■ being susceptible to psychological triggers such as building relationships, authority, status and reciprocity.

The victims are not able to walk away. They read and reread even when they feel uneasy. Avoiders don't pore over the decision; they tear it up. Are schools equally vulnerable? Sometimes going into a school and trying to persuade them to invest in the learning to learn journey feels like trying to sell a non-existent timeshare off the coast of Dubai. Except that the product is entirely ethical!

So, back to the question: How do you persuade others to take the 'risk' of going with you on the learning to learn journey or on a skills and competencies based approach? If we take the profile identified above of those vulnerable to a scam, then to operate ethically we need to make sure we:

▦ provide full information about the approach, how it works, who is using it and the evidence for success

▦ are realistic about the context of the school – some are starting a long way back

▦ give it proper time so no one is 'bounced' into a commitment

▦ put decision makers in touch with others who have experience of using the approach

▦ be clear about the relationship of any learning to learn approach and the relationship with statutory requirements and current national strategies

▦ enrol as many stakeholders in the planning process as possible.

Some schools are *ready* and well positioned for moving to a skills or competencies based approach, others need a more *steady* platform before making a whole commitment to this approach. At the extremes we can see the differences and just why it can be so difficult to make any change. Again, the promise of a sudden and quick fix which at a stroke will remove all of these obstacles by replacing them with something more positive and forward thinking, may be very tempting for some but the reality is that it is a cumulative process.

Schools which need to be steady	Schools which could be said to be ready
High or exceptionally high external pressure	Managed and welcomed external pressure
Wide mix of abilities in staff	Development culture
Uneven motivation in staff	Clear lines and levels of accountability
High internal variability	Internal consistency
Exclusive focus on results	Focus on learning and results
High staff turnover	Stability without sclerosis
Pessimistic culture	Optimistic culture
Problem preoccupied	Solution focused
Inconsistencies within systems	Coherent systems
Lack of clear leadership	Clear leadership
Poor use of data	Effective use of data
Curriculum with built in obduracy	Curriculum with built in flexibility
Fear of abandoning strategies even if they don't work.	Willingness to abandon strategies if they don't work.

It is because schools are at such widely different starting points that the concept of a journey is so helpful. We argue for five year strategic plans with learning at their core; schools reclaiming and so owning their core purpose; communicating and selling the benefits of that core purpose; testing everyday decisions against it; landmarking the journey points; and, as Jim Collins says in his book *Good to Great*, being clear about who is on the bus and who is not on the bus. Mystery tours are great entertainment but if you want to get somewhere it's better to have a sense of your destination.

> *No matter how dramatic the end result, the good-to-great transformations never happened in one fell swoop. There was no single defining action, no grand programme, no one killer innovation, no solitary lucky break, no wrenching revolution. Good to great comes by a cumulative process – step by step, action by action, decision by decision, turn by turn of the flywheel – that adds up to sustained and spectacular results.*
>
> Jim Collins[45]

The journey stages we talk of are *adopt*, *embed* and *spread*. The idea is that schools that are ready for a whole school learning to learn approach go there quickly; others may take longer and may need to evolve through stages. Before we describe the characteristics of each of these stages, let us look a little more at the psychology of 'buy in'. What sorts of things can and should we do to enrol the commitment of others?

Influencing strategies to nudge change

Seek consistency. People will wish to act in ways which are consistent with what they believe about themselves – just as a teacher, observing misbehaviour, can say to a child 'I know you are not really like that' in the anticipation that the child will agree that he or she is 'not really like that' and adjust accordingly. We can appeal to an individual's beliefs about themself as a learning professional. When individuals are asked to behave in ways which are inconsistent with what they hold to be true and of value we can get dissonance. Dissonance is a psychological tension; it's difficult to remain in such a state for any length of time and we naturally seek a resolution. So, the first strategy is to appeal to a wider set of beliefs about the importance of learning, about being there for the students and about the staff role in supporting *our* agreed core purpose. In small scale research conducted using mirrors, employee theft was reduced. On a other occasion, when at Halloween sweets were left to tempt young people who came to the door, with the householder inviting youngsters to take *a* sweet before then leaving them alone, 33.7% took more than one sweet. When a large mirror was placed so that they had to look at themselves as they took the sweets the numbers dropped to 8.9%.[46] The issue is one of accountability and there is no one to whom you are more accountable than yourself. The mirrors, like name badges and photographs of teachers in the reception area, are devices *to remind you of who you are* – so if we are learning professionals why would we choose to behave in any way which did not advantage the learning of the children in our care?

Use the power of the peer group. Social compliance is an extraordinary persuader. When, at what was Stamford High School in Tameside in 2004, a Year 7 group undertook a learning to learn programme, their behaviours in and around the school improved for the better. Staff who until then had been sceptical about involving themselves in the initiative, noticed the difference in this group in their own lessons and slowly offered to get involved. For most of us, being outside but very close to the peer group is too lonely a place. Informal networks are profoundly influential so choose who you trust with a pilot programme carefully. Include a balance of enthusiasts, weathered sceptics and evidence gatherers. Mavens are also influential. In his book *The Tipping Point*, Malcolm Gladwell used the term to describe those who are intense gatherers of information and impressions, and so are often the first to pick up on new or emerging trends. He also suggested that when combined with a connector – those people who have wide network of casual acquaintants by whom they are trusted – then we get a powerful synergy. So allow influential others to sell the benefits of the shared journey.

Give something first. The psychology of 'reciprocity' means that people feel beholden when confronted with a personal favour which has been done for them without expectation of return. The more personalised you feel the gift, the more likely you will feel obliged and so respond positively. This is why junk mail is festooned with free gifts – address labels, calendars, diaries, key rings, plant seeds – which usually bear no direct connect to the product being touted. They make a subtle change to the nature of the relationship. Small favours earn big returns. Research with memos sent to employees found that by attaching a sticky note with nothing on it responses went up; with the addition of a short handwritten comment they went up dramatically. Don't expect staff to be endlessly altruistic – make some personal concessions. You could start by deleting some of the tiresome, off the point tasks.

Exploit scarcity. Being the first, the best or the only has an appeal. Scarcity attracts and that's why when a street seller gets out the perfume on Oxford Street it is always the last batch, it is iffy and he may have to pack up and run for it at any time: 'So to you, my dear, £20.' Ask what it is you have around you that is unique. What can you do via this learning to learn journey or skills and competencies based approach that will make you the first in your area, or the leader in the field, or the only school of its kind? The offer of going somewhere or having something that's a bit different is compelling.

Choose your emissaries. People do more for those they like or admire. The more we like people the more we want to say yes to them. Who are your learning to learn emissaries? Do they have status? If not, are they very well liked? In a process which involves us seeking the validation of those we respect we become suggestible, sometimes dangerously so. The downside to this is compliance and unquestioning adherence to authority figures, a not entirely healthy situation for an organisation that may need to change. We may need to question our role models, the rituals with which we surround ourselves and some of the everyday routines we take for granted. If we can get the balance right then we can carry staff with us.

Breakthrough strategies to force change

Roger Bannister, Dick Fosbury and Chris Hoy are athletes from three generations of sport. An Englishman, an American and a Scot, they have all achieved remarkable breakthroughs which have left a permanent mark on their sports. The stories behind each of their sporting breakthroughs provide insights into what could be done in education. Bannister's success was built on the support of others. He was a genuinely amateur athlete who was dependent on *enrolling* others to forgo their personal ambition to help secure the record. Fosbury, also a student and amateur athlete like Bannister, achieved a phenomenal success by *rethinking* what he was doing, going back to first principles and so coming up with an entirely new approach. Hoy, a professional athlete in the modern era, if only so as a result of subsidies, was so busy *focusing* on what he needed to do to achieve that he escaped the pandemonium that preceded his record-breaking ride.

Our three breakthrough strategies are to (1) enrol others in sharing your dream and working to achieve it, (2) if it's not working have the strength to change it and start over and (3) focus on what is possible and stay focused to the end.

Enrol others in sharing your dream and working to achieve it

The four-minute mile had never been achieved. It was the Everest of athletics. Once it had been achieved it was as though a dam had burst. On a cloudy day in Oxford in 1954 on an old fashioned cinder track with pools of water only just having been cleared after a sudden shower Bannister, supported by two friends Chris Chataway and Chris Brasher, finally broke the barrier and came home in 3 minutes, 59.4 seconds. To do so he needed Chataway to pace the first two laps, Brasher the third and then, for the last quarter of a mile, he was on his own.

Bannister's success created a new mindset. Just 46 days later, the Australian John Landy broke it again. Over the next 50 years over 1,000 different runners from around the globe have done the same. On one event in August 1980 in London, 13 men ran sub four minutes. By the end of the 20th century, the record had been lowered to 3:43.13 by Hicham El Guerrouj of Morocco in 1999.

The message for school leaders and those who wish to introduce a learning to learn approach is to enrol others who share your vision of success and allow them to help you.

If it's not working have the strength to change it and start over

Dick Fosbury was a high jumper who, when a young athlete in the US, took a dislike to the dominant style of the day which at that time was an upright straddle method. He began experimenting with the old fashioned scissors and eventually refined it so that it looked like nothing ever done before. He ran at the bar, turned his shoulder at the last minute and flopped over face and chest up, legs trailing. Reporters quickly labelled it the 'Fosbury Flop' and the name stuck. Using his new technique, Fosbury succeeded at the US Olympic Trials.

At the 1968 Olympics in Mexico City, he flopped to the gold medal, amazing the world and setting a new Olympic record at 2.24 metres (7 ft, 4.25 in.). Other jumpers were sceptical, but the innovation had shifted thinking forever. Four years later in Munich, 28 of the 40 competitors used Fosbury's technique. By 1980, 13 of the 16 Olympic finalists used it. Of the 36 Olympic medalists in the event from 1972 through 2000, 34 used 'the Flop'. Today it is the most popular technique in modern high jumping.[47]

The message for school leaders and those who wish to introduce a learning to learn approach is to ask the question, 'Is what we already have in place working?' – and if the answer is 'no', change it.

Focus on what is possible and stay focused to the end

Chris Hoy, who won three gold medals at the Beijing Olympics, is Scotland's most successful Olympian and a world champion in four different disciplines. Steve Peters is a forensic psychiatrist who worked with the British Olympic cycling team and with Hoy to help prepare him for the 2004 Olympics in Athens and the kilo which, at that time, was the world's most demanding aerobic cycling event. Flat out for 1,000 metres. This is how author Richard Moore, described their method:

> They worked through various scenarios, all relating to the high-pressure environment of the Olympic kilo. 'What's your biggest fear?' he would ask him. 'What's unsettling you as you sit there?' It could be your own ego; the fear of failure; it could be the size of the crowd; it could be the idea of letting your parents down. You have to define what's going through the mind and then determine where it's coming from.
>
> How would you react to a fast time by one of your rivals while you're waiting to go? How would you react to a world record? You have to visualize these scenarios. I have to dig into a person's mind to do this. But the part of your brain I want to work is the logical part. The part of your brain I want to turn off, or control, is emotional. Your emotions aren't rational. They create irrational thoughts that can mislead you.[48]

It was put to the test on 20 August 2004 in Athens when his 15 opponents went on before him one after another in a packed, hot velodrome. Whilst all of this is going on Hoy sits in the middle, headphones on, oblivious to what's happening, focused on what he needs to do. The Olympic gold finally comes down to the last five riders. Kelly of Australia completes the four laps in 1 minute, 1.224, a sensational new Olympic and world sea-level record; the Aussies in the 6,000 strong crowd go mad. Nimke, the German, goes next and gets 1 minute, 1.186, even better and faster than Hoy has ever done in his life. Bos, the Dutchman, fluffs it so its Hoy's oldest adversary, Tournant of France, next. Tournant gets the first ever sub 61 seconds at sea level – 1 minute, 00.896, a time which is superhuman. Then it's Hoy, last up, his mother and father watching from up in the stands. He explodes out, going really hard at it, giving it his all, years of preparation focused on one moment. As he goes through the line the time goes up – 1 minute, 00.711 – it's the best Olympic cycling performance of all time: phenomenal.

The message for school leaders and those who wish to introduce a learning to learn approach is to focus on what you are doing and need to do, avoid being distracted and see it through to the end.

Adopt, embed, spread – your learning journey

> Most change theorists and practitioners agree that significant changes should be attempted, but they should be carried out in a more incremental, development way ... Large plans and vague ideas make a lethal combination ... Significant change can be accomplished by taking a developmental approach, building in more and more components of the change over time. Complex changes can be pursued incrementally by developing one or two steps at a time.
>
> *Michael Fullan*[49]

Building in a plan for progression is vital. There are two aspects to this. The first is the strategic development of the approach and how to best sit your chosen approach within your own school context. The second is about building clear progression for students.

The concept of a journey implies that success is all about arriving at the destination. In our model of adopt, embed and spread it's also about recognising where you are starting your journey from. It is not necessarily better for your school to be striving to get as quickly as possible to your chosen destination. More haste means things get left behind, fellow travellers get overlooked and arrive feeling disoriented and badly prepared. Plan carefully.

Students can quickly tire of 'building their learning muscles' if, for three years, they are asked to do the same or very similar things, using the original inventory and checklist. Similarly there will be a dramatic drop off in enthusiasm if they are expected to use the same thinking tools, from a limited selection chosen by their teachers, in every lesson across the school. Thought needs to go into planning how the students' experience will be managed over an extended period of time. In this respect it's as important to plan for concluding aspects of the approach as it is to plan for their initiation.

The suggested features of the adopt, embed and spread stages we provide in the following tables are intended to give a sense of what may be possible and no more than that. They are not exemplar outcomes nor are they must-do's. We have structured them together to help keep your thinking as divergent as possible without diving into the detail. The following headings come with prompt questions and we have set out some responses of our own.

Intent. What is your strategic intent at this stage? How does this intervention serve your core purpose?

Pedagogy. What are the defining features of the teaching and learning which will be taking place? How will you recognise that you are securing the pedagogy you wish for?

Student knowledge. What sorts of things are students expected to know about learning and their part in it at this stage?

Student attributes. What personal qualities or attributes will students develop at this stage?

Student skills. What skills will students develop at this stage?

Student experience. What additional opportunities will be provided for students to enrich their understanding of learning?

Assessment. How will progress be assessed? Who will be involved in assessment? How will students share responsibility for assessment?

Reporting. What will be reported to parents? What data will be collected? How will it be collected?

Staffing. How will staff become involved in the approach?

Progression. Will the approach be accredited in any way?

Staff development and continuing professional development (CPD). How will staff training needs be met? How will staff development needs be met?

System rigour. How will the approach be given status? How will the approach be monitored? Who will do this? How will progress be evaluated?

Typically, though not exclusively, schools that are new to these ideas and ways of working, that are more steady than ready, may be well advised to start modestly. In the adopt stage it may be that a limited pilot is what is best.

Adopt					
Intent	**Pedagogy**	**Knowledge**	**Attributes**	**Skills**	**Experience**
Limited pilot, possibly as a discrete course, in order to test the approach and pump prime the process	Increasing use of 4 stage cycle across school Teachers modelling facilitation behaviours Use of process investigators in classroom lessons Much enhanced awareness of process	Students know about learning 'preference' Students stretch their learning preferences with help of others Team protocols and behaviours Basic language of learning Learner journals identify processes used for learning	All students know the 5R's: ▓ Resilient ▓ Resourceful ▓ Responsible ▓ Reasoning ▓ Reflective Understanding of how the attributes apply to all areas of life	All students know the basic thinking tools and the way they are used: ▓ Knows ▓ Organises ▓ Judges ▓ Transfers ▓ Innovates Metacognition regularly features as part of review Students understand and can apply 4 stage cycle	Independent research activity Authentic presentations to real audiences Team challenge Participation in a themed event such as a 'well-being day' Student podcasts or blogs

Adopt (cont.)					
Assessment	**Reporting**	**Staffing**	**Progression**	**CPD**	**Rigour**
Three dimensional success criteria in use to brief and debrief in all learning to learn lessons and some beyond Students using Success Mats to learn self and peer assessment skills Electronic profiling with debriefing on outcomes	Parental meeting: What is learning to learn? Parental guidance sheet: What is learning to learn? Why is it important?	Selected group of staff who are, at very least, curious about the approach and open minded enough to adjust their classroom teaching	Learning to learn increasingly applies the new knowledge, skills and attributes Expectation that some transfer will occur Content of 'lessons' becomes more demanding Themes progress from individual to teams and communities to applications	Learning to learn teacher team training and evaluation of resources Concentration in staff training on four part lesson planning, review, debriefing, three dimensional success criteria Feedback to all staff on learning to learn approach Learning to learn bulletin for all staff	Features in School Development Plan (SDP) Senior member of staff accountable for approach Home learning part of discrete course Student questionnaires at start and end of year Student interviews with portfolio of work Teacher questionnaires – learning to learn and non-learning to learn teachers Evaluation based around the 12 essentials

All staff understand the positive benefits of this approach. We may have a mixed economy with a thriving discrete course alongside themed whole school experiences, use of some of the techniques in all lessons, systematic use of the learning cycle for planning learning, and some reporting to parents using the 5R's, all with clear leadership and direction.

Embed

Intent	Pedagogy	Knowledge	Attributes	Skills	Experience
Approach is now a permanent feature of the school's thinking, well understood and received by staff	4 stage learning cycle is used across the school	Students and their teachers are applying work done on memory, similarity and difference, exam preparation, decision making	All students, teachers and wider school community know the 5R's	All students know their way around the thinking tools and the way they are used	Space for independent research activity that is given status
	All teachers know about the worth of varied teaching methods including those which are facilitative	Student learning goals and targets are recorded and shared	5R's built into lesson success criteria	Thinking tools feature across the school	Termly authentic presentations to real audiences
	Students are skilled and active in briefing and debriefing	Team protocols are consistently applied across the school	5R's feature in reporting to parents	Electronic Thinking Tools and Electronic Learning Wall is accessible in every classroom	Structured themes such as resilience day or which require team working
	Much enhanced awareness of process across the whole school	Teachers and students use a shared language of learning	Learner Passport featuring the 5R's is used to debrief informal learning experiences such as work experience	Metacognition features as part of review with learning journals used for this across the school	Student podcasts or blogs integrated into learning and shared with others
			Rewards system reinforces 5R's		Lead Learner responsibility at whole school level

	Embed (cont.)				
Assessment	**Reporting**	**Staffing**	**Progression**	**CPD**	**Rigour**
Three dimensional success criteria used to brief and debrief in all lessons Students applying self and peer assessment skills Outcomes from electronic profiling used to inform target setting Work uploaded to Electronic Learning Portfolio	5R's feature in reporting to parents 5R's reporting is conducted in a pilot that is limited to core subjects Parents can independently access an online support programme (PAL) to help them help their child to learn. This is accessed via the school website	Significant time and resources devoted to approach Cohort of staff actively involved in teaching learning to learn is widened All staff know and understand the learning to learn pedagogy, its outcomes and the 12 essentials All staff contribute to or are involved in themed events	Phase 2 of the L2 approach Individual and team challenges more demanding and sustained Evidence of more independent learning Electronic Thinking Tools used across the school Common approach to lesson planning Standardised learning display in classrooms	Training for all staff in 12 essentials Mini-research groups follow through each of the essentials Learning to learn team meeting regularly Lesson observation programme introduced using 'L2 Observe' Electronic Observation Tool Learning to learn bulletin for all staff	Clear accountability Home learning now integral to learning to learn Accreditation – internally or externally sought Student questionnaires' outcomes evaluated Evaluation based around the 12 essentials, classroom observation, student interviews

Eventually, there is no separate learning to learn *course*. Every teacher is skilled in the methods, there is an assessment and reporting system which reinforces the student outcomes we seek, parents are involved, students know and understand more about their responsibilities in learning and the school recognises the worth of a well thought through systematic whole school approach.

	Spread				
Intent	**Pedagogy**	**Knowledge**	**Attributes**	**Skills**	**Experience**
A well thought through systematic whole school approach with all staff trained and involved	Common, well informed understanding of and approach to learning design	Students and their teachers can apply learning to learn knowledge in different contexts in and out of school	All students, teachers and the wider school community understand and use the 5R's	All students use a variety of thinking tools and can explain their choice	Progressively demanding independent research activity with authentic outcomes built into the timetable
	All teachers applying a balance of well considered teaching methods	Learning protocols – team working, coaching, peer assessment, research strategies – are consistently applied across the school	5R's built into lesson success criteria and used to observe against	All teachers know, understand and use a range of meta-cognitive interventions	There is a balance of learning to learn opportunity: some discrete lessons, some use of the approach in subjects, themed events, days or weeks
	Students are encouraged to co-construct		The Electronic Learner Passport is used to assess work against the 5R's	Electronic Thinking Tools and Electronic Learning Wall is part of the virtual learning environment	There is a Web 2.0 L2L school community
	Whole school processes are in place and are successful	The school community shares a language of learning	Rewards system reinforces 5R's	Students can independently conduct purposeful peer review sessions	Lead Learners are an active component of student voice

| | Spread (cont.) | | | | |
Assessment	Reporting	Staffing	Progression	CPD	Evaluation
Tracking of 5R's built into Electronic Learner Portfolio (L2 Passport) Students applying self and peer assessment skills face to face and electronically Outcomes from electronic profiling used to inform target setting Students more active in recording evidence	5R's are used to report to parents 5R's reporting is across all learning experiences Parents are using the 5R's at home A high percentage of parents regularly access the online support programme (PAL) via the school website	Time and space is used flexibly All staff have experience of the learning to learn approach The 12 essentials are integral to what the school does Thematic, enquiry and student led 'events' provide opportunities for the school community to evidence learning to learn	All phases of the L2 approach Independent learning is evidenced through the enquiry approach which allows proper space and time to exhibit KAS There is a hosted environment with a range of sophisticated electronic learning tools	Ongoing development around the 12 essentials Mini-research groups reporting Learning to learn team meeting regularly Lesson observation outcomes integrated back into development Learning to learn support now in an electronic environment	SLT have the approach as a standing agenda item Home learning remains integral to learning to learn External accreditation in place Ongoing monitoring and evaluation is fully aligned to inspection criteria and is helping to inform future thinking

The school experience of the 12 essentials

L2L Essential 1: Three dimensional success criteria

Creating a coherent approach to learning outcomes in three dimensions shifts staff thinking across the whole school. In the schools where we have worked the instigation of success criteria for each lesson has, in itself, succeeded in pushing teachers towards clearer thinking about outcomes and this sometimes goes beyond lesson planning, for example, departmental meetings which agree on broad outcomes before looking in detail at any agenda items. In schools where they go further and insist on three dimensional success criteria we see more questioning of decision making processes via *what*, *how* and *why* questions.

There is always a tension between respecting the professional freedom of individual teachers to instigate learning based on their own accumulated experience and insight versus the benefits of an across the piste approach. The judgement is made more complex when you are faced with a mixed ability and mixed motivation community of teaching staff which is, in some instances, led well and in others led very badly. Formulaic solutions are inherently problematic. That said, some interventions, judiciously made, have an exponential value: we believe consistency in the use of success criteria to be one of those interventions.

Take something which appears small: terminology. There are a plethora of terms used in various ways to describe the final 'product': learning intentions, outcomes, consequences, skill, success criteria, competence, attainment level, capability. Each provides a recipe for confusion. Stick to one agreed set of terms and use it throughout. Simplify it down as far as possible so that everyone – students, staff, parents and other adults – has an easy understanding. Now use the same success criteria – this is what we will learn (do); this is how we will do it; here is how we benefit – for every school process. Use the criteria to test each decision.

L2L Essential 2: Process sensitivity

Encourage staff to become process detectives – remember this is our Trojan mouse! Invite reflection on the processes used to arrive at decisions. How do we make choices which affect the learning of our students? If we ask them to take responsibility in our classrooms do we provide them with any responsibility in the bigger questions which affect their learning?

At the macro and micro levels, scrutinising decision making processes provides a radical challenge to integrity. Every decision needs to stand up to the core purpose test: How will this decision help us fulfil our core purpose?

An enquiry, rather than advocacy, based decision making culture allows you to ask hard questions around core purpose. Hard questions provoke discussion and debate and make people feel slightly uncomfortable in doing so. This is no bad thing. It's the dissonance which can arise when what we say is not consistent with what we do. Here is a sample of some hard questions:

- Are our lessons worth behaving for?
- Do students understand and value success criteria?
- Whose welfare is most important to us?

- As a staff what do we celebrate with most enthusiasm?

- What do we want our learners to leave with?

- Do we know what great learning looks like?

- In school, what do we spend our time talking about?

- Who are our staff role models? Why?

- Do we accept well intentioned failures? If so, why?

- Where does the comfort of staff sit relative to the needs of students?

- Who owns the standards – the individual teacher or the school?

L2L Essential 3: Learner behaviours that are well defined

If we have consensus on what it is we want our students to know, how we wish them to be and how we want them to think, we can design an approach to help us deliver these things. We, as educationalists, can design systems which can help students to become better at learning. To do so we need first to have agreed on the outcomes we seek, then we need to provide a curriculum and a set of experiences to deliver those outcomes. For each of the broad outcomes we seek it is important to break them down further and isolate any under-pinning features – so, for example, if we want to develop 'responsible' learners what do we mean by that?

Responsible means different things to different people. For one teacher, it may mean 'doing what I told you to do', for another it may mean 'following the school rules' and for another it may mean 'showing initiative'. So it's important to nail it down. In the context of learning to learn and for us it means 'looking after yourself and others', so the responsible learner knows right from wrong and makes good choices, manages him or herself, helps others and plans ahead.

If we assume too loose or too flexible a definition then we inhibit the opportunity for progression in student understanding. If it seems fairly straightforward for a teacher to develop 'responsible' learners then think again. The first feature is that 'the responsible learner knows right from wrong and makes good choices'. If we open this up we could ask about 'knowing right from wrong' *for whom* and *in what circumstances*? What would then be a 'good' choice? It becomes important for the teacher to help students by engaging them in discussing the complexities of being guided by these learning attributes. This means revisiting the discussion over time and after different lessons have played their part in adjusting the students' experience.

Learning will be enhanced when we get specific about what constitutes great learning behaviours. Being specific helps students revisit learning experiences and make worthwhile comparisons. It helps students measure progress because the before and after differences are not so far apart. Learning to learn experiences should not be random and unplanned. Progression of experience needs to be thought through carefully. To help the students, they need to have strong sense of structure or, *nearly but not quite the same*. Near-sameness helps the learner plant stakes and measure out progress.

A school wishing to promote a set of competencies or skills, or in our case the 5R's, must ensure that they are well understood, that there is a shared starting point or definition, that they are revisited (hopefully in variety of contexts), debated and discussed by students as to what they might mean in practice, that opportunities for them to be seen being used are found and, finally, that the competencies or skills are capable of being built upon through experiences which have what we call 'near-sameness'.

In the midst of this, if the school strategy to develop competencies or skills includes the tracking of student experience, care is needed to keep the exercise within reason. There is a potential problem which can lurk up ahead like an iceberg: run into this and it can puncture all your good intentions below the waterline.

If we have five attributes or R's which we consider essential and each 'R' has four underpinning features, that's 20 features to consider. If we wish to stake out progress and pay respect to the principle of near-sameness that must be at least three progressions, possibly more. With three progressions, let's say A, then B, then C, we have a possible seven positions: up to A, A, between A and B, B, between B and C, C, beyond C. Seven possible positions for 20 features leaves us 140 potential assessment points and a large headache. That's demanding enough. However, the QCA has six Personal Learning and Thinking Skills (PLTS). Each has six sub-categories with one having seven; that's a total of 37 sub-categories for a teacher to consider. Give them three progressions and we have a possible 259 separate boxes which could be ticked. That's what could be called a big ask!

Whilst it's desirable to monitor progress against the outcomes we seek, it's unreasonable to turn teachers into auditors and ask them to spend large amounts of time ticking checklists. A balance is required otherwise the real learning opportunity will be lost. For us the real learning opportunity lies in layered discussions around the student experience. What this means is that students, parents and carers, teachers and other influencers can have structured and purposeful dialogues around each of the 5R's.

Students can gather evidence and reflect on that evidence as it appears in their paper based learning passport or, if it's in the Electronic Learning Portfolio (L2 Passport), tag the 5R's as they are used. Parents can learn about the 5R's through the Parents as Learners (PAL) programme on the school website, download and follow shared activities with their children. Teachers can plan learning experiences and lessons with

built in 5R's tracking so that each lesson builds on what went before. Schools can observe classroom teaching to itemise the extent to which the 5R's are actively developed.

On a more mundane level, placing definitions in the staff handbook, the student planner or homework diary, which are then replicated in posters in each classroom acts as a reinforcer. We don't have to spend time denoting each and every progression to know that we are being successful.

L2L Essential 4: Language of learning

In schools we want to create more opportunities for students to be able to express their views on their progress, doing so in an informed way, and also be able to sit what they do at school in the wider frame of personal ambition and aspiration. Through a combination of the use of tools – some of which are very simple – utilised to provide a structured record of formal and informal learning with a variety of occasions for students to talk to others, we can build confidence, reinforce their view of themselves as self-directing learners and continue all the while to build their vocabulary.

In our primary schools' Building Bridges learning to learn programme, we use a very simple Learner Passport. We take the idea of the children being on a learning journey where there are countries to be visited. A country can be visited lots of times. The more times you visit, the more familiar you become with the country. With each visit the passport is stamped.

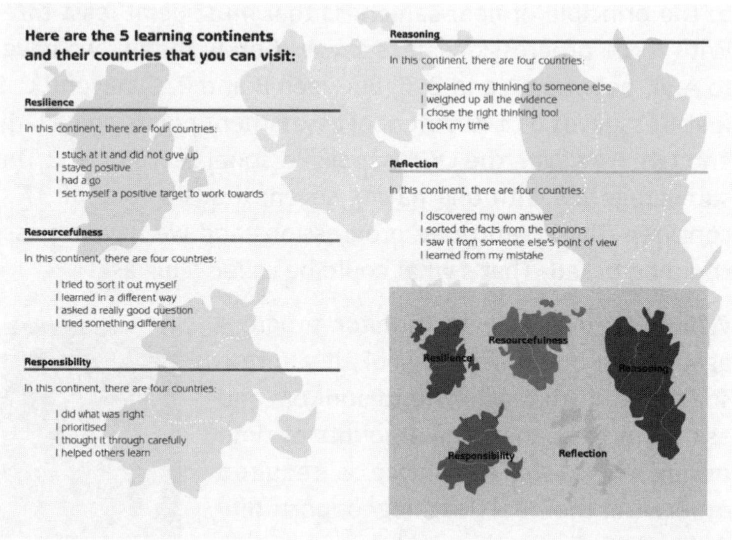

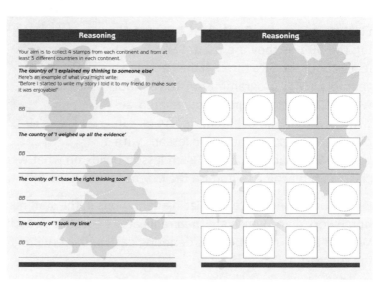

Figure 3. Primary Learner Passport

Because we are looking for evidence that the country has actually been 'visited' we might ask the primary children to talk us through the details. To help this along we encourage the pupil to take the passport with them at home and at school. At the end of the week we would go through a review process. Children would sit in pairs to go through the 'evidence', asking questions, perhaps using the Kipling Question prompts:

*I have six honest
serving-men
(They taught me all I
knew);
Their names are **What**
and **Why** and **When**
And **How** and **Where**
and **Who***

Then in groups doing the same process and then as a whole class we would gather up good examples of how a pupil plans to use their learning and how they might do things differently and better next time

Figure 4. Evidence page from the Primary Learner Passport

around. Should the school have consultation sessions with the parents or carers, the passports would always be used as a tool to help the child structure their thinking.

In primary classrooms, Success Mats are also used to build vocabulary as well as teach process skills. In Figure 5, the Success Mat helps introduce pupils to peer assessment and has four components. The first is a process which pupils in pairs are encouraged to follow. It is positioned in the centre of the mat so that it is noticeable. The process is simple, one of many, and takes the pupil through five steps. On the left hand side are tips, again no more than five, and on the right are some ideas to try out which we have called tools. Along the bottom, we list the simplest of assessment vocabulary.

The laminated A3 Success Mat is drawn from a bank of mats on different topics, placed between the pupils or in the middle of a table for a group, referred to and used as a resource to prompt thinking and discussion. Some schools create their own based on our simple model. We have also designed electronic interactive versions which are used by the teacher and displayed on a whiteboard or on a screen for impact.

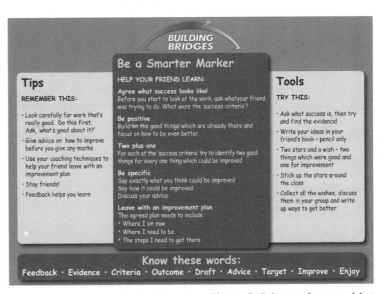

Figure 5. Primary Success Mat

For older students, we have Success Mats in Coaching, Team Working, Asking Really Good Questions, Independent Enquiry, the Learning Cycle and Presenting Skills (see Figure 6). Each of these Success Mats has an electronic and a paper based version. Through their use students become more attuned to process and will talk confidently using accurate descriptors. Because they are such simple generic resources they provide opportunities for the skills to be transferred into different disciplines and to be used in informal learning situations.

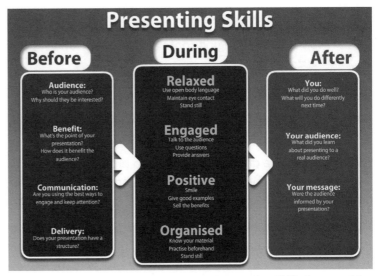

Figure 6. Presenting Skills Success Mat

L2L Essential 5: Systematic debriefing and reporting

If we take care to define the knowledge, attributes, skills and experiences that we want our learners to leave with, and the delivery of this combination is driving our core purpose, how do we know if we are being successful? How do we assess a student's progress in achieving them?

One of the most succinct and readable summaries of these issues was the *Developing and Accrediting Personal Skills and Competencies: Report and Ways Forward*, published in the UK by Futurelab on behalf of the QCA in 2007. It talks of the power of skills and competencies to transform:

> *What is clear is that the acquisition of skills and competencies was often seen to require new relationships between teachers and students, a greater focus upon personal development and progress against individual goals, and an increased emphasis upon formative, personalised and ipsative assessment practices.*[50]

The authors argued for a new set of assessment principles in the context of developing personal skills and competencies. Assessment, in their view, should:

- provide a stream of easily understood and relevant information
- be integrated into learning processes
- be sensitive to context and complexity
- promote self-worth and development
- be meaningful to and owned by learners
- act as a bridge and currency between learners and diverse communities
- enable multiple comparisons and lenses
- recognise collaboration
- be flexible and evolutionary
- be responsive to changing context/knowledge and subject domains
- be manageable by students and teachers.

This is as good a summary as we would be capable of providing and so it is worth using the most significant elements of it to ask what each might mean in a learning to learn approach and, of course, if there is anything missing from the list.

Assessment, to be of real value needs to provide *a stream of easily understood and relevant information* which is timely, is in the hands of the right person(s) and is capable of being actioned.

For assessment to *be integrated into learning processes* there needs to be a shared grammar which allows teacher and student to be in dialogue about the same things. For peer and group assessment to occur in any meaningful way there would need to be some basic skills training for students on how to give, receive and act on feedback. We use our Questioning, Coaching, Marking and Goal Setting Success Mats as an integral part of learning of these processes.

Assessment which is *sensitive to context and complexity* is conducted in such a way as to be developmental but challenging. Some experiences, like some products, are inherently more difficult to evaluate and pass judgement on. By planning for structured triangulation in assessment – self evaluation, teacher evaluation and peer evaluation – in a safe yet challenging learning environment, and with participants who are clear about success criteria, we preserve integrity.

Assessment which does not *promote self-worth and development* is not worthwhile assessment in our view. High stakes testing can, some say has, lead to a diminution of formative assessment. The Primary Assessment, Curriculum and Experience (PACE) project, a longitudinal study that followed a cohort of primary school pupils for eight years starting before the introduction of national tests for 7-year-olds, found that after the introduction of the tests, teachers' own classroom assessment became more summative.[51]

Assessment should be *meaningful to and owned by learners*. It is impossible to commit to the latter part of this aspiration, other than offer that students should be actively involved in as many component features of the process as is practicable. It will never be wholly 'owned' by the learners. Without reference to the Secretary of State it would be difficult to remove a requirement for assessment, but given that it takes place it should do so in a way that is of mutual value. Meaningful feedback that can be actioned and integrated into planning is key to this; so is what is done with advice and guidance. Our assessment model builds in personalised student guidance and target setting; it is complemented by the use of an electronic portfolio – the L2 Passport – where students create an inventory of their work annotated by the comments of others.

If assessment is to *act as a bridge and currency between learners and diverse communities* then it must be easily understood, easily accessed and be enabling for the learner. By using a range of opportunities, some of which are face to face, others of which are electronic, assessment which permeates the learning experience will *enable multiple comparisons and lenses*. It will, however, be important for the individual student that advice and guidance becomes coherent and provides a sense of progression. Too much advice, or advice which is conflicting, requires space and time to be worked through.

Any meaningful assessment which attempts to develop skills of working with and on behalf of a team or group ought to have mechanisms built in to *recognise collaboration*, or more specifically the nature of contributions made in collaborative work. Contributions could be face to face but also, in an age of wikis and online simultaneous gaming, be remote and electronic.

The best assessment systems derive from well considered principles but retain some capacity for growth – they need to be *flexible and evolutionary.* This is particularly so when they have to work across different subjects, in and out of school and in formal and informal learning. Obvious examples are assessing work experience, contributions to 'learner challenge days', voluntary or paid part time work. In such cases assessment must be *responsive to diverse context/knowledge and subject domains.*

Finally, and it is worth saying again, any assessment system worth investing in *must be manageable by students and teachers.*

L2L Essential 6: Coherent structure to learning

The 4 stage accelerated learning cycle of Connect–Activate–Demonstrate–Consolidate is a coherent model of learning. Its use provides the school community with a mechanism for sharing understanding about the component processes of learning. By planning all classroom lessons and many of the other learning experiences using a common framework it allows students, staff and parents to talk the same language. There are obviously other models but we favour this one for its simplicity.

1. **Connect**

   Connect to the learning and to the students' understanding. Provide an introductory experience which simultaneously provokes thinking, challenges and connects what's gone before to what is to come

   i. **Outcomes**

      Share the outcomes at this stage. Use the three dimensional model: this is what we will learn, this is how will learn it and this is how we will benefit.

2. **Activate**

   Provide problems to be solved rather than information to be remembered, rehearsed and then regurgitated. Provide access to the information needed to begin to solve the problem or guidance as to where to look for it. If necessary, do so through an experience, a reading or viewing, authentic source or sources to get the process going: the more engaging the better.

3. **Demonstrate**

   Provide opportunities for learners to 'show they know' through several rehearsals and in multiple modes. Allow students to share what is being learned in a variety of groupings. Provide opportunities for peer and teacher feedback especially around learning process and about content improvement. Give learners the opportunity to construct their own meanings in a variety of group situations.

4. **Consolidate**

   Reflect on the success criteria: What has been learned? How have we learned? How will we benefit?

Our learning to learn lesson plans, which we call learning cycles, are all written for 60 minutes and are broken down into the 4 stage cycle. In an electronic format we build in tracking to the 5R's and include hyperlinks to all the resources. Teachers designing their own can customise the tracking should they wish and can hyperlink to any resource which is in a file format: video, audio, PDF or web-link. Coherence across the school is one of the great benefits of using a common learning design. It doesn't manacle the teacher because there is still a great deal of freedom within the structure.

L2L Essential 7: Engaging experiences

Designing engaging learning experiences is about creating a balance between the ability of the student and the level of challenge. Success in an activity should be almost out of reach for the student.

The US based academic Mihály Csíkszentmihályi developed a theory for this describing the moment as 'flow'.[52] It occurs when individuals are so involved in an activity which for them is deeply absorbing that time seems to fly by; no other incentive or reward is necessary because the experience is fulfilling enough. Csíkszentmihályi described flow as deep absorption in an activity that is intrinsically interesting. Flow occurs at the point of balance between the challenge inherent in the task at hand and the skills required to accomplish it. The challenge for the teacher is to shift students into the top right hand corner of the box below.

High-skills with low-challenge	High-skills with high-challenge
■ Challenges of learning are too few in relation to skills ■ Unable to identify how they can make the experience more challenging ■ Students disengage because they see little relevance in what they are asked to learn	■ Students generally feel that their skills and the challenges of the tasks they are asked to perform are in balance ■ These are the students that would frequently experience *flow*
Low-skills with low-challenge	**Low-skills with high-challenge**
■ Students feel apathetic about learning ■ They find themselves in situations where they have low skills and the tasks they are asked to perform are of low-challenge ■ These are students who tend to opt out because school work is inconsequential	■ Students are more likely to feel worried in learning situations because they have low confidence in their skills ■ The tasks they are asked to perform are perceived as too challenging ■ Students will challenge the task

Learning to learn should be the repository of engaging experiences. Under flow theory, the conceptualisation of student engagement is the culmination of concentration, interest and enjoyment, as opposed to boredom or apathy.[53]

L2L Essential 8: Thinking fluency

Visit a psychologist or counsellor for treatment and the expectation is that you begin to get better between the hours not during them. In our learning to learn approach we provide tools and techniques to support our suggested learning experiences. We do not want teachers and their students to 'do' the tool. We want them to be able to use a tool or a technique as and when it is appropriate. Doing the tool is a bit like taking a spanner to serve the pasta: because we've bought a nice new spanner, a tool of which we are proud, we mustn't blind ourselves to its limitations. The real learning can come between the spaces. We think that schools need to work hard to create those spaces and this requires:

■ Whole staff understanding of thinking approaches

■ Recognition of the integration of cognitive, meta-cognitive and affective domains

■ Provision of a variety of contexts

■ Opportunity for enquiry perhaps shaped by driving questions or what some call 'rich tasks'

▓ Time for debriefing and reflection built into learning

▓ Student reinforcers such as visuals, electronic tools, teachers modelling the use of techniques.

Thinking fluency is the ability to move between social or learning contexts and, when confronted by a dilemma, to choose to act appropriately. We hope that what guides the choices is shaped by experience and contributing to that experience will be opportunities we have provided to practise problem solving in or near to similarly 'real' situations.

Learning contexts might be formal or informal, in or out of school, high tech, low tech or no tech. Each requires a self-assurance borne of familiarity. A mind that recognises, anticipates and selects having done so many times before. When we teach the tool but only ever in one context we do the learner a disservice. Different contexts require constant re-adjustment.

L2L Essential 9: Team and personal challenge

We may not know what jobs will be available to young people ten years from now; we do not know what knowledge they require to ensure they will have a productive, lifelong career. But to the extent that teenagers have had experiences that demand discipline, require the skilful use of mind and body, and give them a sense of responsibility and involvement with useful goals, we might expect the youth of today to be ready for the challenges of tomorrow.

Mihály Csíkszentmihályi[54]

Many, maybe most of, our learning to learn lessons have a team or personal challenge built in. Often the structure is to start with individual and paired challenges which are modest but related to the wider topic before expanding the activity to group challenges. The characteristics of great challenges are: a degree of authenticity (perhaps a real solution to a real issue presented to a real audience); personal involvement (does it matter to me?); extended so it's not a one-off easily forgotten moment; at a level of difficulty which will stretch but not disable; and with time for a meaningful review.

L2L Essential 10: Co-operation skills

Clubs, team games and small group activities can, and do, foster co-operation skills but what's the benefit of co-operation? Why not encourage more competition? Isn't there too much fear of competition?

The two positions are not mutually exclusive. It is obviously worthwhile learning to collaborate towards a mutually beneficial goal. It happens in some form in most areas of life. One of the most interesting expressions of the dilemma posed by the conflict between self and mutual interest is in the prisoner's dilemma. The dilemma is along these lines:

> Two students are suspected of serious misconduct in school. However, the head teacher has insufficient evidence to punish them even though she knows of their guilt. She separates them both and then visits each of them to offer the same deal. If one 'squeals' on the other and the other remains silent, the squealer goes free and the one who keeps quiet receives a week's detention. If both remain silent, both are given one evening's detention. If each betrays the other, each receives a three night detention. Each

student must choose whether to squeal on the other or whether to remain silent. Each one is assured that the other would not know about the betrayal before the end of the investigation. How should they act?

We are not suggesting you do this, but you can see it's a classic tug between selfishness and selflessness. Researchers use this and similar dilemmas to explore the concept of co-operation. Co-operative behaviours include:

- listening – trying hard to understand the other's position

- envisaging – being able to see a mutual benefit

- forgoing – being prepared to give something up

- committing – doing it for real

- re-invigorating – looking at the relationship to make sure it's working.

What drives co-operative behaviour? There has to be a common interest, a likelihood that the consequences of collaboration will stick, an understanding of each other's motive based on previous experience and a willingness to give something up – if only temporarily. Then perhaps, co-operative behaviours might flourish.

L2L Essential 11: Independent enquiry

If you are going to take the time to develop independent learners then you must also find the time to allow them to practise being independent. We described independent enquiry earlier as a 'learner superhighway'. Many, maybe most, of the major national and international project initiatives detailed later in this book have an element of independent enquiry as an integral part of their offer. They vary in how they are presented, though there are obvious similarities: closed enquiry, negotiated enquiry and personalised enquiry; residential projects; progressive challenges; creative projects, research projects and rich tasks.

Independent enquiry is just that – an enquiry or investigation which is chosen by the individual and for which there is no given set of off-the-shelf solutions. At its worst it would be completely closed and teacher directed, without any sense of planning or structure and ending up in a tsunami of copying and pasting. At its best it would be completely open and would put the skills acquired in the learning to learn experience to the test.

At Cramlington Learning Village significant time is being given to a model of student enquiry which is, to some degree, open ended. Students are asked to pursue a line of enquiry inspired by a 'driving question' and to find, sort, organise and present a considered response.

Stimulus material is everywhere around us! A good example is one provided by Canadian singer Sarah McLachlan's 'World on Fire' video depicting global poverty. In the video made for $15 on a home movie camera she illustrates how she spent the $150,000 given to her for the video by the record company. The driving question would be, 'How do we begin to end world poverty?'

An Australian calling himself Juan Mann showed a video of himself on a street in Sydney with a large placard held above his head. On the placard it said 'Free Hugs'. The video showed how people on the street responded. The YouTube community responded with 27 million views worldwide. The driving question would be, 'What should be done to build trust amongst people?'

MadV's video 'One World', also posted on YouTube, asked viewers to write a simple statement on their hand and show it to the world. It was the most responded to video in its history with millions of young people sharing positive, highly moral messages shown on the palms of their hands. The driving question would be, 'What message is worth sharing with the world?'

Some other possible driving questions might include:

- Is the sky blue?

- Does competition make us better?

- Is there such a thing as love?

- Are wars inevitable?

- Can anyone win a talent show?

- Is it right to keep a pet?

- Can you have a happy school?

- Are humans greedy?

- Can we save the planet?

- Should we have zoos?

- Is knife crime endemic amongst young people?

- Should parents be limited to only one child?

- Will athletes continue to improve on world records?

- Is art a luxury?

- Is school the best preparation for life?

- Are some people born to succeed?

- Is there such a thing as a just crime?

- Can you ever overpay talent?

- Have books had their day?

- Are we all musical?

In the Cramlington model there are a number of characteristics of such driving questions which are at the core of a trans-disciplinary project. They list the desired features of the trans-disciplinary project as:

- A 'driving question' is anchored in a real world problem and open to a variety of solutions

- Opportunities for students to make their own active investigations that enable them to learn concepts, apply information and represent their knowledge in a variety of ways

- Collaboration among students, teachers and others in the community so that knowledge can be shared and distributed between the members of the learning community

- The use of ICT to aid research and support students in the representation of their ideas

- High levels of choice, advice and feedback

▓ Assessment which is public and celebrated

▓ Two or more disciplines are involved (trans-disciplinary).

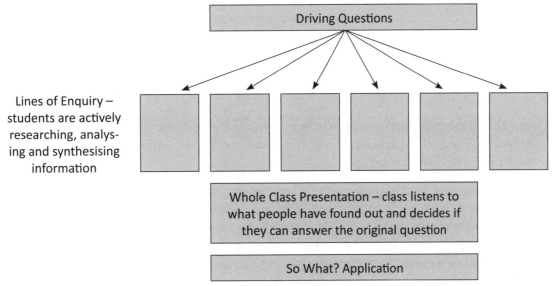

Lines of Enquiry – students are actively researching, analysing and synthesising information

Driving Questions

Whole Class Presentation – class listens to what people have found out and decides if they can answer the original question

So What? Application

Figure 7. Independent enquiry

The 'driving question' has a number of characteristics which make it powerful. Without these characteristics the level of challenge would be insufficient, so the question must be:

▓ open – in principle does not have one definite answer but several different ones (through which students' opinions can be valued)

▓ rich – important to understanding the world; impossible to answer without careful researching; tends to break up into sub-questions (lines of enquiry)

▓ charged – having an ethical dimension, and so likely to generate a range of strong emotions

▓ practical – a question about which information is available to students

▓ multi-disciplinary – needs two or more disciplines to answer.

A number of possible lines of enquiry arise from the driving question. The Cramlington model looks like the one in Figure 7.

Differentiation occurs in a number of ways. The Cramlington model suggests:

▓ The frequency and intensity of questioning, advice and feedback are obvious ways to differentiate

▓ Differentiation occurs through input of resources

▓ Remember that a real life problem may exist at the school, community, regional, national or global level so 'scale of problem' can be used for differentiation

▓ Through a real problem students can move outside the classroom and/or be introduced to a variety of outside sources or opinions – either real or virtual. This affords another opportunity to differentiate

▓ Assessment rubrics are differentiated with different levels of guidance from novice to expert level.

Progression is possible by scaling the challenge. Their list suggests:

- Increasing authenticity – its scope and scale

- Increasing complexity – projects can be increasingly complex by making them multi-dimensional, requiring students to probe, search and connect ideas, information and resources. We can build in requirements (through our rubrics) for higher order thinking skills such as analysis, synthesis and evaluation

- Increasing command of resources – extending the usual definition of resources to embrace human, community and expert resources

- Increasing the degree of co-construction – ultimately students could design the project with you, set their own quality standards for presentations, write their own rubrics and facilitate their own debriefing.

On a practical note this approach will be used with a total of 700 13 and 14-year-old students. Students work on authentic and engaging projects driven by the rich questions described above, they have access to and learn from 'experts' in the community or from visits to local amenities, and present their learning to a live audience at the end. Every Wednesday afternoon will be devoted to this sort of learning. Students can choose to either work on-site or at home. The Project Wednesday cycle will repeat several times over the course of the year.

In order to get this right, senior staff from Cramlington visited 15 different Australian schools which specialised in enquiry based learning. As you can see it's more than just sending students to the library with a worksheet!

L2L Essential 12: System rigour

For any learning to learn approach to have worth it needs to have significant leadership support. There are certain minimum requirements which take it out of the ghetto of 'timetabled last, staffed last, roomed last and resourced last' and into an approach which will have legs.

We would expect any learning to learn, skills or competencies based approach to feature in the school development plan and to have a designated member of the senior leadership team taking responsibility for its day-to-day oversight. Progression and focus in the form of three to five year planning are vital with a clear expression of what it is and isn't so that there are levels of accountability built in. Support is anticipated, planned for and budgeted. Staff teams are given time and space to meet, evaluate what they do and plan for improvement. The approach is visible in that it is actively promoted. It has a presence and senior staff are involved. It is talked about and promoted amongst the school community, the e-newsletter gets sent, the blog is updated regularly and the television screens in the foyer describe the theme of the week.

Finally, when a programme is accredited, when staff are expected like any other subject discipline to provide home learning and when it is reported to parents, it gains life.

The 12 essentials	Sample whole school intervention	Whole school behaviours	Whole school strategy	Whole school benefit
Three dimensional success criteria	CPD to develop use of briefing and debriefing	All staff reflecting on better use of success criteria	Use of the same structure for all learning opportunities – including meetings	Clarity over learning processes used to secure benefits
Process sensitivity	Use of students as Lead Learners	Students in each year group are trained to facilitate a process	Student roles are recognised across the school	Entire school community is more aware of different ways of learning
Learner behaviours which are well defined	Use of 5R's as part of assessment	All staff create reports	Outcomes are reviewed to see where there are generic areas for development	Shifts focus away from exams and content coverage
Language of learning	Prominent display of learning vocabulary	Learning word of the week	Glossary of terms in school planner, homework diary and website	More 'informed' student reviews
Systematic debriefing and reporting	Parent sessions on the 5R's	5R's discussed with parents as part of reporting and consultation	Reporting systems now include 5R's	Practical involvement of parents more likely
Coherent structure to learning	All lessons planned using the same learning model	Shared lesson planning software based on agreed model	Shared resources, feedback and reporting systems	Increased co-operation between staff with more effective use of time

cont.

The 12 essentials	Sample whole school intervention	Whole school behaviours	Whole school strategy	Whole school benefit
Engaging experiences	CPD used to explore alternative opportunities to enrich learning	Reflective practitioners in problem solving groups	Sustained and planned programme of staff development attached to accreditation	Better all round learning
Thinking fluency	All classrooms have 'learning walls'	Teachers use the wall as a prompt and resource	Contents of the wall are replicated in staff handbook, student planner, website and other public spaces	Provides a simple baseline of easily applied thinking tools
Team and personal challenge	Personal challenge week	Students negotiate challenges which will motivate them	Student involvement debriefed daily using Learning Passports and 5R's	Whole community performances on conclusion of week
Co-operation skills	Time given for development of skills	School identifies the core co-operation skills to be developed	Lesson time extended across the school	Fewer transitions and more attention to quality of learning
Independent enquiry	Thematic approach to the curriculum combined with more imaginative use of time to allow for independent enquiry	Subject areas planning together	Major curriculum review	Refreshes thinking about the what, how and why of learning

The 12 essentials	Sample whole school intervention	Whole school behaviours	Whole school strategy	Whole school benefit
System rigour	Learning to learn is given prominence	Senior staff involvement	Key feature of school development planning with resource attached	Acts as a lever for improving all round learning behaviours amongst staff and students

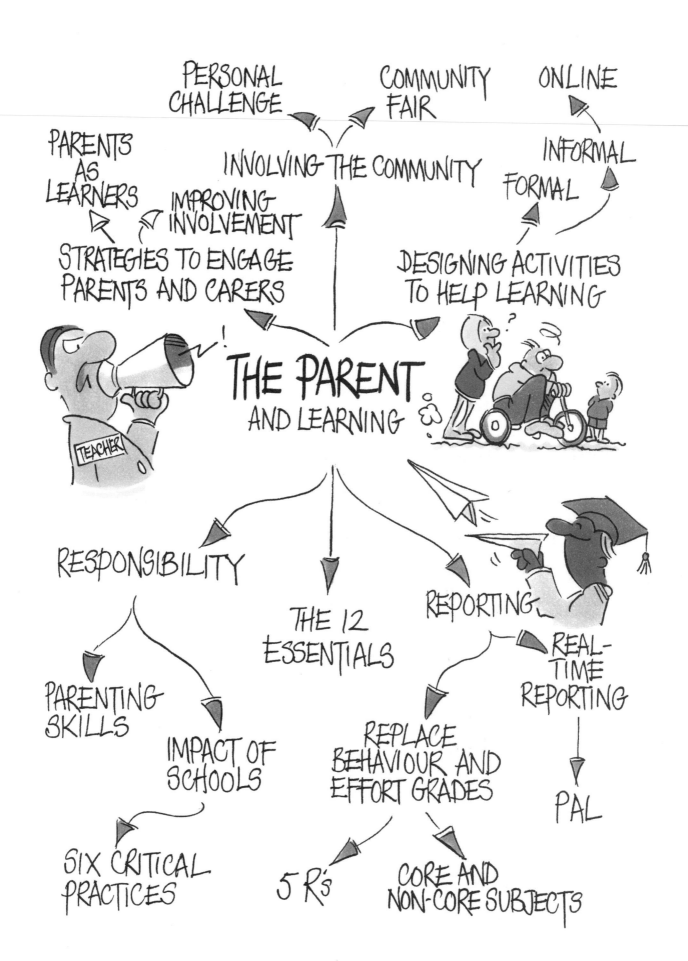

PERSONAL CHALLENGE

COMMUNITY FAIR

ONLINE

PARENTS AS LEARNERS

INVOLVING THE COMMUNITY

INFORMAL

IMPROVING INVOLVEMENT

FORMAL

STRATEGIES TO ENGAGE PARENTS AND CARERS

DESIGNING ACTIVITIES TO HELP LEARNING

THE PARENT AND LEARNING

TEACHER

RESPONSIBILITY

THE 12 ESSENTIALS

REPORTING

REAL-TIME REPORTING

PARENTING SKILLS

IMPACT OF SCHOOLS

REPLACE BEHAVIOUR AND EFFORT GRADES

PAL

SIX CRITICAL PRACTICES

5 R's

CORE AND NON-CORE SUBJECTS

Responsibility **Parents** Community Diversity
Reporting **PAL** Designing **Activities** Rifles
Effort and Behaviour Grades
Direct **Personal Challenge Week**
Parenting Style

6. The parent and learning

In this chapter we:

▪ Ask questions about responsibility

▪ Provide strategies for involving parents and carers

▪ Introduce Parents as Learners (PAL)

▪ Examine the parent and community experience of the 12 essentials

▪ Provide an alternative to effort and behaviour grades

▪ Explain how Personal Challenge Week works.

And ask the following questions:

▪ What do we have to do to involve parents?

▪ How I do engage meaningfully with a diverse community?

▪ Can I get more from my community involvement?

▪ What improvements can I make to reporting?

Responsible citizens

There's a lot of great learning that takes place formally and in school and maybe much more that takes place informally and out of school. During all the years that I went to school my parents didn't. They helped me become a learner but not by going to the school. The research tells us that parental involvement in learning activities 'in the home' is closely associated with being smarter, particularly when we are young. Parental involvement in school, helping out, going to meetings, listening to teachers tell you how your child is doing, confers little or no real benefit on the individual child. As the child gets older, the impact of parents on school achievement diminishes. At the age of 15 what's going on in school is more important. There's a bit of a job to be done to help parents help their children, and to help schools marry up to life – but maybe it's always been that way.

> From the standpoint of the child, the great waste in school comes from his inability to utilise the experience he gets outside ... while on the other hand, he is unable to apply in daily life what he is learning in school. That is the isolation of the school – its isolation from life.[55]

After about the third time of my eye being hit by the sight of the rifle it started to swell and close up. It was becoming difficult for me to see the target 300 yards away and the tears and the drizzling rain were not helping. I was starting to tire. The barrel of the Lee-Enfield .303 was becoming harder and harder to keep steady. Each time I pulled the trigger the full force of the gun was thudding back into my shoulder. It was powerful, a gun of the type used in the First and Second World Wars with a range of over 600 yards: potentially deadly. I'd been out there firing for nearly an hour before I shot my final round. It was to be the last round I ever fired in anger. I was 15 years of age.

I was only a young boy. I was part of a team from Scotland competing at the National Rifle Championships in Bisley, Surrey. We were from a small town on the edges of the Highlands where everyone knew everyone else's business. To get to the competition, we had travelled overnight on a rail sleeper from Edinburgh Waverley, one adult and four youths. We came with 300 rounds of .303 ammunition and four rifles hidden – for security purposes – in a golf bag with a towel over the top. We lugged the guns, the bolts and the ammunition across the London Underground, and took a train out through the suburbs to Surrey. Nowadays we would have been arrested before we got to the bus stop!

As an adult over 30 years later I am amazed at how little we thought of going fully armed on a train down to the nation's capital. Four young boys and a 54-year-old man, who as it happens, was my father. We went out, shot against adult teams in a national competition, did our best and came home. No big deal.

As Air Cadets, the following week, we would be gliding or powered flying or orienteering or playing football: again, no big deal. Most I ever learned of lasting value took place within those years of my life. It was a time of finding responsibility, discovering independence, coping, team working, learning new skills and practising them – all of it at the weekend or on Monday or Thursday nights at the Drill Hall. School couldn't compete with this rich feast, so I didn't go very much.

Then as now if you wanted to get a Double First from Oxford, Edinburgh or St Andrews you had to go to school. Once you were at school you had to knuckle down and conform. That wasn't to be my lot. In the last two years of my secondary schooling I went fishing, played snooker, set off on bus trips and listened to records at a girlfriend's house. Curiously the school never seemed to know I wasn't there.

School at that time in Scotland had taught me stuff. Some of it was OK, and there were teachers who did their best for me, but most of the time it wasn't OK. Stuff wasn't what was to help me subsequently. What helped me most was developing the confidence to take risks, to travel to unknown places, to have conversations with strangers, to tolerate and learn from failure, to appreciate the beauty of experience and always know you could inch forward by degrees.

My own parenting moved between authoritarian and authoritative but by 15 it was, through no fault of either parent, in disarray. In studies of parenting styles three generic types are talked about. They are permissive, authoritarian and authoritative. Authoritative seems to work better. We know that there's a powerful association between parental involvement and student achievement and attainment but we also know that's largely shaped by the nature of the relationships at home. Schools cannot change home circumstances but we can have a small influence on some of what goes on there. Parents who can have positive relationships as a consequence of being better informed about their child's learning, and so have an inkling of when and when not to attempt to help with it, will be more likely to break a vicious circle of low expectation and ill preparedness. As far as the home is concerned, it seems it is expectation – communicated through everyday interactions, comments about the value of education, sharing of war stories and the like – which more than social class, income or educational background impacts on a child's attainment.

In a recent publication on engaging parents and schools the authors boldly stated that 'developing and sustaining effective partnerships between the home, the community and the school is, without question, the most important component of school improvement'.[56]

Another researcher in the field[57] identified six critical practices for schools to put in place:

- Help parents with ideas to establish a positive learning environment at home
- Improve communications about school programmes and student progress
- Encourage participation and volunteering at school
- Give ideas to help with learning activities at home
- Involve parents in school decision making and governance
- Provide parents with access to community resources that increase students' learning opportunities.

In a meta-study of parenting styles where ten separate studies involving 24,826 families were scrutinised the findings showed high expectations correlated to enhanced achievement. Students' perceptions of parental expectation correlated to achievement and perhaps even more important than the expectation itself, authoritative parenting seemed most effective.[58] We take the view that it would be a good thing for schools to help parents and carers better understand how their child learns and what, if anything, they can do to help. In one study, a meta-analysis of 29 studies over a ten year period, the academic achievement of students in 91% of the groups where parents were involved in training programmes was superior to that of students in the control groups.[59] This seems to chime with our own instinctive response.

PAL – a strategy for involving parents and carers

Our own learning to learn programme for parents and carers we call Parents as Learners or PAL. It comes in two formats, both of which are electronic – one in which an agency such as a school or a Local Authority runs parent sessions and the other where the parent accesses it direct. The latter is usually sited on a school website as part of a parent portal. The thinking behind PAL is that most parents or carers want to help their child but don't always know how to, many are time poor and some are fearful of the institution and won't respond to any formal invites no matter what font appears on the letter.

We wanted to try our very best to create something which would appeal to the parent who needed lots and lots of encouragement. We knew it had to be easily accessible, contemporary in look and feel, with minimal – if any – reading and writing and capable of being translated into the most prevalent languages after English in UK schools.

There would always be a tension between an experience which anyone with any level of education could and would want to access, and being patronising. We didn't need an online masters degree in parenting but at the same time we wanted to make it useful to as wide a group as possible. The experience we had in developing an online programme is one worth sharing. Take as many of our ideas as are useful to you! Should you wish to organise a programme of sessions for parents our current session outline may help you get started with your planning.

Each of the 20 sessions can be delivered as a group session of 40 minutes. Parents accessing PAL directly log in and can then graze for as long as they like. The features which we decided upon included structured sessions planned around our 4 stage learning cycle. Each session had a variety of activities designed to ease the parent into and through the topic. Use our sessions to help you plan your own.

What you need to know about learning:

- Then and now
- Knowing your child
- How your child learns
- Helping your child be a better learner.

Developing a love for learning:

- What makes a great learner
- Overcoming obstacles
- Help your child succeed
- Learning in your family.

Key skills for learning:

- Planning and preparation
- Gathering information
- Asking great questions
- Organising thinking.

Positive parenting:

- Knowing your parenting styles

- The basics of self-esteem

- Building self-esteem

- Family values.

Testing times:

- Understanding marks and grades

- Preparing for exams

- Revision techniques

- Handling tests.

To build a sense of affiliation amongst our parent group we created 12 individuals with very different experiences of parenting. These 12 characters we assembled in a visual collage on our home page. By clicking on the individual you could listen on a short audio file to their take on parenting. These characters were our attempt to convey the diversity, complexity and messiness of parenting. It was our attempt to get away from 'teacher knows best' and to invite people of equal status to share their thoughts. The characters, who are entirely fictional, stimulate a great deal of discussion.

We also organised the resources so they were searchable through topic. This allowed parents to go at a different pace and in an order of their choosing. The topics included things like Family Life, Exams and Tests, Understanding Schools, Understanding Your Child, Skills for Learning, Motivating Your Child, Understanding Assessment, Help with Homework, Improving Behaviour and Better Communication.

For those parents who wanted to find a specific resource – such as a questionnaire, checklist, slide show, audio file or maybe even a poster for the fridge – we made it possible for them to go direct.

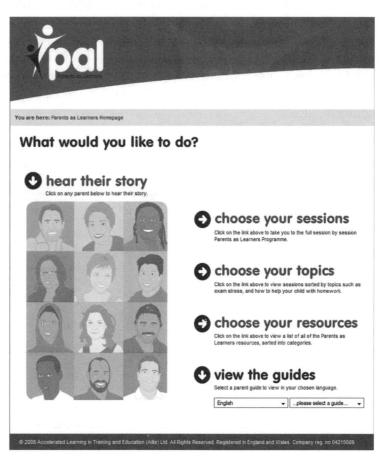

We also decided to produce simple one page A4 guides in 12 languages on core topics which every parent has anxieties over. These are downloadable and topics include: Healthy Living,

Staying Safe, Building Positive Friendships, Help with Home Learning, Help with Maths, Help with Reading, Internet Safety and several others. By putting them into Arabic, Bengali, Guajarati, Polish, Portuguese, Punjabi, Somali, Tamil, Turkish, Urdu and Welsh we hoped to make the learning to learn message more widely available.

Designing activities to help parents understand how to help their child learn

Your parent community may have significant numbers who do not have English as a first language, may have no or incomplete education, may not like the thought of 'being back at school' or may lack confidence, so designing resources to help them help their child is a complex task.

We wanted to encourage parents and carers to feel their experience is of value, make it safe for them to take time and share the detail of that experience so that we could then, collectively, extrapolate some shared learning from it. Designing a means of doing so was our first challenge.

From an early design stage we committed to creating case studies which could be woven into the fabric of the PAL experience and which became the life stories of a group of typical – and there is no 'typical' – parents who were struggling to have a full family life, whatever the configuration of their family, and help their child enjoy and be better at learning. Our 12 characters have different learning biographies: some had lots of education, others had little or none, some loved it, others couldn't leave quickly enough, some saw helping their child learn as the school's responsibility, some were guilty, others a little too forceful. The plan was to help parents, whether online or in a school hall, to feel that their issue was also someone else's.

The individual character's image has an audio file which sits underneath and is activated by a click. Once activated the character tells their story. We meet the character again and again and eventually some patterns emerge and inevitably, those parenting 'patterns' are seen to impact on the child.

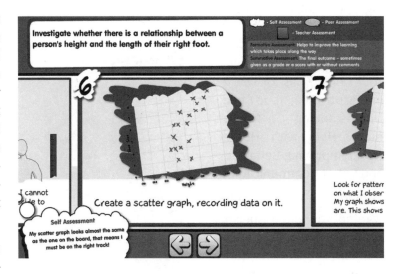

Some of the information which the parents and carers need is explanatory and to do with some of the detail of their children's classroom experience. This can arise because some things we do in schools are now counterintuitive and at odds with parental expectation of what schools do and should be doing. For example, assessment. The idea that their child may self assess or be assessed by another student can seem, on the face of it, almost to be dereliction of duty on the part of the teacher. Formative assessment needs some explanation at the general level before diving into the detail.

Providing interactive models which follow the separate timelines of a maths, English and a science assignment allows us to have a go at explaining the contribution self and peer assessment makes to learning. It also allows us to explain the difference between formative and summative assessment. By showing how their child is credited with drafting and redrafting, thinking things through for themselves but also checking it out with others, the parent can see that it's not about shortcuts to the correct answer. Knowing about the process gives an entry into helping their child.

We also wanted the parents and carers to be able to take specific things away from the PAL experience which would help them better understand their child and how they could help their child to learn.

This needs a gentle touch. It was best in our view to start with something which could be completed with the child and if necessary shared with the rest of the group. We say, if necessary, because there is a danger of parent sessions being hijacked by extended eulogies or by a Dutch auction of horror stories. Whilst this may be needed to get us going, what we really want is to move the dialogue on to learning and what is best done to help with it.

The 'How well do you know your child?' activity is one of many which could be used by a group facilitator or separately by a parent or carer sitting alongside their child. (Copies of 'How well do you know your child?' and the spinning wheel activity are provided on the CD which accompanies this book.)

The spinning wheel activity for encouraging discussion of approaches to practical problem solving

The electronic spinning wheel can be used in a group session on screen or by a parent accessing it remotely.

The wheel spins when it's clicked and then lands on an activity. You then discuss how you would go about the activity.

The activities are very simple and include things like doing a jigsaw, finding an address, cooking a meal, texting or wiring a plug.

Planning a special event

We would finish the session by applying what we have learned to our own child and ask, what does he or she do? How can we help them be better?

The differences which then emerge cluster around preparation, organisation, problem solving methods, motivation and task completion.

By discussing the process each of us favours to complete simple everyday activities we begin to uncover some personal differences. The fact that there are differences then leads into some further input on learning.

Tips for getting parents more involved with schools

Where students are enrolled as co-researchers and contribute to the process of engaging other students in finding out what would help parents liaise more closely with the school 'the potential for improving practice is greatly enhanced'.[60] Here are some of our thoughts about different strategies for increasing involvement.

- Send a personal invitation either via letter or e-mail or text message. You could also ask children to make an invitation for their parent or carer

- Consider the barriers that may exist and work to overcome them: for example, offer childcare or out of work sessions

- Provide appropriate refreshments

- Provide transport to and from the venue

- Encourage 'parent peer' support and peer recruitment

- Try coffee mornings

- Respite time with younger children being looked after

- Create teacher free zones

- Have sessions which are attractive because they don't appear to be like school – so a focus on healthy lifestyles and build in sessions on healthy diet, work–life balance, handling stress

- Invite them to bring a partner or friend along for support

- Take your programme to a 'neutral' ground such as a community centre, function room or leisure centre

- Translate your essential guidance documents into different languages

- Where necessary, offer sessions in other languages, and be sensitive to cultural differences (e.g. some cultures may consider it disrespectful to teachers to become involved in schooling issues)

- State that dress should be casual and comfortable to avoid parents feeling that they may not 'look the part'

- Consider gaining sponsorship so that parents can be rewarded for attending – supermarket vouchers, leisure centre vouchers, mobile phone vouchers or similar

- You have the facilities and expertise in your school to offer a wide range of interesting activities to your parents! Offer an incentive such as free computer training, use of sports facilities, textiles clubs or language tuition

- The most popular session run by one school for parents was 'How to make money on eBay.
- Separate male and female events
- Car club – building and racing model cars was how one school attracted lads and dads
- Grandmas and granddads event
- Create a class blog
- Focus sessions on helping with maths, helping with reading or helping with organisation and planning
- Help your child with …
- Provide parents with a learning to learn handbook: have your students write it
- Put a parent portal on your school website
- You said … we did!
- Damascus – Don't Assume Most Adults Still Can Understand School!

What do I do to get to 2?: a modern alternative to effort and behaviour grades

At Past Times High located towards the bottom end of Old Think Street in Any Town, UK, teachers still give effort and behaviour grades. Three times a year every one of the students is graded by every one of their teachers on the basis of what the teacher judges to be the net sum of their efforts and whether or not they have behaved sufficiently well to remain in the good books.

A score of 5 for effort means you are powering your way towards pupil of the year standard and a laminated plaque beckons. A 5 for behaviour means you are as good as gold and never a problem to the teacher. But, a score of 1 for effort means you are at Blackadder levels in your skulduggery and deviousness and, heaven forbid, a 1 for behaviour proves to all you are indeed a felon in all but name. A score of 3 in either of these categories means that the teacher is not quite sure who you are and is playing it safe as these grades are reported to parents.

Quite clearly Past Times High is an anachronism in an era where people use words like personalisation, assessment is for learning and the latest must-have is a bespoke virtual learning environment! Believe us, it happens and not just in our fictional Any Town. It happens in struggling comprehensives hidden in the midst of the most challenging estates; it happens in schools in shire towns where selection is by house price; it happens in grammar schools where they select; it happens in independent schools, state schools, primaries and secondaries. Stop doing this!

Have you stopped to think how useful these grades actually are to parents and students? If you score 1 for effort, where do you go from there? Do you really try harder and what does trying harder look like? If you score 1 for behaviour, which aspects of behaviour will you try to improve? How will you know you are making progress? *What do I have to do to get to 2?*

In our learning to learn journey schools we are working hard to help modernise reporting. In Cramlington Learning Village, one of our journey schools, they have replaced effort and behaviour grades with the 5R's: resilience, resourcefulness, responsibility, reasoning and re-flection. Mark, who is Deputy Head Teacher at the school, takes up the story:

Each of the 5R's is broken into four parts; for example, Resilient learning behaviour is broken down into the following parts:

▪ Stick at it

▪ Have a positive attitude

▪ Find and sustain interest in what you are doing

▪ Set targets and practise.

Each part has a statement describing what this looks like at bronze, silver and gold level. These statements describe growing independence from bronze to silver.

Bronze level 'sticking at it' is described as follows: 'You stick at some things for short periods of time. You are prepared to ask for help when things get difficult and then will have another go.' At gold level the same attribute is described thus: 'You stick at it until you have succeeded – if things are difficult you explore different ways to overcome this. You always finish what you started to a high standard.'

The grading system is as follows: 1 means a student is working towards bronze level, 2 means a student is at bronze level, 3 means working towards silver level statements, etc. By allocating a statement to each level students can see what they need to do differently and teachers can begin to have a dialogue with students around developing effective learning behaviours.

Click on a character for details of a parenting situation they are dealing with at the moment. In the box that appears you will see which of the 5Rs are needed to deal with this situation effectively. For more information on each of the 5Rs simply roll over the Rs to the left.

In the core subjects of maths, science, English, and humanities, teachers award a grade for each of the 5R's, three times a year for all Year 7 and 8 students. In non-core subjects a grade is awarded in Review One (end of term one) for just one of the R's, Responsibility

– we thought this was the most important one to focus on at the beginning of the school year and with a new cohort (Year 7). Also in non-core subjects, teachers don't see the students often enough to be able to grade each of the 5R's in any meaningful way. In Review Two (end of term two), non-core subjects report on Responsibility and Resilience, and in Review Three (end of year) all subjects report on each of the 5R's. The illustration below shows an example of a report to parents generated by the school's managed information system showing grades against the 5R's.

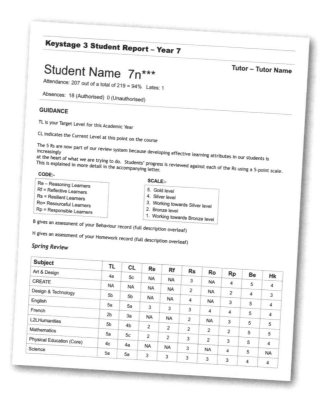

Keystage 3 Student Report – Year 7

Student Name 7n***   Tutor – Tutor Name

Attendance: 207 out of a total of 219 = 94% Lates: 1

Absences: 18 (Authorised) 0 (Unauthorised)

GUIDANCE

TL is your Target Level for this Academic Year

CL indicates the Current Level at this point on the course

The 5 Rs are now part of our review system because developing effective learning attributes in our students is increasingly at the heart of what we are trying to do. Students' progress is reviewed against each of the Rs using a 5-point scale. This is explained in more detail in the accompanying letter.

CODE:-

Re = Reasoning Learners
Rf = Reflective Learners
Rs = Resilient Learners
Ro= Resourceful Learners
Rp = Responsible Learners

SCALE:-

5. Gold level
4. Silver level
3. Working towards Silver level
2. Bronze level
1. Working towards Bronze level

B gives an assessment of your Behaviour record (full description overleaf)

H gives an assessment of your Homework record (full description overleaf)

Spring Review

Subject	TL	CL	Re	Rf	Rs	Ro	Rp	Be	Hk
Art & Design	4a	5c	NA	NA	3	NA	4	5	4
CREATE	NA	NA	NA	NA	2	NA	2	4	3
Design & Technology	5b	5b	NA	NA	4	NA	3	5	4
English	5a	5a	3	3	3	4	4	5	4
French	2b	3a	NA	NA	2	NA	3	5	5
L2LHumanities	5b	4b	2	2	2	2	2	5	5
Mathematics	5a	5c	2	2	3	2	3	5	4
Physical Education (Core)	4c	4a	NA	NA	3	NA	4	5	NA
Science	5a	5a	3	3	3	3	3	4	4

A letter goes out to parents explaining what each of the 5R's means and why the school thinks it is important for students to make progress in these attributes of effective learning. There is further explanation on the school's website (www.cramlingtonlv.co.uk) where there is a short video explaining how grades in each of the 5R's are determined.

Replacing effort and behaviour grades across the school took three years and was accomplished in a number of steps.

The first step was actually to create a progression matrix for each of the 5R's. This was done by creating statements at bronze, silver and gold level for each 'aspect' of each one of the R's which described growing independence. These were trialled in the first instance within the discrete learning to learn course.

The second step was to trial the process internally, with just the core subjects reporting on and getting used to the criteria, the data being analysed within the school.

The third step was to make the system part of the reporting to parents' schedule, which is where it really began to have teeth with both staff and students. As soon as we started to report to parents and it became part of the school's reporting system it moved from something we were trialling to something we had to take seriously. It began to underpin and support the school's learning to learn approach, and classroom practice had to shift to provide opportunities in lessons for teachers to have conversations with students about their learning.

We are in the first year of running the new system and have not completely replaced behaviour grades yet – some teachers were reluctant to 'let go' of this last remnant of 'old think'. We will move towards this over the next few years though as teachers and students become more confident with the 5R's and the criteria. As pedagogy continues to shift and we move to a more enquiry based curriculum there is increasing opportunity to have dialogue with students about their learning, and we will begin to make use of technology to move towards 'live' reporting – these things will help.

We need to make greater use of the data now and perhaps recreate our pastoral intervention teams around the 5R's. For example, we could focus on a group of students who have scored 2 or less for Resilience across a number of subjects over the course of the year – an intervention team could take this group of students off timetable for a week and work intensively around a Resilience programme which involves their parents. Similar 'interventions' could be developed around Responsible behaviour or 'becoming more Resourceful'. This would begin to personalise learning and target intervention at developing learning behaviours.

Our rewards system has also recently come in line with our approach to developing the 5R's across the school. Students receive 'stamps' in their student planners for Resilient behaviour or Reasoning behaviour, etc. The number of stamps is counted every two weeks and students can choose to cash them in for prizes (displayed in a glass cabinet at the front of the school) or 'stash' their stamps to be cashed in later for bigger prizes.

We need to continue to work on consistency with both the awarding of grades for the 5R's in our review system and with the stamping in students' planners within lessons, but we are already beginning to see benefits with both staff and students now talking about developing effective learning behaviours and our students (and parents) understanding what progress in these learning behaviours looks like, and what they need to do to get to the next level.

The parent and community experience of the 12 essentials

L2L Essential 1: Three dimensional success criteria

Many parents will have long since stopped asking their child 'What did you do at school today?' because being told 'nothing' is too dispiriting. This is not the fault of the school or the child but probably the fault of the question. A better question would prompt a more rewarding answer. How about 'What did you learn in school today?' With three dimensional success criteria you are more likely to get a sensible answer. In school the student is expected to be able to answer these questions: 'What will you learn?' 'How will you learn it?' 'How will you benefit?' They are good sensible prompts for any parent–child discussion. A parent can instantly get to the purpose of a home learning activity by asking these questions.

By focusing on 'benefits' the parent reinforces the message that learning is a productive worthwhile activity. The research affirms the worth of a home environment which is cognitively stimulating, with parental involvement in children's activities and high aspirations mediated through everyday behaviours.[61]

L2L Essential 2: Process sensitivity

I remember as a young man being introduced to the wonders of the internal combustion engine by my father, a skilled mechanic. His teaching method was to allow me to hang about long enough to become a nuisance and then put me to gainful activity on some mundane task. Then when a one-off moment such as the removal of the rocker cover arrived, I would be allowed to take part by degrees. Measuring tappets became a process of scientific precision. To learn it I had to watch him as he explained what he was doing in a sort of 'live' commentary. I then had to explain it back to him before I was allowed to start and as I undertook the task I too had to provide the running commentary and, in this way, he knew that I knew what I was doing. Years later I found out that this was called pole-bridging and I think it's a great way for any parent to help their child learn. Get them to talk it through aloud as they do it.

At the community level many an honest endeavour has run onto the rocks because of a lack of process understanding. I include amongst this the Schools Appeals Panel which lasted five times as long as it should have because the committee chair did not attend to the processes of the meeting; the village hall debate which ended in a near-fight because of naivety over protocol; and a rash decision by the playing fields committee because they were ignorant of an appropriate process to evaluate cost-benefit.

As our students and their parents become more sensitised to processes the benefits will spill out.

L2L Essential 3: Learner behaviours which are well defined

Using the 5R's at home is a great way to prove that real learning also occurs outside of school. Any shared endeavour which contains an element of challenge can stimulate thinking around the 5R's. To be frank your children will become bored of it eventually but not, we hope, before their behaviours have begun to be more positive.

L2L Essential 4: Language of learning

Talk to your children! The research work of Betty Hart and Todd Risley showed that by the age of 3 there were remarkable differences in the spoken vocabularies of children. Hart and Risley compared 42 families over a three year period analysing the words spoken between parents and child.[62] They compared professional, blue collar and welfare families. In their research by the age of 3 the child in the welfare family would have heard 8 million fewer words than the child in the professional family who would have been exposed to 11 million. At 3 years of age the spoken vocabularies of the children from the professional families were larger than the parents in the welfare families. The differences stuck and were closely linked with educational attainment later in life. Without language doors close and without a language to discuss learning then again, our gains will be limited.

An enhanced language of learning can change the nature of consultations with parents and carers. It can bring life to student mentoring. More importantly, it will act as an accelerant for dialogue around learning at home.

L2L Essential 5: Systematic debriefing and reporting

Once a parent has a more robust home-friendly report then he or she can use it more pro-ductively. For example around the 5R's there are some prompts:

- What are you most pleased with?
- Where do you think you can improve?
- What might you do differently next time?
- What steps will you take to improve?
- Let's think of a way to remove that obstacle?
- What one thing would make the biggest difference?

Once you have something like a report on the 5R's there are also some practical things which any parent can do to help their child directly.

To help your child be more resilient:

- Encourage them to complete a challenge even if it means coming back to it a few times
- Help them to stay positive by encouraging their efforts
- Share activities which reward sustained concentration such as board games
- Encourage them to set their own targets and practice.

To help your child be more resourceful:

- Explain to them that getting stuck is not a problem but staying stuck is
- Where possible, help them use different methods to do things
- Encourage their questions
- Remind them to involve others, including you if necessary, in learning.

To help your child be more responsible:

- Insist they take responsibility for organising themselves for school
- Help them with plans and to-do lists
- Give them the job of looking after someone or something
- Encourage them to think things through and weigh alternatives before jumping in.

To help your child be more reasoning:

- Ask them to explain their thinking
- Write down the pros and cons of any decision
- Encourage them to explain the thinking tools they use at school
- Delay a big decision.

To help your child be more reflective:

- Do things together which are out of the ordinary

- Raise their awareness of patterns and sequences – for example, events which led up to an argument
- Listen
- Share experiences you have had and what you learned from them.

L2L Essential 6: Coherent structure to learning

Parents will notice differences. The curriculum offer may be described in terms with which they are not familiar, the timetable may now comprise blocks of time used in a more imaginative variety of ways and reporting may now include more than the statutory progress report accompanied by the standard comment on effort and behaviour. As the school 'opens up' its new ways of working there will also be a need to explain some of these changes.

L2L Essential 7: Engaging experiences

Learning something new together is a great way to show a child how much you value learning.

L2L Essential 8: Thinking fluency

When students are confident enough in the use of thinking tools the ideas behind them can be shared at home. Avoid paper where possible – a thinking tool is not a worksheet so we don't want to reinforce a negative association. Thinking tools are intended to guide students away from unhelpful patterns of thinking; however, this can be undone at home. Everyday thinking mistakes include:

- Partial – too concerned to show authority
- Quick – too quick to judge
- Easy – too ready to generalise
- Vague – too blurred to give direction
- Trite – too shallow to be useful
- Narrow – too focused to be balanced.

If a parent can encourage the child to practise using a thinking tool, then everyone at home benefits. Here are some possibilities.

- Finding out about your family tree by using a classification tree
- Deciding on a new purchase by using a Venn diagram
- Planning a trip away by using a flow chart
- Organising a busy weekend by using a priority ranking
- Choosing a party venue by using a weightings chart
- Helping find dad a new job by using an enquiry tool.

L2L Essential 9: Team and personal challenge

The model we describe for Personal Challenge Week encourages students to respond to some great questions. Questions like, 'What would you really like to do?' Then, through the agency of the school, Personal Challenge Week helps the student to achieve it. Interestingly, the school has no truancy issues over the six days. It's the sort of thing that brings learning to life. The basic goal setting model used in learning to learn is simple. It can easily and usefully be replicated at home, maybe not in elaborate language but certainly in sentiment: What is it you want to achieve? How will you go about doing it? What will you give up to get started? When a parent has sufficient confidence to talk a goal through with a child it encourages forward thinking and the sort of 'growth' mindset we described in Chapter 2.

L2L Essential 10: Co-operation skills

For parents who are locked into a competitive frame of mind, a school prepared to educate their child in seeing the benefits of being able to switch between modes might be an eye opener for them.

L2L Essential 11: Independent enquiry

If you are going to become really great at learning then you are going to have to find time to practise on your own. Parents who can exhibit interest in and curiosity about the extended project help the school and help the child. Parents can act as a test audience for ideas; they can encourage and cajole by degrees; they can pretend to be really interested in medieval medicine, polar bears or the solar system.

L2L Essential 12: System rigour

A school taking its learning to learn, skills or competency based approach seriously will exhibit that intent to its parents and to its wider community. It will do so in a number of ways but at the very least it will have considered a structured programme of home learning activities, explored possible avenues for accreditation, provided progress reports and explained how the parents can support their child in this work.

Involving the community through Personal Challenge Week

The leadership team at Cramlington Learning Village decided to replace activities week with Personal Challenge Week.[63] The difference is important. Activities week is often about staff putting on things which reflect their own interests, with a best guess at what some of the students would like and a feel for what would be good for them. Many schools, of which Cramlington is one, have turned this on its head. By asking students to think of something that they would like to have achieved or wanted to be good or even better at, the motivation shifts.

Students are surveyed as to what personal challenge they think they would like to undertake. This follows students having experience of a learning to learn programme where team and personal challenge is built in and where goal setting and performance review occur as a matter of course. Their suggestions emerge from their learning to learn experience. Staff then take the responses and aggregate them to come up with what looks the best offer. The latest list of 32 choices is shown opposite.

What then happens is that students opt in, negotiate and agree groups for their chosen activity where they are needed and are then briefed on the challenge. They can change their mind after the briefing but only once. They are advised that over the course of the five day experience they will be expected to show evidence of significant learning and that a debriefing looking at the attributes they have needed will take place each day. This is Monday to Friday. On the Saturday morning each group shows their learning in a public performance which takes place at the school. The parents and members of the community of the town of Cramlington are invited.

The activities are carefully chosen to appeal to students with very different abilities, interests and motivation but the expectations are high. Take for example, the brief for Fairground Attractions:

> Have 'traditional' fairground attractions had their day? Where would you find out about fairground attractions? Which are the most popular? Could you put together and run a number of 'fairground' attractions to entertain the people of Cramlington on our Exhibition Day?

> Your challenge is to design, build and run a number of fairground attractions for our Exhibition Day which will take place on Saturday 27 June.

This is quite clearly a huge practical task involving a group who must not only exhibit team and planning skills but do so with a real deadline and a demanding audience. The brief for Stand-Up Comedian has a different emphasis:

> Who makes you laugh? What do you laugh at? Is there a science behind comedy? Is there an art to the way comedians perform? Are comedians born or made? Can you make people laugh? Could you stand up in front of an audience and make them laugh? What skills would you have to learn? What would you do if you weren't funny? How would you deal with the hecklers? Your challenge is to take comedy to the people of Cramlington.

> You will plan, market and perform a comedy show for our Exhibition Day. Leading up to this will also perform live to Year 7 and 8 students during the week. You will also produce a DVD of the best moments that you will have available for purchase after the show.

To be successful requires huge individual courage and great confidence with a lot resting on the performance. The brief for Helping Hands would appeal to a different sort of personality:

> Have you ever thought what it is like to be old? At what age do you become old? Have you ever imagined what it is like to live in a care home? Do you know of anybody who does? Can you entertain people who are elderly?

> You will be asked to visit a care home for the elderly and ask them what they need or want. You will then design and produce a wonderful magazine to meet their needs. This will be presented to them at a coffee morning held in school complete with entertainment such as bingo games.

Each of the activities is supported by an adult or team of adults, many of whom are from outside of teaching but all of whom are from the local community. Debriefing takes place each day but also in the week following the experience.

How are you going to deal with the physical pain of cycling 160 gruelling miles across Britain? What training will you need to do? How are you going to change from couch potato to elite athlete? How are you going to raise money to fund the event? What happens when you are hundreds of miles from home, hungry, cold and home sick? Will you have the drive to keep going?

You will be asked to plan and participate in a huge physical test of mind over matter. During the week you test your physical fitness and willpower by completing a coast to coast bike ride from the Irish to the North Sea. You will be away from home for five days. You will be expected to raise money through sponsorship to support you over the 160 miles.

Would you like to help save lives? Would you know what to do in an emergency? How would you respond? What skills and training would you need? Could you develop the leadership skills required? Have you ever thought of a career in the uniformed services?

Do you love magic? Have you ever wondered how people do tricks? How easy would it be to learn? Could you learn some amazing tricks and perform them to a real audience? What skills would you need?

Your challenge is to learn how to be a magician and entertain a real audience at our Exhibition Day. You will need to promote your magic show and maybe produce a DVD of your top ten best magic tricks.

Personal Challenge Week student choices

*Music Festival
T-Shirt Designer
*Extreme Physical Challenge
Own a Pony
*Food Glorious Food
Computer Game
Mosaic Art
*Uniformed Services
Dance Performance
Nature Reserve
Green Fingers
The Apprentice
Phoenix FM Radio Station
Outdoor Survival
Perfect Puzzle
*Magician
Fashion Show Designer
Multimedia News
Hit Decks
Cycling Promotion
Helping Hands
Film Makers
Photography
Ladette to Lady
Fairground Attractions
Dog's Life
*Crazy Science
*Ground Force Building Project
Model Your Town
Secrets of Beauty
The Stand-Up Comedian
World Music

Have you ever grown your own food? Would you like to grow your own food? Would you like our school to serve the food you have grown yourselves? How will you do that? What will it cost? Should you make a profit and what will you grow?

You will be asked to create a sustainable allotment in school. This will be produced to a budget and will be a long term business venture which could supply the school and local community with vegetables and flowers.

How will you bring live music to the people of Cramlington? What will be your inspiration? What bands? What music? What venue? Who will be your lead act and why? How will you inspire the people of Cramlington, give them a great time and leave them wanting to come back for more?

You will be commissioned to run a music festival. You will run auditions and select acts from talented students, staff and beyond. You will plan all aspects of the festival from marketing, rehearsing, budgeting, promoting and staging. The festival will be the focus of huge attention on Exhibition Day.

So what crazy science do you know? How could you turn the people of Cramlington on to science? What would you show them? What would you need to find out and where would you go to find it out?

Are you good at building things? Have you ever wanted to build something you could be proud of and something that would benefit other people in Cramlington? What sort of thing would you build? Where would you build it? What would you build? What skills would you need? How would you develop them in time?

The Personal Challenge Week model exhibits much of what we think is the best learning to learn practice. For example:

- the activities are student initiated
- adults other than teachers are actively involved
- everyone's experience is briefed and debriefed around competencies, particularly attributes such as the 5R's
- the contexts are real
- the challenges are open ended – there's no teacher doing it for you
- students deploy a range of communication and practical problem solving skills
- success requires some degree of transfer from classroom learning
- there are authentic presentations or performances in a variety of appropriate formats
- it extends over a period of time
- it is recorded in different formats
- it is validated by the community
- it is hard but rewarding work
- it is a transforming life experience.

As we said in Chapter 5, very few of us experience flow in our lives but most students are lucky enough to experience it during Personal Challenge Week.

The 12 essentials	Sample parent intervention	Parent–child activity	Parent–child dialogue	Benefit
Three dimensional success criteria	For any home learning check the success criteria	Ask questions about the success criteria	'What will you learn? How will you learn it? How do you benefit?'	Provides a sense of structure and can motivate
Process sensitivity	Talking through what you are doing aloud	Listen as child talks through a process	'Talk me through the steps to ...'	Improves sequential thinking
Learner behaviours which are well defined	Use the 5R's at home	Agree some examples of 5R's family behaviours	'Let's think of a time when we had to be resilient ...'	Proves that real learning also occurs outside of school
Language of learning	Parent asks child to explain meanings and give examples	Look together at the learning words in the planner	'What would I be doing if I were ...'	Opportunity to learn together
Systematic debriefing and reporting	Parent or carer consults 5R's profile	5R's discussed with parent or carer beforehand	'What do you think you could do more of to be better at ...? How could I help you?'	Direct opportunities to help at home without being disadvantaged by their own education
Coherent structure to learning	Child explains the stages in any lesson	Parent discusses which stage helps the child learn best	'Which stage was most difficult? What could you do differently next time?'	Dialogue is not about content or 'events' but about learning
Engaging experiences	Doing something enjoyable	Learning something new together	'What would be a fun way to do this?'	Embeds the message that learning is best when it's fun
Thinking fluency	Parent asks child to help with a family decision	Child explains how to use a suitable thinking tool from a selection in the school planner	'Show me how this tool works ...'	Reinforces good thinking habits *cont.*

The 12 essentials	Sample parent intervention	Parent–child activity	Parent–child dialogue	Benefit
Team and personal challenge	Child is encouraged to set a goal	Parent talks through goals with child	'What is it you want to achieve? How will you go about doing it? What will you give up to get started?'	Encourages forward thinking and a 'growth' mindset
Co-operation skills	Child is encouraged to volunteer or take part in a club	Parent encourages and is positive	'What's going well?'	Development of social skills
Independent enquiry	Curiosity and interest in the extended project	Parent acts as a test audience for ideas	'What progress are you making? What's next? How will you know you are successful?'	An opportunity to explore a personal interest in depth
System rigour	Reviewing home learning	Ten minutes together once a week	'Do you need any help?'	Regular opportunity to talk about progress

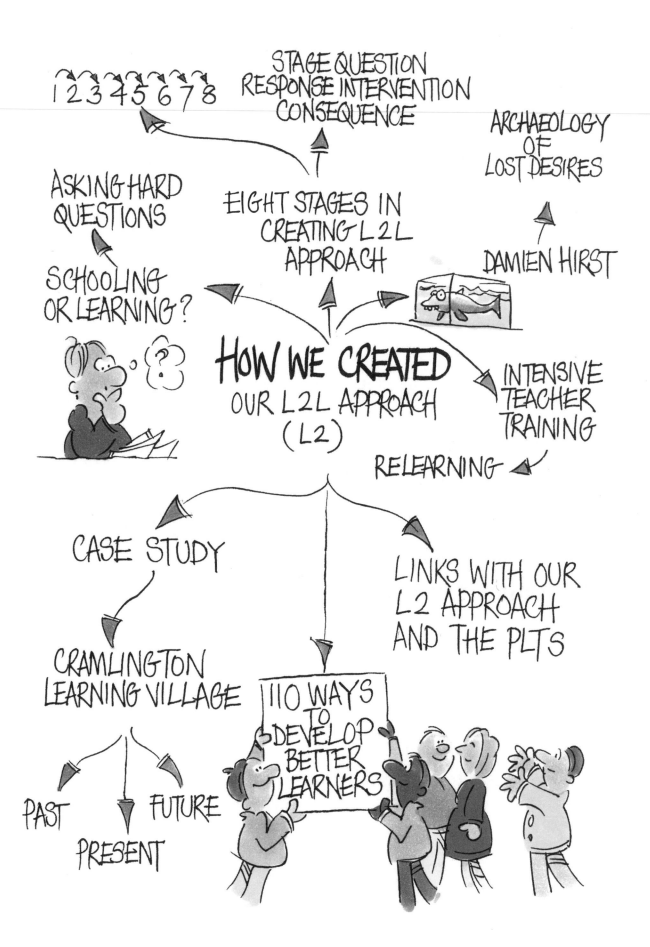

Damien Hirst Exploration KASE Orientation
Definition *San Diego* Specification
Realisation Evaluation Consolidation Lovatt
Support Intent *Outcomes*
Starting Journey Mindfulness Disputation

7. How we created our L2L approach

In this chapter we:

- Ask you to envisage an ideal of schooling
- Provide a planning template
- High School to Learning Village in five years
- Describe our 5R's in detail
- Link the 5R's and the Personal Learning and Thinking Skills (PLTS)
- Provide 11 ways to develop the 5R's.

And ask the following questions:

- If you did this again what would you do differently?
- Who? What? Why? Where? When? How?
- Is there a school like mine?
- What help might be available?
- What can we do straight away?

Learning Village

The 13 year stretch

Imagine going to a party. It's in a fashionable area of New York just before Christmas 2007. There are 600 guests. You are going to the first night of an exhibition. It's an exhibition to do with schools, or at least that's what the title of the exhibit suggests. The main exhibit is called *School: The Archaeology of Lost Desires, Comprehending Infinity and the Search for Knowledge*. The guest list doesn't seem to have many teachers: there seem to be lots of society names, actors, musicians, artists, dealers and even some politicians. There's no signing in at reception and no name badges with this lot.

When the shrouding is pulled back what greets you is a room and a 'class' of 29 dead sheep in formaldehyde filled tanks arranged in rows, a dead shark lurks at the back, 300 sausages, two sides of beef and a dove. On each side of the room are 15 medicine cabinets filled with thousands of empty boxes and bottles with labels for antidepressants, cough medicine and other drugs. At the front in a huge tank is the white dove 'flying' in a metal cage; the cage hangs above a teacher's leather armchair, worn and faded. All the clocks around the room run backwards.

It is however an expensive build and certainly not PFI funded – to you, my son, the installation is US$10 million and welcome to Damien Hirst's view of schooling. Some love it:

> *I think he's got this nailed. The loss of identity, uniformity, submergence and deadening of life, the classroom. The sheer tedium of it all – an 11, soon to be 13, year minimum sentence. The religious imagery of the caged dove as the teacher caught in a pseudo-religious preaching role. The shark is the lurking bully and the ever-present air of frightening violence that is typical of the school experience. Like the students the teacher is merely a larger trapped, farmed animal. The classroom is the mortuary of lost desires. The search for knowledge only emerging after you recover from its leaden effect.[64]*

You may, or you may not, agree with Donald Clark that Mr Hirst has got it nailed. The view that the classroom is the mortuary of lost desires perhaps says more about Mr Clark's experience of school than it says about schools. Ironically there is something very tired and clichéd about this view of schools and schooling. All three authors – with nearly 80 years of shared experience of being in and around schools – think that at this time contemporary schools are exciting places to be and educationalists amongst the most innovative of thinkers. And yet, in the wider world, schools are still perceived by many as factory farms.

When we set about creating our own 'antidote to schooling' we did so by asking lots of hard questions. Some of these were of the 'Are our students more than dead sheep in formaldehyde?' type. Most were about a different and ultimately more useful solution.

How we created our own learning to learn approach

We used, what on reflection turned out to have been, an eight stage planning model – though it was a more messy process than this might suggest. We certainly would not have been aware of an eight stage model at the time. The stages were:

1. Disputation

2. Exploration

3. Orientation

4. Definition

5. Specification

6. Realisation

7. Evaluation

8. Consolidation

Change often arises from dissatisfaction and, in our case, we felt that we needed to take our work on accelerated learning further, making it more student focused. We felt we had a very good practical understanding of what worked in individual classrooms, what engaged and motivated students and what teachers could do to bring energy to their teaching. We now felt the need to build upon that and create a more systemic approach which schools in very different circumstances could take and adapt for themselves. We wanted to help them shift the balance towards learning and away from teaching.

Phase	Question	Response	Intervention	Consequence
1. Disputation	Is everything we currently do good enough?	No, it's too teacher centred	Seek agreement on the need for a major review	Start to explore
	Do we need to make any changes?	Yes, we need to have a radical shift	Agree to find out what's out there that's better	We visited the United States and Australia and looked at brain based learning, thinking skills and co-operative learning

Ten years before the publication of this book five of us from four different UK schools met in San Diego, California where we had all travelled to a learning conference. At this conference we were exposed to a number of approaches, some of which were compelling – Arthur

Costa's Habits of Mind, Ellen Langer's mindfulness – and some less so. However, based on the premise that sometimes 'you have to get out to find out' we felt we were able to come back with a blueprint for moving forward.

At the same time in the UK, lone voices with whom we felt an accord – such as Guy Claxton who had just published *Hare Brain, Tortoise Mind* – were being drowned out by the national strategists and the clamour for performance improvements. The Campaign for Learning had just initiated its first Learning to Learn project. We knew of Daniel Goleman's work on emotional intelligence, Howard Gardner's on multiple intelligence, Carol McGuinness's report on metacognition and thinking skills, the work of the Assessment Reform Group, the publication of Paul Black and Dylan Wiliam's *Inside the Black Box* and Chris Watkins's work on constructivist approaches.

Alistair's work on accelerated learning wasn't universally liked – one academic described it as a sneaky space invader, another to this day talks about 'tinsel on an old tree' and 'learning to learn lite' – but it had played a big part in opening up the debate and taking it away from academics arguing amongst themselves to a wider community. It was a very rich time.

Our next phase involved gathering up what we had found out. Because we were practical people and not academics we had to go on teaching, or in Alistair's case training, whilst we tried to meet and argue the relative merits of different models. This period was like intensive teacher training for us all.

Phase	Question	Response	Intervention	Consequence
2. Exploration	Who or what impresses us?	Forward thinkers from different disciplines	Stay involved with what's happening in worlds outside of education Monitor websites and blogs	▪ Subscribed to www.TED.com ▪ Attended G100 conference ▪ Attended leadership and management events ▪ Worked with clients outside of education

Phase	Question	Response	Intervention	Consequence
	Who or what should we pay attention to?	Ellen Langer Carol Dweck Art Costa Guy Claxton Robert Marzano John Hattie Jim Collins Peter Senge	Ensure that we know and understand the key messages and use their thinking to test ours	▪ Attend SSAT conferences ▪ Involvement with Leading Edge Project ▪ Remain involved with NCSL
	Who or what should we ignore?	Theorists whose models have no practical applicability Shift happens!	Need to remain open minded for whilst we may not have liked some of the interventions we saw being advocated, we needed to be open to what schools thought	We ensured that the best of what we had done over the years in our work on accelerated learning wasn't lost

In order to design our offer we needed to ask what we wanted our learners to leave with. What interventions can our schools make to help them be better prepared for the challenges of the world they will actually inherit, not the one we would have liked them to inherit?

This was where KASE became important for us. Specifying the learner knowledge, attributes, skills and experiences in considerable detail allowed us to create the platform upon which the learning to learn approach would be based. We took what we knew about great learning activities from accelerated learning and structured them into a coherent whole based on the 4 stage learning cycle, in order to deliver KASE – our 21st century outcomes. That was it: great activities plus great coherence plus great outcomes.

Phase	Question	Response	Intervention	Consequence
3. Orientation	What demands will 21st century life place on our students?	■ Problem solvers ■ Adaptable ■ More than just IT literate ■ Communicators ■ Team players ■ Global in outlook ■ Require 'soft skills' ■ High efficacy	Take the latest contemporary thinking and attempt to distil it in a way which is meaningful to educators	Make sure we did more than create endless lists of what students might need in the future – lots of agencies seemed to be doing this – and actually think through how we might deliver
	In this context, how do we prepare them?	Use a simple KASE planning model	Sit down, work out what and specify in detail knowledge, attributes, skills and – later – experiences we want to guarantee	Very specific itemisation of learner outcomes – down to detailing behaviours
	So what do we want our learners to leave with?	Leave 'qualified' by having the right certificates and the right balance of personal characteristics	Create easily understood, accessible outcomes at four levels: students, staff, school community and parents	Approach needs to be more than really engaging lessons
	How do we do this and meet our other responsibilities?	Ensure that our approach aligns with the more significant national strategies, e.g. Electronic Curriculum Map	Stay close to national strategies and statutory and non-statutory requirements	Judgements about the degree to which we would be absorbed by, align with, or ignore intervention such as PLTS, SEAL, AFL

Our next phase was to attempt to distil what we had discovered about effective learning into a workable framework which schools could adapt. To do this we had to agree a common view on learning and particularly when it was 'great' what it would look like.

A significant difference is, of course, that we were designing a commercial product which would have to have a broad appeal. We did not have the leisure of a large funded organisation behind us so we needed to make very careful decisions at each stage.

In your case you would be concerned with your own school but we feel our phased approach can easily be adapted.

Phase	Question	Response	Intervention	Consequence
4. Definition	In our approach what will great learning look like?	Engaging learning activities plus coherence and structure in their delivery plus well considered KASE outcomes	Use this model to design all learning to learn experiences whether they be lessons or longer events	We now have a template in place which can be put into an electronic format with useful features such as clear learner outcomes, 4 stage cycle, customisability, tracking, hyperlinks to resources
	What principles of learning should underpin our approach?	'Nail down' the 12 essentials	Integrate the 12 essentials throughout our approach	We publish our 12 essentials
	What's the most effective way to intervene?	Be sensitive to different schools capacity for change	Design a range of resources, learning tools, support systems and guidance so schools can pick and mix	Create a journey school model of adopt, embed and spread
	Who are our clients?	UK state schools with a student centred holistic focus	Market to, and organise events for, these schools	Stay close to clients

Test out everything in 'partner' schools |

The phase we call specification is the equivalent of being locked in a room to do the school timetable, except it never was as mechanistic as that. By asking ourselves questions which on the surface seemed bound by practical issues, such as how will it be delivered, we once again had to revisit the whole area of change management. We had to ask ourselves what sort of models would be most advantageous to levering change in schools. Our shared experience of lots of schools suggested a distribution curve which, if anything, was slightly skewed towards a traditional teacher centred pedagogy with an emphasis on coverage and being readied for testing. Most schools we had visited to support learning and teaching were more trailing edge than leading edge. In our judgement to insist that any worthwhile intervention had to be immersive and whole school was therefore to miss out the vast majority of UK schools who were in need of radical change but not geared up to produce it.

At around this time, under the guidance of David Hargreaves, the Specialist Schools and Academies Trust (SSAT) were exploring the concept of gateways as levers of school improvement. There were nine such gateways. Later the gateways were organised into a structure of four 'deeps' – deep support, deep learning, deep leadership and deep experience. Deep learning, first coined by John Dewey, involved an intimate marriage of student voice, assessment for learning and learning to learn. Undoubtedly this was a powerful model. The thinking behind it was excellent and in turn, through the reach of the SSAT, it became influential in the thinking of many leading schools. As we visited schools we could see it was beginning to gain attention.

We also found that in many schools the organisational structure showing the interactions between the deeps on a poster pinned up behind the head teacher's desk did not always reflect what was happening on a day-to-day basis in the classroom lessons we observed. This for us was the issue. We did not see enough systematic thinking to ensure that the concept drilled down into classroom practice and, in this way, was limited by being a top down model.

Changing the organisational structure did not necessarily change the teaching habits of the workforce and it was there that most impact was going to be felt. It became important to have capacity to drill down change. For that reason we opted for a 'journey' school rather than a 'deep' school model. We felt it was important to help schools start from where they were at; deep is desirable but for many starting modestly was the reality.

Phase	Question	Response	Intervention	Consequence
5. Specification	What's the approach?	A balance between a course (discrete) and whole school immersion (diffused)	Create a range of possible ways forward from which schools 'cherry pick'	Deliberate design of some resources which are basically one hour lessons and others which are generic whole school tools
	How will it be accessed?	Through both low and high tech	Provide two versions: one which is server based, the other web based	Contract software designers Employ web designer
	How will it be structured?	Around three themes: individual, team and community, 21st century learner	Commit to three years of a core programme: year one (60 hours); year two (60 hours); year three (60 hours). A total of 180 hours of one hour lessons which can be added to or changed	Considerable project management challenge involving 'keeping the plane flying whilst we build and rebuild it' Teams comprising project manager, author, designer, illustrator, web designer
	What's the best way to grow it?	Growth strategy will be shaped by school's capacity for change	Provide guidance documents: ▪ Five year plans ▪ Financing L2L ▪ Aligning with national initiatives ▪ Do's and don'ts Broker visits to other schools	Create a space on our website to host these documents for this community

The realisation phase involved creating complementary resources. Lessons for discrete programme delivery came with whole school tools such as the Electronic Profilers, Learner Passports and Success Mats. Later we developed Electronic Thinking Tools and an Electronic Learning Wall which was a giant interactive poster which allowed teachers and students instant access to thinking tools, classroom protocols and the 5R's progression grid. Teachers could minimise this on a whiteboard and call it up when needed.

L2 students come from every possible starting point. Our ultimate aim is to create content and a suite of customisable learning tools so we can move towards a personalised provision. Personalised learning is just not possible without the right technology but now we have it we must ensure that educationalists design the learning tools with software programmers and not the other way around.

L2 teachers also come from every possible starting point. Some want paper based lessons; others turn their noses up at anything without a plug – so it's a demanding clientele. Some learning to learn programmes are basically teacher training on the job with the materials written for teachers with all the concomitant dangers of reading levels being too high, the concepts too abstract and the work of designing appropriate learning challenges given over to the teacher. Fine in some circumstances but, we judged, insufficiently respectful of the different needs out there.

L2 schools are better off in the long run if they can construct their own learning to learn programme to help deliver their local needs. Many, probably most, don't have the capacity to do so to a sophisticated level and so want to fall in with programmes they feel they can trust to help them get to where they need to be.

L2 parents do not, in the main, get formal guidance on how their child learns. Many schools do liaise well with parents but most do not engage them on understanding learning.

Phase	Question	Response	Intervention	Consequence
6. Realisation	What do we provide for the student?	Active, engaging and relevant learning experiences organised thematically	▪ I Learner ▪ Team Learner ▪ Independent Enquirer ▪ Peak Performer ▪ Learning Alongside Others ▪ 21st Century Learner ▪ Developing Thinking Skills ▪ Well-Being and Happiness ▪ Independent Enquirer – extended project	Need for constant review and a graduation across to an entirely hosted provision
	What do we provide for the teacher?	Support for a change in classroom practice Practical activities and guidance	Need for a meaningful programme of teacher support and development most of which will be in-house	Provide guidance materials Review the learning processes we commend as well as the content we provide
	What do we provide for the school?	Structures, guidance and resources to allow for a change in classroom teaching	Access to a national database and a national support network of schools on the learning to learn journey	Set up local networks and link them together

cont.

Phase	Question	Response	Intervention	Consequence
	What do we provide for the parent?	Guidance on how their child learns and how to help: PAL	Remotely accessible programme to help their child learn	Large commitment of time and resource

Evaluation threatened to become the elephant in our room. We wanted to be able to say that these approaches worked and 'here is the evidence' but it was problematic. It's a very difficult thing to do in a single school with one tightly defined intervention, and it's extraordinarily difficult to do with over 800 schools and loosely interpreted interventions. We have since embarked on a programme to support schools in doing their own evaluations though this is a specialist field and where it seems to work best is when schools are very clear about what they want the process to do for them.

One thing you will not be able to do with any certainty is to say that following any learning to learn approach will result in a given percentage rise in attainment. What we were able to offer were the views of lots and lots of stakeholders, the broad performance patterns with and without a learning to learn approach, case studies based on teachers' own experience and our own observation reports having visited many schools. Some individual schools have gone a step further: Cramlington used a university researcher; de Ferrers is one of a number which have used Pupil Attitudes to Self and School (PASS); Blessed Edward Oldcorne had staff that completed MA research on the impact of L2; and in various Ofsted inspections learning to learn has been cited directly. As we go to press we have developed an electronic classroom observation tool for schools which can be linked to inspection criteria and which will aggregate up data so that patterns of strength and weakness can begin to be seen across different departments and specialisms, thus allowing CPD to be aligned directly with need.

Phase	Question	Response	Intervention	Consequence
7. Evaluation	How do we evaluate?	Not possible to do so effectively on behalf of our entire community	Compromise: - Give guidance on self-evaluation - Create evaluation tools - Evaluate our control group of journey schools	Quality evaluation becomes an on-going challenge

Phase	Question	Response	Intervention	Consequence
	How do we develop?	Shift the model gradually from 'done on behalf of' towards 'done alongside'	Create local learning to learn hubs centred on journey schools with learning champions	As a result of a shift in relationship we become more focused on developing electronic products which are instantly accessible, personalised and user friendly
	How do we support?	Establish a national network	▪ Support events in and around journey schools ▪ Provide ongoing support for champions	Both virtual and face-to-face support which must be scalable and guaranteed into the future

For us there are two issues around consolidation. One is about improving what is already in place and the other is about innovation around newer approaches.

The personalisation of learning agenda is one which for the first time ever can begin to be addressed seriously. Without intelligent ICT it is just not possible to achieve personalisation of learning. Differentiation is not personalisation, nor is mixed ability teaching, nor is one-to-one support, nor is a new textbook every term. However, with intelligent ICT it is possible to enter into a whole new environment of connected support.

Looking forward our personalised learning solutions are all electronic. This doesn't mean an end to schools, teachers or lessons but it means more wrap-around individualised support informed by choice and a better understanding of particular need. The student gets a Formula 1 pit stop service. When they need support suddenly everyone and every system is there at the point of need, they are topped up and off they fly.

Phase	Question	Response	Intervention	Consequence
8. Consolidation	How do we sustain?	Stay very close to the end user and very close to the prevailing technologies	Liaise with those involved in creating software solutions which emerge from an understanding of learning not programming	Virtual learning environments (VLE) driven by learner need and not school administration needs or commercial availability
	Where do we go next?	Personalisation of what we offer Imaginative use of ICT solutions but built entirely on an understanding of great learning	Web 2.0 tools Careful design of electronic tools which 'talk' to each other. For example: L2 Plan – Lesson Planning tool, L2 Pass – Learner Passport, L2 Profilers, L2 Thinking Tools, L2 Classroom Observation Tool, L2 Share – Assessment Tool	Merge great content with great tools in a modern ICT environment to genuinely personalise learning The technology tail must not wag the learning dog

High School to Learning Village in five years

Mark Lovatt tells the story of how his school adopted, embedded and now is spreading learn to learn.

Cramlington Community High School (now Cramlington Learning Village) first introduced a learning to learn course in September 2002. At the time we were a 13–18 school and the course was introduced with Year 9 students, our intake year group.

Our first attempt at a learning to learn course was homemade and fairly simplistic – for example, we did some lessons on the brain and memory, we taught mind mapping, and the students did very basic questionnaires on learning styles. We even had a 55 minute lesson called 'Building a confident future' which was taught in week 7 – imagine being off that day; you would have gone through the rest of your life with hopelessly low self-esteem.

The course was taught by a team of 12 or so teachers who had time 'left over' on their timetable in rooms that were 'available' after the important subjects were accommodated. Learning to learn was allocated one hour per week of precious timetable space.

Looking back now it seems naive that this course would successfully teach students the knowledge, attributes and skills they needed to become independent and effective learners, or that students would begin to transfer and apply these skills within their other subject areas. However, 'even a journey of a thousand miles begins with a single step' and for the first time learning to learn appeared on student timetables and we had taken our first tentative steps towards developing independent learners.

In September 2004 we launched a new learning to learn course which had been co-developed with Alistair. We decided that if we really wanted to develop learners capable of working more autonomously and taking greater responsibility for their learning then we should really do things more thoroughly.

We decided to give the course some proper curriculum time – four 55 minute periods per week (the same curriculum time allocated to English, maths and science) and to ask some of our best teachers to deliver the course. We were also able to transform what was an old social block to create three new classrooms. These were large learning spaces, nearly 85 square metres. We installed circular tables, eight in each classroom, and around each table were four chairs and on each table were four slide-out drawers, and on each slide-out drawer a laptop computer. The idea was to encourage group learning: each table would sit a home team of four students, students would have access to ICT (via the slide-out drawers), however ICT would not dominate and computers could be slid out of site underneath the tables when required.

In each room we also provided alternative spaces to learn and even provided a number of brightly coloured bean bags. The bean bags would give a different feel to the rooms, students would be allowed some choice about how and where they learned – you could choose to work on the bean bags (students loved these) if you could behave responsibly – 'earned' autonomy. The space in the rooms allowed for a number of different configurations, from home teams to whole class review, and allowed a greater flexibility in terms of movement around the classroom.

We also had a much more sophisticated learning to learn course. Instead of the 'tips and tricks' of the previous course – this one was designed to develop the attributes of successful learners – the 5R's: Resilience, Resourcefulness, Responsibility, Reasoning and Reflection.

We had over 60 hours of lessons and resources in three modules called: I Learner, Team Learner and 21st Century Learner.

We thought that the new course and the way it was taught could also provide the impetus to further develop teaching and learning throughout the whole school. This would be the beginning of a learning to learn approach that we planned to eventually spread to all subjects.

During the first year of the course we ran open days for teachers from around the country who were interested in developing a learning to learn approach of their own – we always included some of our own teachers on these days, so that by the end of the year, 18 of our own staff (apart from those already teaching the course) had spent a day immersed in the learning to learn course and its environment and seeing for themselves the skills and attributes students were developing. In this respect the course was not only teaching our students how to be better learners but numbers of our teachers were increasingly becoming more sensitive to the processes of learning. We used the course as a training opportunity for both students and staff.

To ensure the new course was successful we did the following:

- Put together a teaching team which included some of our best teachers – in other words, staffed the course first.

- Provided sufficient curriculum time to cover the materials.

- Provided training on the course materials for the team of teachers delivering the course.

- Held regular (teaching) team meetings to review the module that had just been taught and to preview the lessons coming up.

- Appointed someone at a senior level to be in charge of teaching and learning and to lead the learning to learn course and learning school wide.

- Rewrote some of the modules and worked with Alistair to create a course which later became L2.

- Wrote and produced a reflection journal used in learning to learn lessons to encourage students to reflect on learning and as something which could be used to show progress through the course. This was a journal that could be collected in and work 'marked' by the teacher – this helped to give the course status in the eyes of the students.

- Linked the course to wider key skills qualifications and about 70% of our students were able to achieve the wider key skill of 'working with others' at level 2 by the end of Year 9. This also helped to give the course status in the minds of students, parents and teachers.

- Evaluated the impact of the course and tried to gauge progress in the development of skills and attributes.

This last point, the evaluation of the course, was carried out by a PhD graduate 'researcher-in-residence' who was jointly employed by the school and by Newcastle University in that for some of the week (two days) he worked for us and for the rest of the time he carried out work on behalf of the university.

The research evaluated the learning to learn course in terms of the extent to which students were becoming aware of (sensitised to) the processes of learning and the extent to which the learning to learn course was enabling them to become better learners. The approaches used were reasonably straight forward – interviewing groups of students and teachers, and asking students to complete an online survey. The difficulty is asking the right questions and being able to analyse the information collected.

The results were encouraging. For example, more than 80% of students stated that they felt they were more resilient learners by the end of Year 9 than at the beginning and many of the students could relate personal anecdotes or incidences where they were able to use what they had learnt in 'learning to learn' in other areas of the curriculum.

This gave us the confidence to take the next step which was to move from a discrete learning to learn *course* to begin a school wide learning to learn *approach*.

The move towards a whole school approach where students were explicitly taught the skills and attributes they need to become better learners within the context of their subjects started in 2006 with the creation of a new course called L2 Humanities. This course ran alongside our discrete learning to learn course and was designed to build on the skills introduced in learning to learn lessons. For example, a learning to learn lesson might introduce the idea of teamwork and roles taken in groups; the humanities lessons would then give students the opportunity to work in small teams on a collaborative project, and the humanities teacher would give students feedback on how well the students were able to work in groups. Students would reflect on this experience through collaboration charts – like a pie chart where students self-assess and divide up the circle corresponding to how much (or how little) each member of the team has contributed.

In other lessons they would use 'responsibility clocks' to plan out the use of time or question stems to build the skill of good questioning. These 'learning' skills – working well in groups, time management, asking good questions, use of thinking tools like Edward de Bono's Thinking Hats or Venn diagrams for comparing and contrasting information, etc. – were a planned, explicit and coherent part of the L2 Humanities course. For the first time students began to transfer their learning about learning and apply what they knew to help them learn in other subjects.

The new course was not without some issues – teachers were unsure about the time they should spend on process skills versus humanities content and would sometimes default into the comfort zone of teaching content and forgetting to emphasise the learning skills being developed. This is a common problem with a learning to learn approach which tries to develop learner attributes and skills through subjects. Teachers are, not surprisingly, generally more comfortable with delivering subject knowledge; this is, after all, where their expertise and training lie.

There is also a culture of coverage – if we are not covering the subject content and 'getting through the syllabus' there is an air of panic. Amidst all this there is a feeling of not being quite sure that developing learning skills/behaviours is actually going to yield any results, especially as we must all worship at the altar of league tables!

What helped us to get through this were a number of important things. Firstly, and most importantly in my view, we started with a discrete learning to learn course. This meant that over the years we had been running the course we had built up a body of knowledge and expertise – we had become more confident with teaching learning to learn strategies and had been able to see that it could be successful. Enough teachers had taught on the course (many of these were humanities teachers) to be able to write these ideas and strategies into the new L2 Humanities schemes of work.

Another thing that helped was having a humanities team of reflective practitioners who were willing and able to try things out and take risks within a school culture which actively encouraged this. The L2 Humanities course was led at a senior level by an assistant head teacher with overall responsibility for humanities and supported by the deputy head with responsibility for teaching and learning. One more thing that gave us the confidence to develop learning to learn still further was our growing success in terms of results – 85% of students were obtaining five 'good' GCSEs compared to about 50% ten years previously. We were in the top 10% for Key Stage 2 to Key Stage 3 for value added and to top it all in

2006 Ofsted rated us an outstanding school where 'learning was not done to the students but with the students'.

In September 2008 we became a secondary school of 2,300 students taking Year 7 and 8 students for the first time. The Local Authority in Northumberland made a decision to change from a three tier system to a two tier system and the first pyramid of schools scheduled for change was Cramlington. This gave us the opportunity to completely rethink the curriculum at Key Stage 3.

We moved our existing learning to learn course into Year 7 and there was an opportunity to write a learning to learn approach into schemes of work in all core subjects in Year 7 and after that all subjects in Year 8. We would support the development of independent learning through an enquiry based curriculum with frequent opportunities for students to work on enquiries or extended projects. If you are going to teach students how to be better learners then you need to provide opportunities for them to practise working independently.

We used a KASE curriculum model to plan each module. The attributes and skills column described whole school learning outcomes. The attributes column was centred on developing the 5R's and the skills column outlined the key learning skills of communication, thinking and collaboration which we wanted students to learn. The knowledge column was the subject knowledge (or skills) that were being developed in that particular module. For example, an English module entitled 'Why do people tell stories?' would have specific subject learning outcomes (in the knowledge column) and teachers would look for opportunities to build elements of one or more of the skills and attributes as well (e.g. opportunities to develop collaboration through team challenges, and/or learning from peer feedback (Reflection)). These activities were explicitly written into the new schemes of work and launched in September 2008.

We are nearing the end of the first year of our new curriculum and due to run our own internal curriculum review designed to evaluate the effectiveness of our curriculum model in developing learner attributes and skills. At present we run a learning to learn humanities course in seven 75 minute periods per fortnight for Year 7 – the first module of this course is I Learner, and is exclusively designed to introduce learning attributes and skills which are then picked up and developed on the humanities course and in the other core subjects of science, English and maths. In Year 8 and 9 there is still a discrete learning to learn course but this will fade out next year as our learning to learn approach builds from Year 7. Next year we will launch a new trans-disciplinary course (the first half term of which will be a module on information literacy called 21st Century Learner) where students will practise what they have learnt and further develop independent learning skills and attributes through authentic and extended projects. In 2009, Ofsted returned and pronounced Cramlington outstanding for a third time, saying 'learning to learn played a significant part in developing a coherent and school wide culture of learning'. We are still on the journey.

Links between the 5R's and the PLTS

There are links to be made between our 5R's and the QCA Personal Learning and Thinking Skills (PLTS). We would not advocate any approach which requires a teacher or teachers to conduct an extensive lesson by lesson audit of where and when each of these skills is delivered; better to use them as a framework for students themselves to discuss progress.

Characteristics of the 5R's	Summary characteristics of PLTS
Resilience ■ Sticks at it ■ Stays positive ■ Stays involved ■ Sets targets and practises	Effective Participator ■ Persists and presents a persuasive case ■ Discusses issues and seeks resolutions ■ Gets involved and identifies practical ways forward ■ Identifies improvements that could benefit themselves and others
Responsible ■ Knows right from wrong and makes good choices ■ Manages themselves ■ Helps others ■ Thinks ahead and plans	Self Manager ■ Organises self and resources ■ Shows initiative ■ Deals well with pressures ■ Responds positively to change, seeking advice and support when needed
	Team Worker ■ Collaborates with others towards a common goal ■ Reaches agreements together ■ Shows fairness and consideration to others ■ Takes responsibility and shows confidence
Resourceful ■ Shows initiative ■ Learns using different learning methods ■ Asks good questions ■ Involves others, including the teacher, in learning	Creative Thinker ■ Generates ideas and explores possibilities ■ Asks questions to extend thinking ■ Tries out alternative or new solutions ■ Adapts ideas as circumstances change *cont.*

Characteristics of the 5R's	Summary characteristics of PLTS
Reasoning ▪ Explains thinking ▪ Considers all evidence ▪ Chooses the best method or thinking tool ▪ Takes time to think things through	Independent Enquirer ▪ Identifies questions to answer and problems to solve ▪ Plans and carries out research ▪ Analyses and evaluates information ▪ Supports conclusions with arguments and evidence
Reflective ▪ Curious ▪ Can describe progress ▪ Listens to and learns from feedback ▪ Learns from experience	Reflective Learner ▪ Assesses themselves and others ▪ Sets goals with success criteria ▪ Reviews progress, acting on outcomes ▪ Invites feedback, deals positively with praise and setbacks

To do this some schools have used RSMA (rarely, sometimes, mostly always) as a quick check. Others use Red, Amber and Green (not yet, about to, always) traffic lights. Students detail their responses to one or more of the PLTS.

We feel there are overlaps within the PLTS framework. They are in part brought about by confusing the definitions of a skill, a behaviour and a personal quality. The resultant checklists are, we feel, clumsily expressed. It is a welcome direction which asks students to reflect on the value of their learning beyond school but maybe there is a little too much going on at once.[65] Our model benefits from attaching four specific behaviours to each of five attributes. We think this is comprehensive enough to be of worth but concise enough to be workable.

110 ways to develop better learners using our 5R's

Developing positive learner attributes is at the core of our learning to learn approach and should be at the heart of yours. You don't need to use our 5R's, but if you should wish to here are 110 quick and easy to apply ideas.

General strategies

1. Value them!

2. Identify what resilient behaviour consists of, break it down into its components, describe it in classroom examples and capture the behaviours as and when they arise. Draw attention to the behaviour – 'Here's a good example of resilience.' Label the behaviour – 'Thank you for being resilient.'

3. Use the L2 posters (which identify each of the 5R's) as classroom learning resources. Share them out, ask pairs or groups to explain them and give examples from everyday life.

4. Use the 5R's posters as the basis of a prominent and permanent quality display adjoining students' examples of what each means in practical terms for them.

5. Create your own certificates so you can give bronze, gold and silver awards for each of the 5R's.

6. Allow students to vote in the 5R's Oscars: 'Best example of resilience goes to … for …' 'R of the week goes to … for…'.

7. Create research opportunities for students to look for examples of each of the 5R's in the biographies of famous people or ask them to interview relatives, friends or neighbours for examples.

8. Send definitions of the 5R's home to parents or carers.

9. Have a 5R's assembly or a series of assemblies or as theme of the week.

10. Use the 5R's as an evaluation tool when reviewing group work. This is especially good when students become skilled at doing it themselves.

11. Have a 'No marks – Only R's' day, week or month where teachers' marks and grades are replaced by the R's.

12. Design a 5R's rubber stamp to allow quick self assessment. The stamp has each of the R's and a space for tick, cross or question mark.

13. Help students to use the R's for peer assessment, particularly for activities which are informal such as theatre productions, work placements or study trips.

14. Evaluate a lesson or a scheme of work with students or staff using the 5R's.

15. Watch an excerpt from a film and evaluate what you see using the 5R's.

16. Choose a character from a play, soap opera, book or comic book and evaluate them using the 5R's.

17. Read a biography of a contemporary character and decide if and when they exhibited any of the five R's.

18. Use the Alite Superheroes cards or make your own based on our ideas.

19. Have students design their own 5R's superhero trading cards.

20. Have students design cartoon strips in only five frames exhibiting 5R's behaviours.

21. Have students create a personal portfolio of evidence broken down by R's and put in any personal reflections, evidence, photographs or messages alongside.

22. Identify how the 5R's will be developed as part of the school development plan.

23. Agree with staff that one or more of the R's will feature in each subject lesson and be debriefed as part of the learning experience.

24. Require departments to briefly outline what each 'R' looks like in their subject areas.

25. Use the R's as the basis for one-to-one interviews and for student goal setting.

26. Use the 5R's to replace effort and behaviour grades.

27. Report on the 5R's to parents.

28. Create classroom observations around the 5R's.

29. Have an assembly around each of the 5R's

30. Have 5R's themed days looking at what it means for individuals, groups and communities.

Specific strategies

Resilient learners

31. Reward for persistence. For example, sticking at a difficult problem, drafting and redrafting, repeating something until it's right.

32. Emphasise the importance of trialling out ideas first.

33. Model persistence within a subject area. For example, artist's sketch books, drafts of a piece of prose, workings behind a maths problem, passages of complex legislation.

34. Identify persistence within the biography of successful individuals.

35. Reward for maintaining a positive attitude, especially with complex problems and tasks.

36. Focus on improving rather than proving. In other words, be specific in feedback on how to improve rather than being specific about grading and raw scores.

37. Use a solutions focus approach – 'Don't come to me with a problem unless, at the same time, you come with two possible solutions.'

38. Reframe: 'How would someone else approach this challenge?' Reframe using known traits: 'How would the optimist, expert or prodigy approach this challenge?'

39. Reframe using known individuals: 'How would Anita Roddick, Bob Geldof or Nelson Mandela approach the challenge?'

40. Change the language. Use learning instead of 'work', improvement instead of 'effort', challenge instead of 'problem'.

41. Help learners see the development and progression of their learning by tracking beginning, middle and end. Ask 'Where have we been? Where are we going next? How should we get there? What are the benefits of getting there?'

42. Review learning using the three dimensional success criteria.

43. Conduct interim process reviews in the style of a press conference.

44. Utilise the Olympic Goal Setting Method – outcome, performance and process – and shift the emphasis away from outcomes-only goals ('I will get 12 GCSEs at A*') to performance and process. Performance and process goals stimulate discussion.

45. Go through goal setting case studies with students so that they can become more skilled at setting more useful goals.

46. Pair students so that they can coach each other through their goals using the Coaching Success Mats.

Resourceful learners

47. Use the classroom walls as a display space to support problem solving. Use three sorts of display for learning: protocols, tools and affirmations.

48. Include amongst the problem solving posters Edward de Bono's Consider All Factors (CAF), Plus Minus Interesting (PMI) and his Six Thinking Hats – also include your version of hierarchy of questions from Bloom or Anderson. Use the Kipling Questions. Make regular reference to these tools and have students choose from them when problem solving.

49. Keep a set of class portfolios of problem solving tools which students can pick up and look through any time they are stuck. To source them use the Alite Electronic Thinking Tools and choose from the 48 which are there.

50. Use 'getting stuck' as an opportunity to rehearse ways of getting unstuck. Draw attention to the 'stuck moment' to model how to cope.

51. Draw attention to and reward initiative in problem solving. Use posters and certificates to help.

52. In planning learning use a model to help you accommodate difference. The simplest is Visual, Auditory and Kinaesthetic (VAK) – remember it is only a model, and there are others which are more sophisticated. If it's helpful to you and your students, ignore the academics who tell you it's unproven.

53. Use classroom dialogue to promote a vocabulary of learning amongst students. The vocabulary should allow them to describe different ways of learning and different moments in the learning experience.

54. Put key learning vocabulary into the back of your student planners.

55. Model good questioning. Talk up the skill of questioning – use our Success Mats to help you.

56. Start lessons with students' questions rather than teacher's answers. For example, 'What would be the best three questions to ask if we wanted to …?'

57. Use artefacts, props, freeze-frame, role play, mystery guest, hot seating or story to engage curiosity at the beginning of learning. Do so before taking registers, agreeing objectives or collecting sick notes!

58. Scaffold the questions you and students ask. For example, 'That's a good question. How can we build on it …?'

59. Model the questioning techniques of clarifying, scaffolding, reflecting and summarising and use the words as you do so: 'So let me clarify what I think you have just said …'

60. Have a large sign on your classroom door which says 'The Give It a Go Club meets here on weekdays'.

61. Make it safe for a student to take a learning risk. Avoid any sort of put-down or anything that could possibly be perceived as a put-down.

62. Declare your classroom a put-down free zone.

63. Explain about comfort zones and the need to move to the edge of them for all of us when we learn.

Responsible learners

64. Build in choice to your lesson planning. For example, homework can be differentiated through core activities and options. Learners have to accumulate a number of points. Core activities generate more points than options.

65. Build in choice to the demonstration phase of learning where students present solutions and findings.

66. Unpick the decision making process – yours and theirs.

67. Model time management by showing you understand student deadlines. Give lots of notice for your own deadlines. Use a visual planner to show how the deadline fits with other possible commitments.

68. Start on time, finish on time and use all the time for learning that is available to you. Don't contradict yourself by allowing 'winding down' or by using time as a reward.

69. Actively solicit the views of students regarding the everyday conduct and management of the classroom learning environment.

70. Avoid putting students into arbitrary groups. Introduce group work by agreeing group protocols, roles and problem solving approaches. Reinforce these each time a group activity is used. Don't allow students to assume any one role – e.g timekeeper – at the expense of their active engagement with the group.

71. Spend time exploring three dimensional success criteria. Show how it works by breaking it down bit by bit.

72. Before any extended group activity, insist that the group agrees its own success criteria. Share their criteria.

73. Build in planning time to any group activity. Ask for their plan.

74. Allow planning time for homework in class. Talk through examples of plans. Ask 'When will you do it?', 'Where?', 'How?', 'For how long?', 'With what success criteria?' Also ask, 'How will you benefit from doing this?'

75. Use a study buddy review system where two students pair up from time to time to review progress. Use the Peer Assessment Success Mat to help frame the dialogue.

76. Lead Learners. Find the six best performers on your topic. Break the class into review groups. Have each of the six learners teach their group the key points.

77. Groups ask 'really good questions'. Incentivise the quality rather than the quantity or frequency of questions.

78. Envoys. Debrief group activities in a variety of ways including envoys. The envoy visits another group and summarises what they have discovered so far.

79. Peer assessment is easier said than done! Using our Peer Assessment Success Mats drives the process.

80. Use ABC to help students understand the part choice plays in everyday success and failure. A stands for antecedent – what's gone before; B for behaviour; C for consequence. Use a timeline to show how A leads to B leads to C.

Reasoning learners

81. Have a 'no hands up rule' which you operate as a general rule but can suspend from time to time.

82. Ask learners to take time to explain their thinking. Encourage the use of, and familiarisation with, the learning vocabulary to help them do so.

83. Allow 'wait time' after asking a question.

84. Use 'chatterbox' before taking any students' responses to your questions. Chatterbox is where answers are explained in pairs or trios before being volunteered to the whole group.

85. Ask open ended evaluative questions.

86. Model the fact that problems can be solved in different ways.

87. Ask for minimal sentence answers. 'At least three sentences about …'

88. Add numbers. 'Who can give me five factors which contribute to …'

89. Start with the answer. The learners come up with the best questions.

90. Ask 'impossible' questions as a starter. 'How many tiles on this roof?', 'What is the most important geographical feature?'

91. Prompt answers using the hierarchy of questions. For example, 'Who can synthesise the arguments for me?'

92. For younger learners, use talk to the alien – who is a green blow-up plastic figure – as a means of students explaining unfamiliar words or concepts. Use 'alien' questions – questions which expose a flaw in thinking.

93. Draw out similarity and difference in your use of everyday examples. Use Continuity Lines, Venn diagrams and Comparison Alley to help.

94. Teach learners categorisation skills to help them make distinctions. Good examples are double bubble, memory maps and classification systems.

95. Replace the word 'plenary' with the word 'debriefing'. Vary the debriefing to include paired, group and class debriefing. Use a thinking tool to debrief. For example, the Kipling Questions.

96. Give examples of reliable and unreliable sources. Try the murder mystery approach where a series of clues leads to a theory, a personality or an event. Put in lots of false trails and bits of bogus evidence.

Reflective learners

97. Present information in the form of a problem or a challenge rather than a set of notes or facts. Allow the students to select from a range of problem solving tools.

98. Present information in the form of notes or facts but riddle it with errors. Point out that these are the only notes you are going to give and they will have to decide what is accurate and what is inaccurate.

99. Begin the learning through a related but obscure activity. You are eating an apple at the beginning of the lesson, they have to guess why. Answer? The lesson is about the geology of earthquakes – surface, core, molten lava.

100. Engage curiosity and learning by posing big questions. Sit down with your colleagues and work out what the big questions for each topic are. How can we make the planet safe? What's the point in learning French? Who invented irregular verbs? Why does lightning go down and not across?

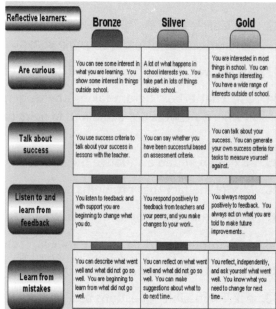

101. Demonstrate the difference between fact and opinion. Use the internet example to do so. How much of what presents itself as reliable information is in fact one individual's opinion?

102. Take a television debate or interview and analyse it for: types of question – based on the hierarchy and opinion or fact – based on what is said, by whom and how!

103. Ask your learners what they want to know about your topic. Collect the questions, revisit them and cover them all over the course of the topic.

104. Model the drafting process. Illustrate how the completed scene, poem, painting or piece of music was, in fact, the product of lots of trial and error.

105. Use 'hot seating' and 'press conferences' to see things from different perspectives.

106. Use timelines to help learners understand simple time and management rules and to understand how to place mistakes in perspective.

107. What's the minority view, alternative solution or outrageous position? How many great ideas were ridiculed at first?

108. Encourage students to build upon ideas first and refute them last.

109. Ensure you always find time to review the learning. Do so by revisiting your learning outcomes. Draw out the content learned, the processes used to learn and the benefits accruing as a consequence.

110. Be intimate with the practical applications of your subject. If you have to teach quadratic equations then be prepared to connect the experience to real life – explain where students come across this in their everyday world.

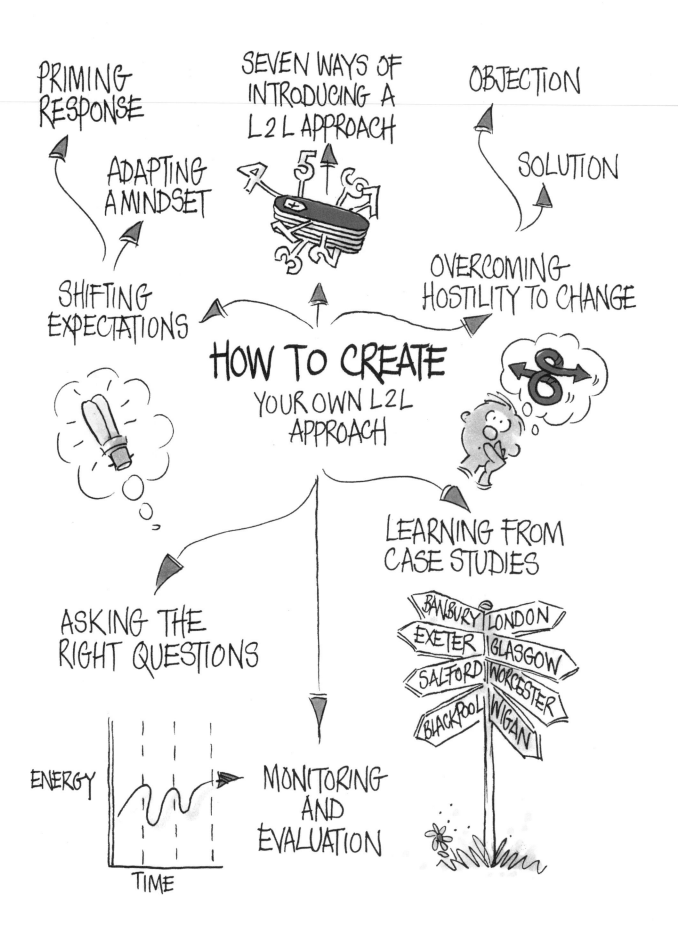

PRIMING RESPONSE

ADAPTING A MINDSET

SEVEN WAYS OF INTRODUCING A L2L APPROACH

OBJECTION

SOLUTION

SHIFTING EXPECTATIONS

OVERCOMING HOSTILITY TO CHANGE

HOW TO CREATE YOUR OWN L2L APPROACH

LEARNING FROM CASE STUDIES

BANBURY LONDON
EXETER GLASGOW
SALFORD WORCESTER
BLACKPOOL WIGAN

ASKING THE RIGHT QUESTIONS

ENERGY

TIME

MONITORING AND EVALUATION

Questions Plan Lead Learners ASDAN
Beginnings Entry Points
People Case Studies Processes Problems
Progression RSA Principles Guilds
Hostility Leaders
The Right Questions

8. How to create your own L2L approach

In this chapter we:

- Suggest how you might deal with objections

- Provide different entry points for learning to learn

- Provide a template for planning

- Learn from the case studies of others

- Outline a way forward for each of the 12 essentials.

And ask the following questions:

- How do I develop my own strategy?

- How do I enrol the whole school community?

- Where should my energies be directed?

- What should drive our development?

- What have others done?

Doing it for yourself

George B. Dantz studied mathematics at the prestigious University of California at Berkeley. Part of his studies included a statistics class. One morning he arrived late for the class. He frantically copied the two problems he saw on the board, knowing that to miss homework was not going to be a good move so early in the course. He found the problems difficult and had to spend more time than he would have liked struggling on them. At the next class he handed them in. What he did not know was that they were not homework problems but examples of unsolvable challenges that the lecturer had been using to demonstrate the complexity and rigour of statistics in the lecture that day. Dantz had approached the challenges in a completely different frame of mind from his classmates. As a result of his efforts he quickly became a celebrity. The story forms the basis of the plot of the film *Good Will Hunting*.

Ellen Langer in her 2009 book *Counterclockwise: Mindful Health and the Power of Possibility* describes an experiment where she deliberately set out to re-adjust the 'social clocks' of a group of very old men. In 1979 she took these men on a residential retreat out of their care homes and cosseted environments and back to a time when they were more independent, youthful and optimistic. She recreated the 1950s and for a week these men were asked to live as though they were 20 years younger. They weren't allowed to talk about anything after 1959. They listened to Hank Williams and Nat King Cole, talked about baseball matches which were coming up. They dressed for the time, read the books and watched films and television from that era. They were given the responsibility of looking after themselves, organising their day and caring for the environment as they had done when they were younger – tending plants, switching off lights, turning down the heating and getting out and about. Langer had a theory that these men might be magically rejuvenated by the change in expectation. She turned out to be correct.

After a week the men were scoring higher on cognitive tests including memory tests, they were physically more upright in the way they carried themselves, they seemed sprightlier and more optimistic. From all the 'environmental cues' which had played a part in winding their clocks back, they had adopted a more positive and more independent take on themselves and on what they were capable of doing. Langer points out that this so called 'priming' effect shifts our response: students were more competitive in a business studies challenge when there was a briefcase close by on a table rather than a rucksack, people tidied more thoroughly when they smelt cleaning fluids, and older women who married younger men seemed to live longer!

Both the 'Dantz moment' and the Langer 'social clock' experiment say something to us about how we make sense of the cues which surround us and most of the time we are unaware of these cues. It also makes us think about how environment can encourage us to impose limitations on what we think is appropriate behaviour in any given situation.

Whilst we don't make naive assumptions that you can think your way out of serious ill-health, stop the process of aging or make yourself into an intellectual by wishing hard enough, you can very easily slow the process of recovery, live an older lifestyle and think yourself out of any intellectual challenge. This 'choosing' of negativity and a tolerance of being surrounded by cues which prime limitations – lowering the ceiling rather than raising it – can be so damaging to success in any school.

What you can do to develop the essentials

Part of the challenge of introducing change is to do with your school 'expectation clock' – what Ellen Langer did with the old men's 'social clocks'.

You can't expect to introduce any sort of learning to learn, skills or competency based approach overnight; it's more of a journey than an epiphany and whilst it would be nice to have a sudden manifestation of a divine learning to learn solution it's better to plan for something more mundane. That's why we use our three stages to the journey: adopt, embed and spread.

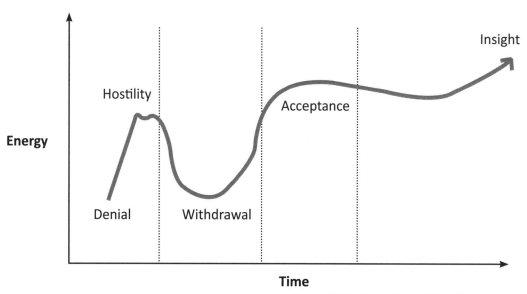

Figure 8. Working through hostility to change

Early in your journey it will become important to identify what great learning behaviours are for you; alternatively, accept ours as we have spent some time in creating them. Next comes the task of designing structured mechanisms for levering up those great learning behaviours in a process – specify, capture, draw attention to, actively promote – which suggests that we get more of what we reinforce.

Inevitably there are new teaching skills which go with this approach so prepare to overcome some resistance which, experience tells us, often looks like Figure 8. It is all too easy to get stuck in the denial–hostility phase, a phase often characterised by energies being displaced into finding flaws.

Perceived obstacle	Typified by	Possible solutions
1. Students	*Students' potential characterised by a weighting in favour of collective staff impressions rather than analysis of objective data*	▨ Challenge staff perceptions ▨ Share student successes ▨ Evaluate data ▨ Look at others' contextual value added *cont.*

Perceived obstacle	Typified by	Possible solutions
2. Parents	*Parents perceived to be disinterested in, or disconnected from, child's schooling*	▦ Re-evaluate what is reported to parents and how ▦ Improve quality not quantity of communication ▦ Allocate 'hard to reach' parents to a nominated team
3. Staff	*Focused on their own area of current expertise, heavily burdened and unable or unwilling to see benefit of alternative approach*	▦ Instigate a disciplined innovation ('adopt' mode) pilot ▦ Sell big picture benefits ▦ Enrol and involve using influencing and breakthrough strategies
4. Leadership	*Locked into maintenance mode*	▦ Provide case studies from similar schools ▦ Identify your school's unique proposition (scarcity influencing) ▦ Join local network activities
5. Inspection process	*Perception that meeting their requirements overrides everything else: the tail wags the dog syndrome*	▦ Establish that learning to learn and positive inspection outcomes can co-exist, i.e. it's possible to do both well ▦ Select case studies from 'outstanding' schools who do learning to learn
6. League tables	*'Must-win games' get low-risk strategies. In other words, the higher the concern about public perception the greater the pressure to play safe*	▦ Need a long term strategy to raise all round performance – not just win a few games and avoid relegation! ▦ Aim to go beyond the mundane ▦ Use the adopt, embed, spread concept
7. Timetable	*An over-emphasis on the needs of the timetable, unimaginative, last minute or poor timetabling can kill creativity*	▦ Earlier planning cycle ▦ Use opportunities to free up space ▦ Get your best brains working together: don't rely entirely on the 'lone fixer' or a software package ▦ Don't use the word 'timetable' – it's for railways and leads to a similar mindset

Perceived obstacle	Typified by	Possible solutions
8. Facilities	*Poor quality, dispersed or over-used classrooms*	■ Solution is integral to imaginative use of time ■ Classrooms themselves should not be a barrier: 'negotiate' access to halls, open areas
9. Equipment	*Common impression that lots of equipment is needed*	■ Laptop, projector and screen, sound system ■ Scheduled use of computer facility ■ Everything else is a bonus
10. Cost	*Little or no funding available*	■ Approach needn't cost in hard cash unless a programme or expertise is being bought in ■ Question may be around what's the real cost of not making a change ■ Could be seen as investment in a long term staff development package
11. Precedent	*Our academic provision is what drives our school and is what appeals to our parents*	■ Illogical to aspire to be leading edge in performing whilst being trailing edge in learning ■ Sell the bigger picture to parents ■ Time to refresh the delivery of academic subjects
12. Culture	*That's not how we do things around here*	■ Says who? ■ Do we undertake systematic review for ourselves and, if so, what is the purpose? Are we actually confronting the brutal facts or jollying ourselves along?
13. Worth	*It's not a priority; we've got too much on our plate and besides we don't get inspected on it*	■ Urgent versus important issue ■ Is there clarity over core purpose? ■ Are we asking the right questions of ourselves?

Some of our essentials may provide a quicker yield than others; for example, three dimensional success criteria is relatively easy to implement and supports frequent classroom process review. Teaching students co-operation skills is also a relatively easy win – many schools use very good commercial systems such as Kagan's co-operative structures to help with this.

Perhaps the most powerful of our 12 essentials is deploying a coherent structure to learning, such as the 4 stage cycle. For some schools a limited trial of these three methods supported by committed professionals would create a sufficient forwards momentum to turn the 'flywheel'.

Starting from where you are at: different entry points for an effective learning to learn approach

A discrete, timetabled lesson for learning to learn

Learning to learn is taught as a discrete lesson in a timetabled slot in the Year 7 curriculum with a team of 'volunteer' and committed staff who deliver the course using a commercially produced programme tailored to the school's context or a school self-developed programme.

Strengths

■ Easy to implement

■ Short lead in time

■ Obvious structure and accountability

■ May prove to be cost effective if a quality experience.

Weaknesses

■ Does not necessarily align with school priorities

■ Learning may not transfer

■ Uneven impact of pedagogy across the school

■ Easily marginalised.

A course integrated within a particular subject or subjects

The ideas, strategies, knowledge, skills and attributes of learning to learn are taught within the scheme of work of a particular subject or subjects. This could take the form of discrete learning to learn lessons taught by subject staff followed by opportunities to practise and use the knowledge, attributes and skills taught within subject-specific contexts and work, or these knowledge, attributes and skills being totally integrated within the teaching of a subject scheme of work.

Strengths

■ Can be grown in a structured and planned way

■ Impactful on student learning

■ Obvious structure and accountability

■ Improves pedagogy across a range of disciplines.

Weaknesses

■ Needs significant planning time

■ Staff need to be trained in the approach before writing schemes of work

■ Conflicts of interest may be difficult to resolve

■ No accreditation or reporting.

A course integrated across the school

In this approach, subjects across the school identify the learning to learn knowledge, skills, attributes and experiences that they can deliver and assess within their subject based curricula and build these elements into their schemes of work and teaching and learning practices. This could begin in Year 7.

Strengths

■ Thoroughly integrated

■ Potential for significant impact on student learning

■ Could improve pedagogy across a range of disciplines.

Weaknesses

■ Needs very large commitment of planning time and a detailed understanding of the essentials

■ All staff need to commit to and be trained in the approach before writing schemes of work

■ May be susceptible to lots of overlap and repetition; student experience may suffer as a consequence of the difficulty of monitoring

■ No accreditation or reporting.

A course delivered within a competency based curriculum framework

Learning to learn can also be delivered within competency based frameworks such as the RSA's Opening Minds and ASDAN's Certificate of Personal Effectiveness (CoPE) Award integrated within cross-curricular tasks, enquiry and problem solving activities that are developed by schools to demonstrate key competencies such as learning, relating to people, managing situations and managing information.

Strengths

■ Accredited and nationally recognised

■ Proven framework

■ Recognised by parents, governors and wider community.

Weaknesses

▪ May not align with school needs

▪ Need to develop resources and audit existing provision

▪ Caught 'between a rock and a hard place' – positioned outside the mainstream of GCSE and similar qualifications yet not locally designed and owned.

As a transition experience

Schools can integrate learning to learn knowledge, skills and attributes within transition projects involving Year 6 and 7 students. Staff in primary schools would start the project work involving learning to learn at the end of Year 6 and this work would then be continued by secondary teachers in the first weeks of Year 7.

Strengths

▪ Motivational and engaging

▪ Provides a focus and helps with transition anxieties

▪ Emphasises skills and competencies approach.

Weaknesses

▪ Not taken seriously

▪ Students miss out on transfer

▪ Benefits could be lost very quickly with a change of school.

As an induction project at the start of school

The first week or two in Year 7 can be used as an induction to secondary education with learning to learn knowledge, skills and attributes integrated within project and enquiry work and taught across the school.

Strengths

▪ Easy to manage

▪ If done well can help students 'get off to a flier'

▪ Could be a good jumping off point for further focus on learning skills.

Weaknesses

▪ Not taken seriously

▪ Students miss out on transfer

▪ Soon forgotten by staff and students who then get on with 'the real work'.

As 'off timetable' days or longer blocks of time

Learning to learn can be delivered and integrated within off timetable days or half days where classes or year groups are involved in real life or subject-specific problem solving and enquiry projects.

Strengths

▨ Easy to manage

▨ Lots of flexibility with an opportunity to be topical

▨ Can emphasise skills and competencies approach.

Weaknesses

▨ Isolated and one-off so less impactful

▨ Little or no transfer

▨ Only involves a limited number of staff.

Of course, some schools use a combination of the above approaches as part of their customisation of the learning to learn approach to their own context.

A whole school approach

A whole school approach is not a recommended entry point – it's more a destination than a starting point. The complexity of having every member of staff marching to the same drum from a given date in the near future is only to be attempted by the most confident. If this is something you remain convinced you wish to do, then bypass adopt and embed and go straight to spread!

A whole school approach is in place with every teacher in every lesson drawing attention to learning processes, using systematic debriefing and also planning engaging learning experiences using an agreed model. In this whole school approach we report competencies or skills to parents using an easily understood framework. We provide whole school tools such as the Electronic Thinking Tools which sit on a virtual learning environment which will in time host a broad range of personalised learning tools. Staff are supported by an imaginative and challenging CPD programme, we review our provision which features on the five year plan and a senior leader heads it up.

Strengths

▨ Impactful and involving

▨ Improves pedagogy across the school

▨ Given automatic status.

Weaknesses

▨ Significant commitment of time and resource especially in planning and development stages

▨ Very long lead-in time

▨ May encounter some subtle and some open resistance if imposed.

Asking the right questions

If a more root and branch approach is needed then maybe the questions we asked in our phases could be useful.

Phase	Question	Response	Intervention	Consequence
1. Disputation	Is everything we currently do good enough?			
	Do we need to make any changes?			

Phase	Question	Response	Intervention	Consequence
2. Exploration	Who or what impresses us?			
	Who or what should we pay attention to?			
	Who or what should we ignore?			

Phase	Question	Response	Intervention	Consequence
3. Orientation	What demands will 21st century life place on our students?			
	In this context, how do we prepare them?			

Phase	Question	Response	Intervention	Consequence
3. Orientation	So what do we want our learners to leave with?			
	How do we do this and meet our other responsibilities?			

Phase	Question	Response	Intervention	Consequence
4. Definition	In our approach what will great learning look like?			
	What principles of learning should underpin our approach?			
	What's the most effective way to intervene?			
	Who are our clients?			

Phase	Question	Response	Intervention	Consequence
5. Specification	What's the approach?			
	How will it be accessed?			*cont.*

Phase	Question	Response	Intervention	Consequence
	How will it be structured?			
	What's the best way to grow it?			

Phase	Question	Response	Intervention	Consequence
6. Realisation	What do we provide for the student?			
	What do we provide for the teacher?			
	What do we provide for the school?			
	What do we provide for the parent?			

Phase	Question	Response	Intervention	Consequence
7. Evaluation	How do we evaluate?			
	How do we develop?			
	How do we support?			

Phase	Question	Response	Intervention	Consequence
8. Consolidation	How do we sustain?			
	Where do we go next?			

Learning from the case studies of others

In this section we look at the experiences of nine different schools focusing on an aspect of their work on learning to learn.

A head teacher told me about his staff in-service which involved all of his Year 6 pupils. They spent a session discussing and recording all the ways they liked to learn. The outcomes were written up on flip charts. At the same time the teachers spent a session discussing and recording all the things they had to teach. The outcomes were written up on flip charts. Then they swapped and for an hour each tried to see if they could engineer the best ways to learn what they had to learn and so solve each others' problem. It could yet turn out to be the perfect form of marriage.

Involving students in their own learning is an aspiration which should go beyond ticking the student voice column. Increasingly we see changes to the structures in schools to open up opportunity for more student contribution. Vertical tutoring takes place in a number of schools with the intent of creating more dynamic communities of learners. Some schools have adopted a guild system. Lipson Community College in Plymouth restructured its tutor groups to build upon the success of the college's vertical guild system. The college's six guilds are like medieval guilds or craft associations: chandlers, coopers, mariners, surfers, players and merchants. Pupils choose their guild according to their interests. The vertical tutor groups sit within the guilds – with a maximum of four pupils per group from each year. The concept is that the student is the most important unit of organisation so everything is built around him or her. This sort of structure benefits approaches such as peer mentoring. It would also facilitate a Lead Learner programme with students assuming learning advocacy roles within their guild.

Lead Learners and learning to learn: St Peter's Church of England Aided School, Exeter

Lyn Bourne, Deputy Headteacher, and Ali Sinden, Lead Teacher for Learning and Thinking Skills at St Peter's School describe their Lead Learner approach.

> Since September 2007, staff and students have been working to implement new strategies for learning and teaching throughout the school. Staff Action Groups and the student Aspire Team started the developments by leading training for staff and students, identifying what we wanted to change and how we might make a difference. Following workshops for staff and students looking at different learning and teaching strategies, we chose to implement a whole school strategy with the new National Curriculum in September 2008 with three strands running through Year 7: a discrete L2L course taught by Lyn and Ali, a common language for learning shared across all departments and a team of student Lead Learners to deliver sessions to practise thinking skills with Year 7 tutor groups every week.

> A Shared Language for Learning is being promoted through: a focus on the 5R's – a different R each half term, the St Peter's Learning Cycle as a framework for whole school planning and the introduction of a single thinking tool across the school each year for three years.

Our core team of Lead Learners started as part of the Aspire Project with Exeter University. The core team of eight students led training for the full team of 72 Lead Learners, identified by their form tutors as enthusiastic, confident and committed learners. The full team were involved in workshops designed to gather students' ideas for school development and raise awareness of the 5R's. The Lead Learners were divided into teams to deliver peer sessions with Year 7 students in a tutor period each week, practising good learner attributes through practical activities linked to the 'R' focus for the term, which had been launched with a presentation in assembly by Lyn, Ali and the Lead Learner Team (Resilience – Autumn; Responsible and Resourceful – Spring; Reasoning and Reflective – Summer).

The teams of Lead Learners were trained by Ali in delivery techniques and the activity they would work on – in mixed age teams of four – with each Year 7 tutor group for 20 minutes on Fridays over nine weeks. Year 7 students have given a very positive response to the sessions and the Lead Learners themselves have shown significant personal development through the experience. Next year's Lead Learner programme will draw on the first graduates of the L2L course in Year 7, the team members from this year who would like to continue and other students who have been identified as effective Lead Learners during the year. The activities will broaden to include presentation assemblies by Lead Learners on the 'R' focus of the term to all other year groups and peer led sessions on L2 in Citizenship and Personal Social and Health Education.

Wicked Wednesday at Lipson Community College and Flexible Friday at Leasowes Community College are occasions when the timetable is suspended to allow a different sort of learning. At Leasowes cross-curricular projects allow for staff to be highly creative and break out of the imposition of short concentrated lessons. No two of the 38 Fridays are the same and the demands of planning and delivering the approach are partly offset by increased time for staff to work together. By breaking out of the traditional silos of time and subject disciplines there is less likelihood of students commodifying knowledge and the schools can tap in to the natural curiosity of their learners.

Integrating L2 into an enquiry based Year 7 curriculum: Blessed George Napier School, Banbury

Chris Martin from Blessed George Napier School explains how the challenge was to integrate learning to learn skills into a new curriculum.

We wanted a model to embrace recent changes in education and technology. Middle leaders received expert training on the new curriculum which was drip-fed back to a dedicated L2 team who, in turn, were empowered to deliver outstanding learning experiences.

L2 was introduced for the first time in September 2008 and immediately prioritised – staff were handpicked and rooms allocated first. Every other week Year 7 are discretely taught L2 in a four hour block providing extended opportunities for problem solving challenges where staff can facilitate learning. Humanities and ICT teaching time has been reduced so particular L2 lessons focus on subject-specific content, skills and themes in these areas.

We are assessing pupil progress against the key learner attributes (the 5R's) and this is reported to parents. Also pupil's self-assess during the course using the 5R's.

Initially, to inform our planning, analysis has been qualitative. L2 has deliberately been over-staffed to enable a programme of peer observation. It is taught simultaneously enabling learning walks to assess delivery across the year group. A deputy head has been removed from planning to enable objective evaluation. Pupils have been interviewed by staff and an external consultant. Quantitative assessment of all pupils, staff and parents is planned.

Our curriculum design has enabled us to create real authentic experiences for the pupils and they have responded incredibly to the extended blocks of time showing creativity and ingenuity.

Some schools have integrated a learning to learn approach which they have customised for themselves and dropped into an existing skills framework such as the RSA's Opening Minds. There is a value in this approach – it can be bolstered by having the support of a recognised body with an existing framework and it allows, indeed requires, customisation.

Integrating L2 into a competency based curriculum: Oasis Academy MediaCityUK, Salford

'The Year 7 Creative Curriculum was designed to support and complement one of the fundamental aims of the Academy; to enable each student to achieve his or her full potential in their journey as lifelong learners,' says Karen Sudworth, Deputy Principal of Oasis Academy.

The curriculum is based on the development of six key competencies:

- Enquiry
- Citizenship
- Learning
- Managing information
- Managing people
- Managing situations.

These are based around the RSA's Opening Minds competencies. Alite's Learning to Learn, Philosophy for Children and SEAL are also integral and fundamental to the design of the course. All learning sessions are planned around the accelerated learning cycle and its principles.

The Year 7 Creative Curriculum makes up 43% of the curriculum time allocation and whilst the development of the students' competencies is the priority, learning modules cover key content from the National Curriculum for Humanities, Expressive Arts, Modern Foreign Languages and Technology subjects.

The Year 7 Creative Curriculum is accommodated in a suite of rooms which provides a 'home base' for the year group. Rooms are decorated and furnished in a uniform way to provide a bright, stimulating and welcoming environment. Staff teaching within the Creative Curriculum are willing volunteers and are only timetabled to teach the subject if they are in full agreement.

Assessment of students is through the six competencies with clear criteria for staff and students on how to progress from one level to the next. Peer and self assessment are integral to the modules, while group assessment for the L2 Team Learner is through a half day Murder Mystery activity for the whole year group.

Regular and on-going evaluation of the course is carried out through data collection of progress, student and staff opinion and focus groups, including special educational needs and gifted and talented. Plans for further development include a greater emphasis on the recording of students' attributes, the 5R's of a successful learner and the development of an Applied Creative Curriculum for Year 8.

Some of the schools we work with are very pragmatic in how they use the 5R's. Our own 5R's have proved very useful for those schools who wish to deliver a skills and competencies type of approach and be able, at the same time, to meet national imperatives without 'flipping' between them.

Embedding the 5Rs: Port Glasgow High School

A school that has the Every Child Matters agenda close to its core purpose, is persuaded of the benefits of a more informed approach to assessment and is simultaneously keen to acknowledge other developments – without allowing them to roll through its curriculum like a heavy truck – uses the L2 approach in the belief that it will meet the other agendas. What seems to be key is permeating the everyday moment-by-moment experiences of teachers and students. Pauline Barclay, L2 Champion at the Port Glasgow High School, says 'we are trying to embed the 5Rs in different ways'.

Port Glasgow High School has dedicated several staff training sessions to exploring the L2 strategies and the ways they can be implemented by teachers in their own lessons. Part of this in-service work has been encouraging teachers to look at the written and verbal feedback they give to pupils and see where it would be appropriate to acknowledge an 'R' attribute. A group of staff members have volunteered this term to focus on the 5R's and report back on ways in which they have been useful to them regarding feedback.

Every teaching area in our school has a Learning Wall display in which each 'R' attribute has an individual poster. As a school we are working towards using these posters to acknowledge when an attribute is required of our pupils in a lesson and also when an attribute has been displayed by an individual or group.

We currently have a working group investigating ways in which we could use the 5R's in reporting and how we would enable parents to access this information in a meaningful way. Teachers this year have been encouraged to use 'R' vocabulary when writing Positive Referral Certificates, if deemed appropriate. These certificates are given out by teachers whenever they wish to recognise and celebrate pupil achievement, positive behaviour or success and are a very important part of PGHS life.

Port Glasgow High School successfully runs two off timetable L2 days for S1 and S2 (Years 7 and 8) respectively. During these days, which are practical and active, pupils are encouraged to notice and acknowledge when their group behaves in a way that exhibits an 'R' quality and staff reinforce when one is required. We have also used the Virtual Work Experience in S2 to reinforce team learner skills and reinforce the 5R's. As this is just our second year delivering L2, our main concern is to have pupils gain confidence with the vocabulary and to allow them class time to speculate and discuss which characteristics are required of them in particular lessons.

Assessing and reporting using the 5Rs: Oasis Academy, Enfield

At Oasis Academy, Enfield, assessing and reporting using the 5R's is taken a step further and involves parents, as Jenny Scott explains.

We run an innovative curriculum which incorporates a framework of five theme based modules across the school year. It delivers L2 through humanities, taught at the beginning of each module. The skills and processes are then embedded within the humanities lessons during the module.

The 5R's are used through learning objectives in every subject and lesson across the school. Students are assessed using the 5R's in both humanities and PE, which are reported at the end of every module. Students are assessed using a framework which has been developed over the last 18 months. This assesses how often they demonstrate the competence using 'rarely, sometimes, mostly, always'.

Success of the 5R's has been evaluated through parent and student feedback and student progress. It has also received positive feedback from Ofsted this year which commented:

The academy is constantly refining its assessment procedures in subjects and for skills across the curriculum, leading to accurate identification of areas of need and resulting improvements in achievement.

Very good attention is paid to developing literacy skills and a range of competencies so that students are well prepared for each stage of their education.

The plans for the future are to set up a levelling system whereby students will be given a level, based on assessment in five different areas: Home (parent passport), Classes (such as homework), Humanities, School (such as responsibility posts) and Community (such as clubs). We believe it is essential to encourage the students to demonstrate the competencies in a number of different areas and contexts. We are also developing our reward system based around the 5R's, enhancing our display throughout the school and encouraging parent understanding through the virtual learning environment.

Involving parents in learning to learn: Blessed Edward Oldcorne School, Worcester

The missing dimension in many learning to learn approaches is work with parents. In most it is not featured and yet, as we have described elsewhere, it is very significant in shaping a child's learning experience. For Greg McClarey of Blessed Edward Oldcorne School it was important not to lecture parents but to provide them with useful insights. 'The focus of all our work is to empower parents and enable them to have a "learning conversation" with their children, rather than "what did you do at school today?"'

The strategies we use to try to involve parents more in their child's learning are:

- A learning seminar for parents in each year group once a year.

- Displays on parents' evenings of learning to learn approaches. There are also standardised learning displays in all classrooms.

- A learning newsletter for parents which focuses on key ideas that the school is developing is published once a term.

- Information about L2 and the approaches that we use in school are posted on the school website.

We tried to involve and educate parents in the ideas and strategies of learning to learn and this shaped the learning seminars:

- Defining the 5R's and using '5R' language when talking to children (e.g. 'You need to be more resilient with your French learning').

- The work of Carol Dweck on the importance of a learner's view of their own intelligence.

- The importance of developing skills and attributes which can be used both in and beyond the classroom.

- How to be a learning coach by accentuating the positive.

- How to help your child prepare for examinations: revision techniques, share the 'Intent, File, Rehearse' model of memory.

We have evaluated the success of these initiatives through parental feedback forms at the end of each learning seminar, through monitoring the number of hits on the parental section of the school website and through questionnaires at parents' evenings. We have learned from our evaluations that parents like to talk to other parents and share their own personal experiences. They are very appreciative of learning to learn input as they recognise that the world that their children are entering is very different to the one they entered when they left school. Parents also like the 'sunshine' phone calls we do in which positive news about a child's achievements is shared.

In the future, we will be introducing the PAL package into our learning seminars and newsletters. We are also planning to run learning seminars for parents from our feeder primary schools as well as developing more parent-friendly curriculum resources.

Harnessing technology: Abraham Guest High School, Wigan

At Abraham Guest High School, Wigan they have used the skills of their design team to customise resources to great effect, according to Gillian Pye, L2 Champion at the school.

The Electronic Learning Wall was developed from an idea we saw at Cramlington Learning Village. It is a way of having a common generic learning display in every learning space in school and can be accessed by all staff and learners. It can be used in all subject areas to reinforce the key learning skills and attributes. It can be used to consolidate learning by encouraging reflection through the Thinking Hats for example. The learning wall also has the 5R's assessment statements on it and can be used by learners in their self assessment reviews each term.

The learning wall was initially being used by learning to learn staff with their classes, but now we are spreading the use of the wall across the school. The IT system logs how many hits on the wall there are and by which members of staff – this has given us a way of being able to highlight where further support needs to be offered.

Complementing the Electronic Learning Wall is a Learning Cycle Mat. The mat is used on learners' desks so that they have a constant reference to the planning and delivery style of their learning. It is our equivalent of a Success Mat.

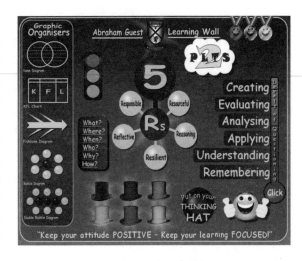

At AGHS we have continued to develop generic planning and reviewing tools to be used across subject areas to reinforce the common learning language and approaches. For example, reflective devices such as the Thinking Hats review and the contribution pie charts.

We want to continue to develop our learners to adopt and embed the key learning attributes and we will be working on a self assessment log where learners will assess and evaluate their own progress in each of the 5R's. The learners will be using the bronze, silver, gold and platinum assessment statements to evaluate their progress and set themselves learning targets.

Involving staff in leading learning to learn change: St Mary's Catholic College, Blackpool

At St Mary's Catholic College, Blackpool there is a strategic view of what learning to learn will do for the school. John Young, L2 Champion at St Mary's says:

Our very first stage was to research and develop a strategy document which identified learning to learn as the way forward for thinking and learning: this was well-received by the school leadership team (SLT) and adopted by the governors. Through this process the SLT became fully committed to the introduction of L2L – a vital prerequisite for success.

The next strategic goal was to present L2L to middle managers in such a positive way that they would accept, welcome and help introduce it. Promoting the benefits of L2L at a practical level needed some evidence: colleagues readily saw that existing approaches produced learners who achieved, within limits, at the ages of 16 to 18 through educational spoon feeding. All acknowledged that this was unsatisfactory and far short of any ideal vision for education. The key to achieving the goal of middle managers taking L2L to heart would be evidence: publicising the experience of Cramlington Learning Village offered a convincing example of L2L effectiveness.

Once hearts and minds were at least positive, practicalities had to be addressed – modelling a new Key Stage 3 curriculum in which L2L would have a significant allocation, and identifying and training staff to teach L2L. Because the prospect of L2L had been welcomed by staff, colleagues in English, history, geography and RE were invited to be the first generation of L2L teachers at St Mary's. All of these had credibility and responsibility as middle or senior leaders. Initial training was preceded by attendance at learning to learn conferences, and followed by a pilot for Year 7 then weekly L2L led by the team for Years 7, 8 and now 9.

Immediate plans for staff development involve further regular CPD using some of the two and half hour slots we have on Wonderful Wednesdays each fortnight, restructuring the senior leadership team and leadership of change through a College Improvement Group and sub-group (working party) to produce an unequivocal and emphatic focus on learning, and integrating the spread of L2L into our developing programme of evaluative lesson observations. The hosting of termly Journey School Events will also be a vehicle for internal staff reflection and development. Positive evaluation of impact will be critical for future staff credibility and enthusiasm.

The key message from our own experience is secure staff backing throughout the organisation, maintain a high profile for L2L and ensure resources and staffing match the high profile words and publicity.

Creating the classroom culture of learning to learn – pedagogy, display, values and expectations: South Shields Community School

It is sometimes said that culture in a school is 'the way we do things around here'. For L2 Champion Karen Tones at South Shields Community School shifting the culture was important. Creating an impact was also important and partly achieved by focusing on the environment.

We have used a range of strategies including a PowerPoint presentation for each of the L2 lessons with the headings of Connect, Activate, Demonstrate and Consolidate. Every lesson starts with teachers meeting and greeting the students and on entry a 'connect the learning' task will be displayed. The learning objectives are then shared with students, split into the attributes, skills and knowledge (ASK) to be covered in the lesson with clear success criteria also outlined.

To further create a positive L2 environment we have developed a range of resources that can support and enhance the learning experience, including the ASK poster, 5R's posters, de Bono's Thinking Hats posters and key questions posters. Each classroom in the school now has a learning wall which, as well as displaying the posters, reinforces key learning language and thinking tools. We are working on our own version of an interactive learning wall which we will use across the whole school.

We also use success/learning mats to support the assessment for learning side of L2 in each lesson. Students are asked to reflect on what they have achieved in the lesson based on success criteria, set either by themselves or the teacher. In addition, we are focusing on developing the student voice. Students are being encouraged use the mats to create their own objectives and success criteria using Anderson's taxonomy in the form of a spider's web.

Before all of the above can occur we, as a department, aim to create a learning environment where students can achieve and feel they can take risks, make mistakes and achieve success with no inhibitions. To create this safe and challenging environment we regularly reinforce our expectations. We focus on the benefits of positive behaviour and how negative behaviour can affect the learning environment. We always challenge negative behaviour with the language of learning focusing on the impact of the student's behaviour on learning rather than the individual themselves. There is a culture of no put-downs, only push-ups – treat others as you would be treated. Each term we ask the students how we can improve the learning environment. Students commented in questionnaires that seeing the work of other students inspired them to give challenges a go and the thinking tools displayed in classrooms helped them to think and focus their learning. Some students even said the learning environment in L2 classrooms felt like home: safe and comfortable!

Monitoring and evaluating learning to learn

Monitoring and evaluation of the learning to learn course needs to be planned for in the same way as course development and progression. The key advice is plan early in the school year and only plan what is manageable and sustainable in your school.

Some ideas for monitoring and evaluation activities might be:

- Collecting student attitudes to learning and perceptions of the effectiveness of learning to learn through questionnaires and videoed interviews of a sample of the cohort

- Collecting teacher perceptions of the course and its impact on learning through questionnaires of learning to learn for trained and non-trained staff

- Interviews with senior leader and a sample of learning to learn trained staff

- Student and staff podcasts on their impressions and successes of the course

- Observations of learning to learn lessons

- Portfolio of student learning to learn work, events and activities

- Portfolio of learning to learn staff course development ideas, as well as more longer term activities that can produce quantitative findings such as:

  - Analysis of assessment and progress data for groups/year groups following the learning to learn course compared with previous cohorts

  - Analysis of GCSE exam results against predictions for groups/year groups who have followed the learning to learn course compared with previous cohorts

  - Analysis of AS and A2 exam results against predictions for groups who have followed the learning to learn course compared with previous cohorts.

It is important to stress that, even if these latter quantitative activities appear to show that learning to learn has had a positive impact on achievement, a direct causal link cannot be directly established due to the range of factors in a school that can impact on achievement.

However, over time if the trend is repeated, schools could argue that learning to learn is one significant influence on improving student progress and achievement. If this data is linked with the more qualitative information collected by activities such as classroom observation, student and staff interviews and questionnaires, it becomes far more powerful.

Some suggestions for the first year of monitoring and evaluating learning to learn

Start of the year

■ Student questionnaire for year group following the learning to learn course focused on attitudes to learning, language of learning, learning attributes, knowledge of how they learn best, learning skills and tools and how much they use this knowledge and skills in other lessons

■ Videoed student interviews with a small sample of the year group on the above areas and their perception of learning to learn lessons.

During the year

■ Classroom observation of staff using this approach

■ Portfolio of student work including photographic/video evidence

■ Sample materials from learning to learn teachers

■ Collection of ideas and evidence of learning display.

End of the year

■ Re-questionnaire students – compare and analyse results

■ Re-interview students – compare and analyse results

■ Collect views of staff teaching learning to learn on the impact of the course on students' attitudes to learning, learning skills and attributes

■ Summarise evaluative findings in short report to the senior leadership team and offer suggestions for improvement/development.

Essential	Adopt	Embed	Spread
Three dimensional success criteria	An example of a 'Trojan mouse' – a small intervention with a massive impact and for that reason best agreed early and worth going for across the school	Continue with emphasis across all staff and all learning experiences	Continue with emphasis across all staff and all learning experiences
Process sensitivity	Small scale trials of process techniques	Agree core learning processes and means of drawing students' attention to their use	All staff know, understand and deploy core learning processes. Student experience is immersive
Learner behaviours which are well defined	Clarity on KASE and, if the model is a small scale trial or discrete approach, then reviewed against these	All staff know and understand the KASE outcomes. Curriculum offer is reviewed against KASE. Students use Electronic Profilers for debriefing	KASE outcomes feature in schemes of learning and are drawn from constructing success criteria
Language of learning	Identify and use core vocabulary in your discrete programme	All teachers encouraged to model use of learning vocabulary. Visual display in place across the school	All teachers model use of learning vocabulary. Visual display in place across the school
Systematic debriefing and reporting	Internal trial in place to see what the issues are around identifying and assessing progress in the R's Use of Learner Passports Debriefing techniques practised extensively within trial	Wide use of assessment for learning tools, appropriate goal setting, debriefing techniques Core subjects reporting on 5R's. Electronic Passports trialled	Extensive use of assessment for learning tools, appropriate goal setting, debriefing techniques 5R's reported to parents. Electronic Passports used across school *cont.*

Essential	Adopt	Embed	Spread
Coherent structure to learning	Another 'Trojan mouse' – a more complex intervention but worth initiating early. Schemes of learning are written consistently. Use the VLE so that all lesson architecture is distinct, easily understood and accessible	Commitment to use in agreed structure across all learning experiences. Programme to put model into every subject area	All learning experiences – formal and informal – show evidence of agreed coherent structure. Taught lessons are all in agreed structure
Engaging experiences	The quality of the learning in the classroom is what matters so use some of your best teachers	Improved engagement across lessons. Supportive classroom observation and monitoring initiated	High internal consistency of engagement. Supportive classroom observation and monitoring fully in place
Thinking fluency	Identify a limited range of appropriate strategies and use in your discrete programme	Agreed thinking skills used across the whole learning experience. Electronic Toolbox used by all students	Co-operation skills bedded in across the whole learning experience. Thematic and enquiry days to apply skills. Toolbox used by all students
Team and personal challenge	Practised within the discrete programme	More commonly used across subject teaching	Used across all subject teaching

Thematic and enquiry blocks or days based on 'challenges' |
| Co-operation skills | Identify a limited range of appropriate strategies and use in your discrete programme | Co-operation skills used across the whole learning experience | Co-operation skills bedded in across the whole learning experience

Thematic and enquiry days to apply skills |

Essential	Adopt	Embed	Spread
Independent enquiry	Practise within the discrete programme	Some time freed up for independent enquiry	Extended blocks of time devoted to independent enquiry
System rigour	SLT responsibility Service delivery plan Home learning Systematically reviewed	SLT responsibility Service delivery five year plan Home learning Reported to parents Systematically reviewed Classroom observation criteria	SLT responsibility Service delivery five year plan Home learning Accreditation Reported to parents Systematically reviewed Classroom observation criteria Changes to school 'day'

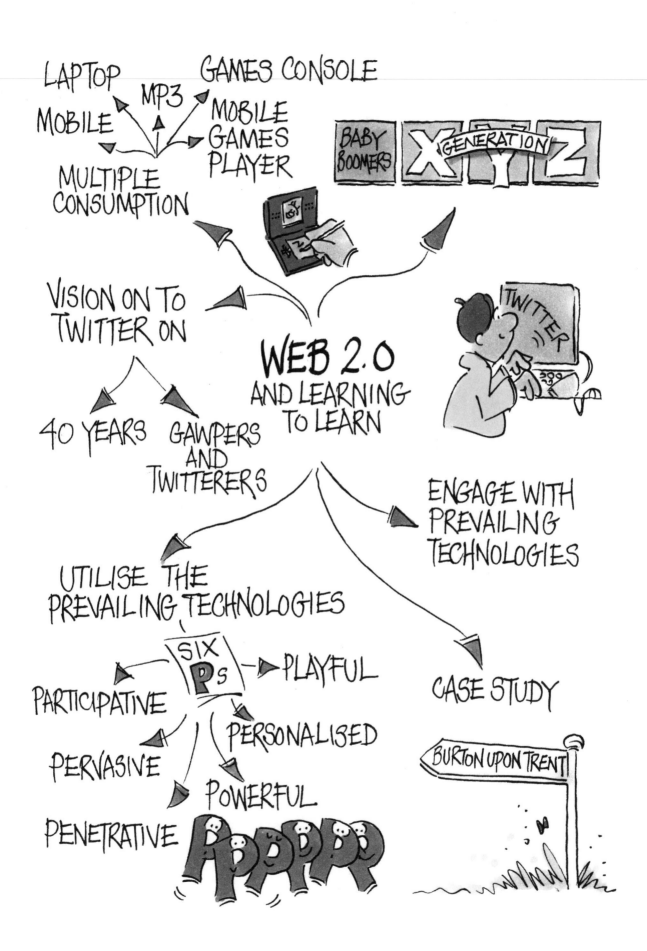

LAPTOP

MP3

MOBILE

GAMES CONSOLE

MOBILE GAMES PLAYER

MULTIPLE CONSUMPTION

BABY BOOMERS

GENERATION XYZ

TWITTER

VISION ON TO TWITTER ON

WEB 2.0 AND LEARNING TO LEARN

40 YEARS

GAWPERS AND TWITTERERS

ENGAGE WITH PREVAILING TECHNOLOGIES

UTILISE THE PREVAILING TECHNOLOGIES

SIX P's

PLAYFUL

CASE STUDY

PARTICIPATIVE

PERSONALISED

PERVASIVE

POWERFUL

PENETRATIVE

BURTON UPON TRENT

235

Technology Paper Platform Generation
BECTA Vision On *Shelf Lives* Blog
Baby Boomer Web X Hosted Y Server Z
Twitter **Web 2.0** *Open Source* YouTube
Facebook **6P's** Google
wiki file sharing

9. Web 2.0 and learning to learn

In this chapter we:

- Go from *Vision On* to Twitter on

- Describe the characteristics of four generations

- Introduce the 6P's

- Describe what schools might do

- Provide a case study.

And ask the following questions:

- What does the information native do which the migrant doesn't?

- How do I overcome the limitations of technology?

- Where is this development taking us?

- What's available?

From *Vision On* to **Twitter on**

Shuffle back in time and away from personalisation – from Twitter, Wikipedia, Google, open source software and Facebook. Go back to the 1970s. The television programme *Vision On* ran from 1964 to 1976. It had a very catchy theme tune. It was memorable for a whole generation – myself included – principally for the endless close-ups of children's paintings viewed to the same accompanying music. The camera panned so slowly from one painting to another you could almost hear it squeak.

In what appeared to be a more innocent age of children's television, families watched a choice of two then three channels, homemade products were celebrated on-screen, programmes finished at the same time in the evening with the playing of the national anthem and a slowly disappearing dot. It was all carefully scheduled, universally consumed and paid for through one licensing system.

Vision On's host, Tony Hart, died peacefully in January 2009 some three days after US Airways Flight 1549, a scheduled commercial passenger flight from New York City to Charlotte, North Carolina crash landed shortly after takeoff in the Hudson River. Within seconds of the plane landing in the river, a so-called Twitterer from Florida, Janis Krums, who was on a nearby ferry, took a picture on his iPhone and immediately posted it on TwitPic. Through micro-blogging and sharing it was seen by 80,000 people all around the world – from China to Iran and Argentina. They saw it before the port authority helicopter had located the downed plane.

Baby Boomers	Generation X	Generation Y	Generation Z
*c.*1946–1964 Digital deniers	*c.*1965–1979 Digital migrants	*c.*1980–1994 Digital natives	*c.*1995– Digital do-ers
Kennedy Cold War Prosperity Conscience Flower power	Thatcher Berlin Wall Boom and bust Individuality Punk	Blair Princess Diana Growth Networking Eco-warriors	Cameron? Climate change? Caution? Collaboration? Entrepreneurs?
Saved first then bought	Payment by instalments	Credit cards	Free downloads?
The Beatles *Top of the Pops* Raleigh Tourer Black and white TV	Sex Pistols MTV Chopper Colour TV	Arctic Monkeys File sharing BMX Satellite TV	Mix your own? YouTube? Wii virtual bike? Hand-held devices?
Log tables	Slide rules and desk top calculators	The BBC 'B'	Brain trainers?

I, you maybe, we perhaps, were 'gawpers' – we sat through Tony Hart's choice of barely discernible paintings at the same time, in the same way, in our separate houses across the country with little or no choice. The students in our schools are would-be 'twitterers'. Their communication is characterised by immediacy and intimacy, with no long tail of scrutiny, adjudication or selection. It's there and it's shared! A potential tsunami of the inconsequential impacting on us all.

It is sometimes said that there are digital migrants and digital natives. We think that we are seeing fine distinctions in how different age groups in the UK have related to contemporary electronic media. For these authors at least there are some defining experiences. Inevitably your defining experiences shape your relationship with technology. At this point in time in our school system it's the generation who are potentially most remote from the prevailing technology that is making most of the decisions about it. It's the Baby Boomers who have been agreeing the strategy, writing the policies, leading the schools and spending the budgets. Generations X and Y have been doing most of the teaching, some of the managing and most of the adapting.

It's been Generations X and Y who have had the biggest task in quickly embracing the digital divisions. They have quickly learned about electronic whiteboards before realising that they are maybe not all that they were expected to be. They pioneered the use of PowerPoint and put all their schemes of work somewhere on the school website before quickly segueing into forums, blogs, wikis, open source software, iPods, MP3 and green screens. Now they find to their chagrin that Generation Z are not that impressed with their efforts!

The prevailing classroom technologies of the age tell us a lot about the learning methods of that age. The classroom technology time trail takes us from my piece of slate to MySpace in less than 40 years. I have two publications in front of me as I write. One is a small book with a red cover and a picture of a BBC 'B' computer. It's called *A Young Person's Guide to BBC BASIC*, published by the National Computing Centre, in 1983. It includes chapters like 'How to Connect Up and Switch On'. In this chapter there are the following guidelines:

> *The BBC computer comes complete with an attached mains lead and moulded 13 amp plug. This plug should not be removed.*

The other publication is a survey from Becta published in 2008, some 25 years later, and is entitled *An Analysis of Emerging Trends Affecting the Use of Technology in Education*. It tells us how far we've come since learning how 'to switch on'.

According to the Becta survey young people have a 'distinctly multi-tasking relationship' with new technologies and a 'multiple consumption' approach to owning them.[66] The following items are what the teens or younger aspire to possessing:

- Laptop computer
- Mobile phone (in some cases more than one)
- MP3 player
- Full-size games console
- Mobile games player.

The research found that young people were in a very strong 'consumer relationship' with these new technologies. The other trends they noted are:

- Since 2007, within the 15–24 age group, there has been a hike in the download of music, films or clips from the internet (52% increase), playing games online (50% increase) and watching video clips and webcasts (45% increase).

- Oldies do not take to games consoles. They are used less frequently as age increases: 60% of 15–24-year-olds have access to games consoles, whereas only 33% of people aged 45–64 do.

- Young people aged 16–24 are the most likely to download unauthorised music and films.

- Nearly seven in ten individuals aged 16–19 claim to upload photos onto the internet, with six in ten being part of a social networking community. Popular user generated content includes blog updates, photos, videos and web pages.

- Young people are the most likely to multi-task with technology.

For the decision makers, as well as those who live by the decisions, it is imperative to enter the world of Generation Z. By doing so we can bring the wealth of what we know about great learning and marry it with great technology. The marriage needs to be one which lasts, so technologies which are ephemeral, which are antagonistic to great learning or which are not readily available, don't get to the altar.

The basic learning to learn kit is low tech. It's the equivalent of your dodgy uncle agreeing to do the disco at your wedding reception for a few drinks. A laptop, projector, digital camera, speakers and screen should be enough for you to get going. For a more enduring relationship with technology which will stand the test of time we need to think ahead.

If it is the case that the prevailing classroom technologies of the age should tell us a lot about the learning methods of that age we need to ask what the features of those technologies are. We have defined the features as the 6P's.

Participative. The dominant 'P', participation is the name of the game. Older students are protective of the communities in which they participate and whilst it might be an example of 'withitness' for teachers to suggest we share our feedback on the form Facebook page many will see that as an undesirable overlap. Whilst protective of some spaces they inhabit, they are nevertheless conversant with the conventions of sharing. Some 10,000 videos – typically of less than three minutes duration and saying nothing very much – get shared every day within the YouTube community. Why? The very best are promoted through sites like Delicious and Digg it, get talked about in blogs and stars are created.

Schools should look to replicate the social networking model to develop co-operation, shared problem solving, mutuality and openness.

Pervasive. Ubiquitous, personally owned digital devices are both an opportunity and a threat to schools. They can offer immediate access to the curriculum anytime, anywhere. They can link to the world beyond the classroom at a click. Parents have the same devices so we can all be connected up. I can text the cancellation of the football match, a reminder about the play and a hyperlink to the real time reporting on our parent portal. But so can lots of other less ethical agencies. Will it be the job of schools to teach safe, responsible and critically aware use of digital technologies? If so how does that happen? As students see technologies as useful tools that help them do what matters, they are not interested in being taught IT. You don't make children fluent and critical readers by teaching the history of printing. As the price comes down and the power goes up more and more children will have technology at their fingertips which will begin to make rooms full of PCs interesting historical curiosities. As we write schools are already anticipating zero capital spend on ICT.

Schools should look again at their ICT strategy and ask is it future proofed? To what extent can you exploit the opportunities that personally owned digital devices bring?

Penetrative. Again Becta reports that at the age of 15, 75% of children own or use an MP3 player or mobile phone. Between the ages of 8 and 11 and again between 12 and 15, a significant increase occurs in the number of media activities carried out, particularly regarding use of the internet (26%), mobile phones (39%) and iPods or MP3 players (24%).

Schools should ask to what extent are our teachers able to exploit this in the design and location of learning resources? Can we host all these learning resources so that they are accessible through a wide variety of portable technologies?

Powerful. Moving information around at the speed of light is big business. By 2006 data centres already consumed more power in the United States than did television sets. Google, one of the big companies at the eye of the storm, has an aspiration to organise all the world's information. That's a lot of ambition but it's worth pursuing because they make their money out of knowing about you and I. In 2007 Google earned US$4.2 billion in net income.[67] It comes from personalising the advertisements it places whenever we conduct a search. The more they know about you and I, the more geared to our lifestyles and interests the ads can become. In order to run this service Google link up thousands of servers across their own data centres. This gives them power, security and speed. Tests they ran on whether consumers would notice a difference between 25 test results in 0.9 seconds or ten in 0.4 showed conclusively that a high number left their site when it took 0.9 seconds. As consumers we have got used to speed and so want it along with high quality graphics. For young people it's graphics before text. Their patience is being conditioned by their search habits.

Schools should ask hard questions about their virtual learning environments and about who is hosting and maintaining their server. For power, security and speed it's maybe best to do so yourself.

Personalised. More and more users want to personalise their digital products and use them in a way of their own choosing. It may be through drag and drop in iGoogle, downloading ringtones, selecting applications for an iPhone, creating your own avatar or using RSS feeds. Providers know this and benefit from it. The system will remember you and the technologies will deliver to the long tail of personalised demand. In the past if I wanted to buy a CD I could go to the Virgin Megastore in Oxford Street and find the popular artists easily. These artists took up a lot of floor space, their music was prominently positioned, marketed with a big budget and hundreds of CDs were in stock. Problems only occurred when I wanted something less 'mass market' and more appealing to my own personal taste. It's unlikely that the store will devote floor space to an obscure folk singer and maybe not have any of their work in stock. My visit would end in disappointment. Now in an online environment the long tail is one where tens of thousands of quirky choices earn as much or more revenue as tens of thousands of the same choice. There's no floor space and advertising needed if I can bring the offer to you direct.

Schools should look at what tools can sit on their virtual learning environment – as a minimum this should include personal electronic portfolios to which students can upload various types of file as evidence of achievement, and shared assessment so that others can go in and make comments, offer advice, edit and add to what's there.

Playful. Research by Demos indicated that children are learning a whole range of skills when interacting with each other, gaming or creating. Informal learning includes the development of digital skills.[68] Demos say that as a consequence of this sort of learning, digital skills are developed including social skills such as collaboration, peer-to-peer learning and risk-taking; cognitive skills such as multi-tasking, logical thinking and trial and error learning; physical skills such as hand–eye coordination; technical skills such as web design and content creation.[69] Marc Prensky, author of *Don't Bother Me Mom: I'm Learning* believes that computer gaming can prepare children for life in the 21st century by teaching them how to collaborate, take measured risks, devise strategy formulation and execution, make complex decisions and respond to moral dilemmas.

One of the best contemporary examples of young people collaborating with strangers in a competitive environment is in World of Warcraft (WoW), a massively popular multiplayer online game. WoW has over 10 million devotees. In WoW, performance is measured in terms of experience points. Players accumulate these by performing a variety of tasks that become more challenging as the game progresses. The better you do the harder it gets, but the time diminishes because you become skilled and you get access to tools. As the game advances, players learn to collaborate and participate in 'guilds' which are teams of players who must work together to achieve the next level of performance. As relationships and trust develop within these teams, everyone is motivated to innovate by the desire not to let the team down. Players naturally organise into guilds as they move on to more advanced levels because they realise they cannot accomplish the tasks without collaborating with others with complementary skills.

Schools should embrace the possibilities that high participation online gaming offers for learning. This can happen in three ways: firstly, by encouraging young people to share their experiences and helping them extrapolate and generalise how those experiences can help them beyond the console; secondly, by investigating the learning opportunities offered by commercial games; and thirdly by adapting some of the principles when designing simple classroom activities, some of which could be web based.

A good example of a school which is attempting to merge learning to learn with Web 2.0 tools is de Ferrers Technology College in Burton-upon-Trent, as Nick Holmes, L2 Champion at the college, explains.

Learning to learn and the Web 2.0 generation: de Ferrers Technology College, Burton-upon-Trent

At de Ferrers, we have developed the use of realsmart to meet some of the needs of the Web 2.0 generation. realsmart is a suite of tools that are designed to develop learning. They include rmap (graphical organiser/mind mapping tool), rweb (website creation), rcast (create blogs and pod/vodcasts) and rpassport (interactive learning passport).

The key aspect linked to L2 is RAFL – a formative assessment tool which is online. Teachers build the self assessments for their students and can also upload guidance for them to follow.

The combination of L2 skills and self assessment by the student is a powerful tool to develop learning across the curriculum. It seemed obvious that the transferable learning skills in L2 are the 5R's: reasoning, responsibility, resourcefulness, reflection and resilience. At de Ferrers, we have added our own sixth 'R': relationships. This is to take account of the SEAL agenda taken up by the Local Authority and also to provide a focus for a new strand to our personalising learning approach.

We have also taken the opportunity of the revised National Curriculum and the demise of SATs to treat Years 7 and 8 as a foundation years learning course. Given the need to rewrite the traditional curriculum content, we have also asked staff to explicitly integrate the 6R's into every lesson. This has been achieved by planning for 'split-screen objectives' to achieve parity between lesson content and learning skills.

So, using the RAFL aspect of realsmart, students are first asked to make a simple self assessment of their progress in that characteristic. This is done using 'smileys': grey for not yet started, red for unhappy with progress and need support, yellow for satisfied with progress but still room for development and green for pleased with progress.

Students are also required to upload evidence to support their assessment. This could take the form of a comment or examples of work in document, picture or media formats. In this way, the student creates an e-learning portfolio which could stay with them during their time at school.

The impact of this focus on L2 and the 6R's has been measured using an online survey, PASS (Pupil Attitudes to Self and School). PASS is a 50 item assessment for each student in Years 7–11 which, at de Ferrers, is delivered online through ICT lessons. The assessment usually takes 15–20 minutes and features automated scoring and profiling. Standardised scores based on rigorous research are provided for nine key education related factors:

Factor 1 – Feelings about school

Factor 2 – Perceived learning capacity

Factor 3 – Self-regard

Factor 4 – Preparedness for learning

Factor 5 – Attitudes to teachers

Factor 6 – General work ethic

Factor 7 – Confidence in learning

Factor 8 – Attitudes to attendance

Factor 9 – Response to curriculum demands

Confidence in learning: de Ferrer's School						
	Boys 06	**Boys 07**	**Boys 08**	**Girls 06**	**Girls 07**	**Girls 08**
Year 7	Average	Above average	Well above	Average	Average	Well above
Year 8	Above average	Above average	Well above	Average	Above average	Well above
						cont.

Year 9	Above average	Above average	Well above	Average	Average	Well above
Year 10	Above average	Above average	Well above	Average	Average	Well above
Year 11	Above average	Above average	Well above	Average	Average	Well above

The impact of L2 and the 6R's has been most evident in Factor 7: Confidence in learning.

10. Learning to learn – a global revolution

In this chapter we:

- Start with a remarkable experiment involving a hole in a wall
- Describe different learning to learn approaches in the United Kingdom
- Describe different learning to learn approaches from around the world.

And ask the following questions:

- Do schools kill curiosity?
- Is there a UK way of doing learning to learn?
- What's happening around the world?

Electronic Computer-literate Europe Wall
Natural Curiosity United Kingdom
Competencies *Risk Taking* Europe Framework
Sociability Ivan Illich
Framework Australia Grid **Philosophy**

The hole in the wall

On the eve of the millennium, January 1999, a director of an IT firm, Sugata Mitra made a decision which would go some way to exploding our preconceptions about technology and learning.

Starting in New Delhi, Mitra installed a computer in a wall of a dilapidated building in one of the poorest slums, a community where children do not go to school, are illiterate and had never previously seen a computer. His research method was to turn the computer on, leave it and wait to see what happened. Activity was monitored through a video camera. Eventually he would do the same in 26 of the poorest communities in India.

Children slowly gathered around this strange television. They touched some of the parts and, apparently by accident, discovered that they could move a pointer on the screen by moving their finger across the touch pad. Gradually other discoveries followed. They told their friends and word spread quickly through the slum area. Within days, dozens of children were surfing the Web, downloading music and games, painting with Microsoft Paint and doing many of the other things that children everywhere do with computers when they have access to them. The children made up names to refer to the computer, its parts, the various icons that appeared on the screen and the activities they could perform with the computer.

For example, one lot described the pointer as a 'needle' and folders as 'cupboards'. Those who did not know English learned key words through their interactions with the computer and their talk with others about it. Children who could read became mavens and took it upon themselves to go off and find out things which would help the group, especially those who were illiterate.

On the basis of various tests given to randomly chosen children who used the outdoor computers, Mitra concluded that the children's abilities to learn in this setting 'seem to be independent of their educational background, literacy levels in English or any other language, social or economic level, ethnicity and place of origin (city, town, or village), gender, genetic background, geographic location, and intelligence'.[70]

Mitra wrote a paper describing this as 'minimally invasive education' – it's the equivalent of keyhole surgery. It is education with the minimal amount of intrusion into children's lives. Mitra and his colleagues estimate that for each outdoor computer they set up, an average of 300 children became computer literate within three months of the computer becoming available. That's 30,000 computer-literate children for 100 computers, within a three month period. The experiments demonstrated that children learned at an amazingly rapid rate with no adult teachers. All that the educators had to do was to provide the tool, the computer. The children's natural curiosity, risk taking and sociability took over from there.

In *Deschooling Society* Ivan Illich wrote:

> *The inverse of (traditional) schooling is possible. We can depend on self-motivated learning instead of employing teachers to bribe or compel the student to find time and the will to learn … we can provide the learner with new links to the world instead of continuing to funnel all educational programmes through the teacher.*[71]

Mitra's story, which provided the inspiration for the Oscar winning film *Slumdog Millionaire*, begs the question as to what we consider to be the ideal learning experience. It really would be 'exploding our shed' if we took the view that teachers cosset their students too much and what would be best would be 'radical absence'. More realistic would be a gradual absence and indeed programmes like Enquiring Minds set out deliberately to remove the teacher from the traditional role.

It's not going to happen in the immediate future, but the idea of 'minimally invasive education' is beguiling and something to work towards. By equipping young people with the right balance of knowledge about learning, positive personal attributes and transferrable skills, and doing so early, we open up a greater opportunity for the teacher to step back and assume a different sort of role. Education systems should not be curiosity killers. They should not remove risk from the challenge of learning nor should they ask each individual to learn in the same way, at the same time, in the same place, with the same resources. We feel heartened that in this country and abroad individuals and organisations, some of whom have been consistent over many years in articulating their view of a skills and competency led approach, are still pushing curriculum innovation forward. We have sampled some of the best for you in the two sections which follow.

Different learning to learn approaches in the United Kingdom

Personal, Learning and Thinking Skills

Personal, Learning and Thinking Skills (PLTS) are now statutory part of the 11–19 curriculum and QCA have provided a framework for describing the PLTS. Each of the six groups of PLTS – Independent Enquirers, Creative Thinkers, Reflective Learners, Team Workers, Self Managers and Effective Participators – has a focus statement which lists the range of skills and qualities involved. QCA argue that these generic skills, together with the functional skills of English, mathematics and ICT, are essential to success in life, learning and work. PLTS are also an essential feature of the new 14–19 Diplomas. Schools are now expected to integrate the PLTS into the curriculum they offer and guidance is given from QCA on how this can be done at a subject and whole school level. The assessment of PLTS is non-statutory and schools are being encouraged to develop their own assessment criteria, often in collaboration with learners, as well as peer and self assessment strategies.

www.qcda.gov.uk/curriculum

Welsh Skills Framework

The Welsh Skills Framework was implemented by the Welsh Assembly in September 2008 as a response to a perceived skills shortage in Wales. The new curriculum, of which the skills framework is a fundamental part, aims to 'focus on and meets learners' needs; is inclusive; provides equality of opportunity; equips learners with transferable skills; is relevant, challenging, interesting and enjoyable for all learners; transforms learning to produce resourceful, resilient and reflective lifelong learners'.[72]

According to Facer and Pykett, 'The skills framework is for learners aged 3–19 and provides a detailed structure for progression taking account of Key Skills, Functional Skills and Thinking Skills.[73] The elements of the framework are: developing thinking across the curriculum (plan, develop, reflect); developing communication across the curriculum (oracy, reading, writing, wider communication skills); developing ICT across the curriculum (finding and developing information and ideas, creating and presenting information and ideas); and developing numbers across the curriculum (using information, calculating and interpreting and presenting).

www.wales.gov.uk

Scottish Four Capacities

The Four Capacities are a fundamental part of the new Curriculum for Excellence in Scotland. This curriculum aims 'to provide coherent, more flexible and enriched education for learners from 3 to 18'.[74] The Four Capacities are designed to enable each child or young person to become a successful learner, a confident individual, a responsible citizen and an effective contributor: 'the experiences and outcomes of a range of curriculum areas are meant to build the attributes and capabilities which support the development of these four capacities'.[75] There are expanded statements that give more detail of the skills and attributes associated with each of the Four Capacities that can be a guide for schools looking to integrate them within the curriculum.

www.itscotland.org.uk/curriculumforexcellence/curriculumoverview/aims/fourcapacities.asp

Northern Irish Thinking Skills and Personal Capabilities Framework

Cross-curricular skills and thinking skills and capabilities are at the heart of the revised Northern Ireland Curriculum at each Key Stage and are embedded and infused into all curriculum areas. Schools are required to assess and report annually each pupil's progress in the cross-curricular skills of communication, using mathematics and using ICT, and also integrate thinking skills and personal capabilities (TS&PC) into the curriculum. In the revised curriculum 'the ability to think both critically and creatively and to develop personal and interpersonal skills and dispositions is essential for functioning effectively in a changing world'.[76] The TS&PC include thinking, problem solving and decision making, self-management, working with others, managing information and being creative at Foundation Stage and Key Stages 1, 2 and 3, and with problem solving, self-management and working with others at Key Stage 4.

www.nicurriculum.org.uk/skills_and_capabilities/index.asp

Social and Emotional Aspects of Learning

Guidance on Social and Emotional Aspects of Learning (SEAL) was sent out to secondary schools in 2007 and builds on the work done in primary schools from 2004 in the area of social and emotional aspects of learning. This guidance sets out a comprehensive approach to the social and emotional skills that underpin learning, giving advice on staff training, discrete lessons that focus on these skills and developing a whole school approach. There are five key aspects of SEAL identified in the guidance: self-awareness, managing feelings, motivation, empathy and social skills. The SEAL approach builds on work on social and emotional issues already taking place in lessons such as PSHE, citizenship, drama and the arts as well as the work on key learner skills and attributes that underpin learning to learn courses in schools.

www.nationalstrategies.standards.dcsf.gov.uk/inclusion/behaviourattendanceandseal

Assessment for Learning

QCA states that 'Assessment for Learning involves using assessment in the classroom to raise pupils' achievement. It is based on the idea that pupils will improve most if they understand the aim of learning, where they are in relation to this aim and how they can achieve this aim'.[77] This initiative, led by the Primary and Secondary Strategies, has had a powerful influence on schools and learning in the classroom particularly over the last five years. Effective assessment underpins good teaching and learning, and approaches – such as sharing learning objectives with pupils, helping them know and recognise standards to aim for, providing feedback that helps pupils identify how to improve, involving pupils in self and peer assessment and giving pupils the opportunity to reflect on their progress – have increasingly become part of schemes of work, lesson plans and classroom practice.

www.qcda.org.uk/4334.aspx

www.dcsf.gov.uk

Opening Minds

The Royal Society for the encouragement of Arts, Manufactures and Commerce (RSA) Opening Minds curriculum framework is different in that it is not an off-the-shelf course with materials or schemes of work, but it is a 'broad framework of competencies through which schools can develop a curriculum that is personalised to the needs of their learners'.[78] The RSA supports schools in their planning of this curriculum through publications, training and consultancy. Another new resource for schools is the RSA Academy opened in the autumn term of 2008. Based in Tipton in the West Midlands it was set up as a centre of excellence.

There are five main competencies: learning, citizenship, relating to people, managing situations and managing information. The learning competency includes:

- How to learn
- Thinking systematically
- Exploring and understanding creative talents
- Enjoy and love learning
- Standards in literacy, numeracy and spatial understanding
- Handling ICT and understanding underlying processes.

Schools have found that learning to learn knowledge, skills and attributes have a direct application to this competence but also contributes to all of the other competencies as well.

www.thersa.org/projects/education/opening-minds

Lancashire Grid for Learning

The Lancashire Grid for Learning is another competence based approach that arose out of a curriculum design project in collaboration with the Primary Strategy with the aim of developing more creative approaches to teaching and learning across the county. It has identified key competencies in terms of learning skills (enquiry, problem solving, creative thinking, information processing, reasoning, evaluation and communication and learner attributes), self-awareness, managing feelings, motivation, empathy and social skills. There is a detailed framework available to guide schools on their self-evaluation in these competency areas and support in terms of curriculum design to deliver courses for pupils that develop and practise these competencies.

www.lancsngfl.ac.uk/creativelearning

ASDAN – Certificate of Personal Effectiveness (CoPE) Qualification Award

ASDAN's CoPE qualification is another competency framework that incorporates a lot of learning to learn knowledge skills and attributes and allows students to progress through staged courses from Key Stage 2 to 5. The competencies include working with others, improving own learning and performance, problem solving, planning and carrying out research, communicating through discussion and planning and giving an oral presentation. Accreditation is based on a series of 'challenges' and collection of evidence of skill development in all six of the competency areas through a student portfolio.

www.asdan.org.uk/cope

Arts Award

Although aimed at a particular area of the curriculum, the Arts Award includes the development of learner skills and competencies. The award aims to recognise the development of young artists and young arts leaders from 14–19. The Arts Award celebrates the creative progress made by young people and not just their artistic skills. It consists of the following units spanning three levels – Bronze (Enjoying the Arts), Silver (Arts Practice, Supervised Arts Leadership) and Gold (Personal Arts Development, Arts Project Leadership).

www.artsaward.org.uk

Creative Partnerships

The Creativity Wheel, developed to support creative development in the primary school classroom, is an important part of the Creative Partnerships initiative that has had a positive impact on many schools a round the country. It was developed as a teaching resource by Durham and Sunderland Creative Partnership. The key competencies – imagination with purpose, originality and value – identified in the wheel are a framework for developing learning skills and attributes as well as assessing creative development. The Creativity Wheel 'allows whole school review of creative development, aims to improve learning by identifying and celebrating pupil success and provides a framework to improve creative teaching'.[79]

www.creative-partnerships.com/area-delivery-organisations/durham-sunderland/resources/the-creativity-resource-wheel-for-teachers,217,ART.html

Duke of Edinburgh Award

The Duke of Edinburgh Award is still popular in schools as a 'programme of personal and social development for young people aged 14 to 25'.[80] As part of its progressive bronze, silver and gold levels it encourages the development and practice of personal and social skills including many important learning skills and attributes. Its key competency areas include service, skills, physical recreation, expeditions and a residential project. Participants work with an adult mentor who helps them set their own goals and plan activities of interest linked with the key competency areas. They record their progress in log books and keep evidence of their achievement as they progress from bronze to gold level.

www.dofe.org

Girl Guides

The World Association of Girl Guides produces an educational framework designed to 'enable girls and young women to develop to their fullest potential as responsible citizens of the world'.[81] The organisation's framework is focused on human development and girls can progress from ages 5 to 25 from Rainbows, through Brownies, Guides and finally the Senior Section. The competence framework covers many learning skills in topics such as healthy lifestyles, global awareness, celebrating diversity, discovery and skills and relationships, including communication skills, conflict resolution, rights and responsibilities, faith and personal values, teamwork, self-reliance and self-esteem.

www.girlguiding.org.uk

The Oxford Global Citizenship Curriculum

The Oxford Global Citizenship Curriculum is designed to be used flexibly by teachers and pupils and to educate students to be global citizens 'who are aware of the wider world and have a sense of their own role as a world citizen'.[82] The competency framework that underpins the course—covering knowledge and understanding (social justice and equity, diversity, globalisation, sustainable development, peace and conflict), critical skills (ability to argue effectively, challenge injustice, respect for people and things, co-operation and conflict resolution) and values and attitudes (sense of identity and self-esteem, empathy, social justice and equality, value and respect for diversity, concern for the environment and sustainable development, belief people can make a difference)—allows students to build learning skills and attributes as they progress from Foundation Stage to Key Stage 5. Guidance is given on how to integrate these competencies into the curriculum and how they can be assessed.

www.oxfam.org.uk/education/gc

The International Baccalaureate

The International Baccalaureate (IB) is becoming increasingly popular with schools dissatisfied with the present range of qualifications offered by exam boards. The IB has three phases: the Primary Years Programme (ages 3–11), the Middle Years Programme (11–16) and the Diploma Programme (16–19). It grew out of the international schools movement and there are now 660,000 IB students in 2,407 schools in 131 countries. In the UK, there are currently 132 schools using the Diploma, seven using the Middle Years Programme and eight using the Primary Years Programme, with many other schools going through the assessment process. The IB is based on a constructivist process led model which stresses the development of skills above content. 'The IB helps students to participate actively in a changing, increasingly interrelated world. Learning to Learn and how to evaluate information critically is as important as learning facts' [83].

One major aim of the IB programme is 'to produce learners who are enquirers, knowledgeable, thinkers, communicators, principled, open minded, caring, risk takers, balanced and reflective'. There is a competency-like framework to support these aims and guidance is given on curriculum design and assessment to deliver these aims.

www.ibo.org

Enquiring Minds

Enquiring Minds is a Futurelab (see below) project and an approach to teaching and learning rather than a set curriculum. It has been developed and piloted with Key Stage 3 students although could easily be used with Key Stage 4 students as well. 'The curriculum is organised around the idea of "enquiry". Students progress from first developing self reflective skills by exploring their own lives with the teacher; second, learning research through a "closed enquiry" led by the teacher; third, developing autonomy, interpersonal, critical and reflective skills through a "negotiated" enquiry agreed with their teacher; finally to a "personalised enquiry" in which they consolidate these learned skills in their own self-directed project. The curriculum aims to develop students and teachers as co-researchers, innovators and knowledge creators'.[84]

www.enquiringminds.org.uk

Critical Skills

The Critical Skills Programme has its origins in the US where in 1981 'a partnership of education and business communities identified a list of skills and dispositions that they thought were lacking at that time in the workforce. They then asked a group of outstanding teachers to design a classroom model that would develop these important skills and dispositions though the mainstream curriculum'.[85] The critical skills that they identified were problem solving, decision making, critical thinking, creative thinking, communication, organisation, management and leadership. The dispositions were owners of lifelong learning, self-direction, internal models of quality, integrity and ethical character, collaboration, curiosity and wonder and community membership.

The critical skills classroom model is 'based on collaborative learning, problem based learning, experiential learning and results driven learning'.[86] A key aspect of the teaching and learning approach is the design and use of learning challenges – complex, open ended problem solving activities which allow for the development of critical skills and attitudes. Thinking tools are also used to teach these skills and attitudes explicitly. Staff are provided with guidance and training on the critical skills approach.

www.criticalskills.co.uk

Philosophy for Children

Philosophy for Children is an approach to the curriculum for 6–16-year-olds developed by Professor Matthew Lipman and his researchers at Montclair State College, New Jersey in the 1960s and 1970s. Lipman developed a new model of learning – communities of enquiry – 'in which teacher and children collaborate with each other to grow an understanding, not only of the material world, but also of the personal and ethical world around them'.[87] This philosophical approach has now spread to the UK and is becoming increasingly popular especially in primary schools. It is argued that this approach enables pupils to evaluate and judge and to think critically about what they learn, and this leads to the development of thinking skills.

A community of enquiry approach in the classroom, 'looks at problems and questions to which there is no obvious answer, and which by their very nature will throw up many more questions. The aim is not to teach philosophy to pupils but to develop their thinking and reasoning ability'.[88] This classroom approach is woven into the curriculum with the aim of developing not only thinking skills but emotional intelligence and spiritual intelligence as well.

www.sapere.org.uk

Thinking Schools

Thinking Schools is an initiative developed between the Centre for Cognitive Education at Exeter University, Imaginative Minds Ltd and Kestrel Consulting to assist schools in developing a whole school approach to the teaching of thinking skills. A programme of training is offered covering such areas as 'use of effective tools and strategies to develop quality thinking, making learning more reflective through philosophy and metacognition, developing a school culture where Habits of Mind such as curiosity and persistence flourish and evaluating teaching and learning for better thinking'.[89]

The Centre for Cognitive Education can provide schools with the means to assess their progress towards becoming a 'Thinking School' and give them a certificate of recognition when they have met assessed criteria. Schools are offered consultancy through their Thinking Schools journey which is likely to last, on average, two years.

www.education.exeter.ac.uk/projects.php?id=29

www.thinkingschool.co.uk

Thinking Through School Project

The Thinking Through School Project was developed by Anne de A'Echevarria and Professor David Leat in 2005–6 and backed by the University of Newcastle and Electric Word plc. It was trialled in schools with Year 7 pupils and the materials were published in 2006 under the title

Thinking Through School. The approach aims to help pupils think about learning and themselves as learners as well as building student voice and more positive relationships between pupils and teachers.

'It is structured as a story which unpacks fundamental issues about learning and being a learner. It follows eLfi and Jaz as they find out about how they learn and what it means to be a good learner. Each chapter of the story includes a narrative and is based around a key idea. Each chapter also includes practical exercises around this theme for teachers to work through with pupils. Then pupils try out activities and investigate an aspect of their own learning building to a community of enquiry where teachers and pupils report back. Each chapter ideally takes two hours to complete'.[90] *Thinking Through School* can be used to complement a wide range of initiatives such as learning to learn, student voice, thinking skills, assessment for learning and personalised learning.

www.thinkwell.org.uk

The Teacher Effectiveness Enhancement Programme

The Teacher Effectiveness Enhancement Programme (TEEP) was set up in 2002 by the Gatsby Charitable Foundation to 'develop a model of effective teaching and learning drawn from available research and best practice. This teacher development and training model is underpinned by elements such as accelerated learning, thinking for learning, assessment for learning, collaborative problem solving and effective use of ICT'.[91] Training stresses effective teacher behaviours in terms of classroom behaviours, interactive teaching, classroom management and variety of teaching and learning styles and encourages use of the TEEP Learning Cycle for planning lessons. This learning cycle has six stages – prepare for learning, agree learning outcomes, present new information, construct, apply and review.

www.teep.org.uk

The Campaign for Learning

The Campaign for Learning, an independent charity, has been involved in learning to learn research in schools since 2000 and is now in its fourth phase of project work on learning to learn. Evaluation of Phase 1 and 2 of the project suggested learning to learn can help 'raise standards of achievement and attainment, boost pupil motivation and confidence in learning and enhance teacher motivation and morale'. The Phase 3 evaluation reinforced these positive findings and emphasised the 'positive impact of learning to learn on learner skills, attitudes and attributes and teacher pedagogy'.[92]

The Campaign for Learning, as part of the research process, has developed its own definition and features of learning to learn along with an approach that emphasises its own 5R's of an effective 'learn to learner': readiness, resourcefulness, resilience, remembering and reflectiveness. Bill Lucas later used the same combination in his book, *Power Up Your Mind*.[93] Earlier this year the Campaign removed 'remembering' and replaced it with 'responsibility'. The Campaign for Learning offers training, consultancy and support on this approach.

www.campaign-for-learning.org.uk

Futurelab

Futurelab is another research based charity that works with a range of partners from government, industry and universities to individual schools on strategies to transform learning, in particular tapping into the huge potential offered by digital and other technologies. It 'develops innovative resources and practices that support new approaches to learning in the 21st century'[94]). The range of projects at Futurelab is broad with the aim of 'incubating new ideas, sharing hard evidence and practical advice, communicating the latest ideas and practice in educational ICT, experimenting and exchanging ideas'.[95] Projects and research focuses include Enquiring Minds, Innovations Workshops, Games and Learning, I Curriculum, Teachers as Innovators, Thinking Skills and Learning Space Design.

www.futurelab.org.uk

Building Learning Power (BLP)

Building Learning Power is an approach to learning to learn that has been developed by Professor Guy Claxton and is based on the principle of 'expanding (students') learning capacity' as opposed to just supporting their learning. This approach is focused on the progress and development of these learning capacities and 'is also intended as a means by which lessons and teaching and learning activities can be planned to develop particular "habits of mind" for particular students'.[96] Claxton identifies these Habits of Mind as the 4R's – resilience, resourcefulness, reflection and reciprocity – and outlines their main elements. He states that teaching and learning activities in the classroom should be 'rich, challenging, extended, relevant, responsible, real, unknown (open) and collaborative'[97]) to develop these Habits of Mind of effective learners. This kind of framework, it is agued by Claxton, 'needs to be part of a whole school approach to learning to learn where developing learning capacity is as important as qualifications'.[98]

BLP is supported by TLO, a commercial organisation that offers consultancy, training and resources that can help schools develop such a whole school approach.

www.buildinglearningpower.co.uk

Different learning to learn approaches from around the world

Definitions and tests: European initiatives

The focus of a lot of recent learning to learn research in Europe has been in two main areas: firstly, arriving at an agreed European definition of learning to learn and secondly, looking at assessing learning to learn key competences through a European developed test.[99]

In 2007 the European Commission Education Committee identified learning to learn as a key competence in the development of lifelong learning in Europe and thus 'education and training needs to provide the learning environment for the development of this concept for all citizens'.[100] The Centre for Research on Lifelong Learning (CRELL) was created by the

European Commission in 2005 to look at education and training and had a brief to define learning to learn and identify a way of measuring this key competence. The European definition that was developed drew on both the social, cultural and cognitive psychological traditions:

> Learning to learn is the ability to pursue and persist in learning, to organise one's own learning, including through the effective management of time and information, both individually and in groups. This competence includes an awareness of one's own process and needs, identifying available opportunities, and the ability to overcome obstacles in order to learn successfully.[101]

The learning to learn test that has been developed again draws on the social, cultural and cognitive psychological traditions and is based on three dimensions of learning to learn, the cognitive, affective and metacognitive.

The European Learning to Learn Test Framework

Affective dimension

- Learning motivation, learning strategies and orientation towards change
- Academic self-concept and esteem
- Learning environment.

Cognitive dimension

- Identifying a proposition
- Using rules
- Testing rules and propositions
- Using mental tools.

Metacognitive dimension

- Problem solving (metacognitive) monitoring tasks
- Metacognitive accuracy
- Metacognitive confidence.

The test has been piloted in eight European Countries: France, Italy, Cyprus, Slovenia, Finland, Austria, Spain and Portugal with 2,310 14-year-olds and the data is currently being analysed.

The Finnish answer

According to the Director General of the Finnish Board of Education, Timo Lankinen, the answer is:

- Ubiquitous technology, ubiquitous opportunity
- Collaborative, social-constructivist learning
- Problem based instruction

- Progressive enquiry, experimental study

- Peer feedback and peer co-operation

- Contextual, authentic learning sites

- Networked local, technological and social forums of learning

- Hands-on, on-the-job, real life learning arrangements

- Online study in virtual environments, through social media, with mobile tools

- Blended teaching methods, hybrid learning resources

- Public–private partnerships.

South Australia – 'A systems approach to learning to learn'

The Learning to Learn initiative in South Australia began in 1999, involves schools covering pre-school to secondary and is now in its fourth phase. What is different about this initiative is that 'it draws on and promotes constructivist learning and systems theory as the most appropriate path to re-thinking learning processes and improving learning outcomes at *all* levels of the educational system – at the policy, administrative and leadership levels as well as for classroom practice'.[102] Another distinction of the South Australian approach is that it puts emphasis on both social and academic outcomes and central to this concern is 'a rich pedagogy – pedagogy which is engaging, challenging and connected to life experience'.[103] The teacher is at the centre of the initiative with the focus on not *what* but *how* they teach and the relationships they build with one another and with the students, as well as parents and the local community.

There are five key elements to the South Australian learning to learn approach: a core learning programme which gives classroom teachers and school leaders access to leading research on learning, curriculum reform and constructivist pedagogies; 'learning circles' where school leaders develop a deeper understanding of how to change the learning culture, systems and processes of their schools; practicums where learning to learn project schools demonstrate and model good practice to staff from other local schools and share strategies and experiences; expo's – large events where staff from across the state share their experiences of learning to learn and project staff gather evaluative data; and project colleague networks – links between learning to learn teachers and the Department of Education and Children's Services (DECS), tertiary education sectors, local universities and educational researchers from around the world.

The impact of each phase of the Learning to Learn project has been assessed using online surveys, analysis of centrally held database records, qualitative data using interviews, case studies and personal narratives as well as 'most significant change stories' gathered from participating schools. The evaluative results from Phase 1 and 2 of the project showed 'improved student engagement and well being', 'enhanced student achievement,' 're-vitalised teacher professionalism and pedagogy' and 'improved system wide learning'.[104] The recent report on Phase 3 of the project talks about:

- 'The positive effect that engagement with Learning to Learn has had on teacher pedagogy in the classroom'

- 'The measurable change to student outcomes influenced by change in teacher pedagogy particularly in the areas of higher metacognitive and thinking skills, tests of problem solving/thinking and tests in literacy and numeracy'

- 'Improved student engagement and well being'

- 'Positive changes in leadership approach, learning cultures and professional identities in participating schools'.[105]

The Project for Enhancing Effective Learning – 'A teacher-led approach in Australia'

The PEEL project based in Victoria was founded in 1985 by a group of teachers and researchers who shared a concern about 'the prevalence of passive, unreflective, dependent student learning, even in apparently successful lessons'.[106] The project was unfunded and not the result of any system level or school level initiative. The aim was to research classroom approaches that would stimulate and support student learning that was active, independent, informed and metacognitive. Teachers got together regularly in their own time, in mini-networks, to share their experiences and ideas. The project was originally intended to run in one secondary school for two years but such was the quality of ideas, learning strategies and action research that arose from the work, the teachers involved refused to let the project end and it spread to other secondary schools in Australia and around the world.

PEEL is different from other learning to learn initiatives in that it does not involve a course or programme but an approach. In 2006, the PEEL collective reflected and identified the characteristics of this approach:

- Having a strategic, long-term learning agenda focusing on multiple aspects of quality learning and metacognition

- Making consistent, persistent and purposeful use of teaching procedures, appropriate teaching behaviours and the principles of teaching for quality learning

- Trusting students and sharing responsibilities and intellectual control with students

- Problematising and purposefully interrogating and developing your practice

- Supporting and being supported by others in a process of collaborative action research

PEEL operates as a network of groups of teachers who take the role of interdependent innovators. Coherence and structure is provided by shared concerns about passive and dependent learning and publications such as *PEEL SEEDS* (the journal of the PEEL collective) and PEEL in Practice (a large database of teaching ideas) where experiences and teaching strategies are shared. Over the 24 years of the project, teachers have aimed to promote what are termed 'good learning behaviours' in their students and they have also identified a number of 'poor learning behaviours' shown by many students and developed procedures to reduce these behaviours.

The impact of PEEL has been to produce a huge repertoire of teaching resources, findings about the nature of student and teacher change, and findings about collaborative development in schools and between schools and the tertiary sector. 'Schools and teachers report substantial changes to teaching practice and classroom. Teachers consistently report much higher levels of student interest and engagement as well as learning that is more informed, purposeful, intellectually active and independent'.[107]

Quality Teaching Initiative – 'An Australian systems approach focused on improving teacher quality'

In New South Wales, the Department of Education and Training has developed a systems approach to improving learning that focuses on identifying the features of effective teaching for learning through professional teaching standards and then providing support and resources to schools to develop and implement these standards. 'The Quality Teaching model first developed in 2003, provides a framework to focus attention on, and provide consistent messages about, pedagogy in schools. This model can be applied across all key learning areas from Kindergarten to Year 12'.[108]

The NSW approach identifies three dimensions of pedagogy that have been associated with improved student outcomes:

▪ pedagogy that is fundamentally based on promoting high levels of intellectual quality

▪ pedagogy that is soundly based on promoting quality learning environments

▪ pedagogy that develops and makes explicit to students the significance of their work.

These dimensions of pedagogy are reinforced in the systems approach by classroom guidance materials focusing on engaging learning activities and learning resources, guidance on planning and designing programmes of work, guidance on evaluation and guidance on leadership and management. Schools and staff are encouraged to be self-evaluative and reflect-ive about the learning they deliver as well as share experiences with colleagues both in an online community and in local networks. The NSW Framework of Professional Teaching Standards reflects and supports the dimensions of pedagogy in guidance on the key teaching elements such as 'know their students and how students learn', 'plan, assess and report for effective learning', 'create and maintain safe and challenging learning environments' and 'continually improve their professional knowledge and practice'.[109]

New Basics Systems Approach – 'Rich tasks, blueprints and pedagogy in Queensland'

The New Basics Project was launched in 1999 by Education Queensland to better prepare their young people for the world of the future – 'a world of new student identities, new economies and workplaces, new technologies, diverse communities and complex cultures'.[110] The project was an educational system response to the changing world and the need to improve student outcomes. It focused on a triad of what is taught (curriculum organisers), how it is taught (productive pedagogies) and how children demonstrate it (rich tasks). Even though the project completed its four year trial in 2003, in 2008–9 some schools continue to use rich tasks, blueprints and guidance on productive pedagogies to structure their curriculum, assessment and staff development.

The curriculum organisers are grouped around clusters such as 'life pathways and social futures' as well as 'environments and technology' and the rich tasks are designed to be intellectually engaging and deal with real world issues. They incorporate learning to learn skills and are the assessable and reportable outcomes of a three year curriculum plan aimed at preparing young people for the challenges of the future. The emphasis is on students demonstrating they can use key learning skills and have the opportunity to demonstrate these skills in front of family and local community. Blueprints have been developed recently in response to teacher demands for more rich tasks which are less prescriptive and allow a wider range of curriculum content and assessment techniques.

Productive pedagogies are a set of teacher practices that have been identified from observation and developed from teacher support networks. They are clustered around four groups: recognition of difference, connectedness, intellectual quality and supportive classroom environment.

Teachers are encouraged to plan together when and how the learning skills, knowledge and understanding will be taught to enable young people to undertake the rich tasks and blueprint activities. Education Queensland produces the systems guidance, resources and support to help in this process.

New Zealand – 'Identifying capabilities for living and lifelong learning'

The New Zealand Curriculum identifies five key competences for living and lifelong learning:

- thinking
- using language, symbols and texts
- managing self
- relating to others
- participating and contributing.

'These competencies are key to learning in every learning area. Successful learners make use of these competencies in combination with all the other resources available to them. These include personal goals, other people, community knowledge and values, cultural tools and the knowledge and skills found in different learning areas'.[111] Learning to learn knowledge, skills and attributes clearly contribute to these competencies which is why schools have adopted a range of approaches to delivering learning skills.

The New Zealand Curriculum identifies teacher action that impacts positively on student learning and there is clearly a strong link with learning to learn pedagogy. Based on extensive evidence, students learn best when teachers:

- create a supportive learning environment
- encourage reflective thought and action
- facilitate shared learning
- make connections to prior learning and experience
- provide sufficient opportunities to learn
- enquire into the teaching and learning relationship.[112]

USA – Habits of Mind – ' Dispositions of intelligent behaviour'

This approach, developed by Arthur Costa and Bena Kallick in 2000, focuses on defining and describing 16 types of intelligent behaviour called Habits of Mind. They argue a Habit of Mind 'is knowing how to behave intelligently when you don't know the answer'. A Habit of Mind means 'having a disposition toward behaving intelligently when confronted with problems, the answers to which are not immediately known: dichotomies, dilemmas, enigmas and uncertainty'.[113] They see Habits of Mind as a composite of many skills, attitudes and inclinations that can be taught, practised and used in schools and beyond. These 16 dispositions include:

- Persisting

- Responding with wonderment and awe

- Thinking and communicating with clarity and provision

- Managing impulsivity

- Gathering data through all the senses

- Listening with understanding and empathy

- Creating, imagining, innovating

- Thinking flexibly

- Taking responsible risks

- Questioning and posing problems

- Thinking about thinking

- Thinking interdependently

- Striving for accuracy

- Applying past knowledge to new situations

- Finding humour

- Remaining open to continuous learning.

The Habits of Mind approach to learning to learn is popular in both primary and secondary schools in countries such as Australia and New Zealand, where this is often taught in a planned continuum combined with an emphasis on thinking skills and tools, as well as the US. Schools are encouraged and given guidance, in a Habits of Mind approach, to explicitly teach the dispositions, give students the opportunity to practise using them and weave the dispositions into the language of learning in the classroom, school processes and the curriculum.

Schools in the UK have also adopted Habits of Mind, and one of our L2 Journey Schools, St Peter's School in Exeter, has interestingly integrated these dispositions within Alite's 5R's, linking for example 'resilience' with 'persistence', 'responsible' with 'managing impulsivity' and 'reasoning' with 'thinking about your thinking' as they found this provided more clarity and ease of use for both students and staff.[114]

USA – Pennsylvanian Resilience Program – 'Building self-belief and the skills of resilience'

The Pennsylvanian Resilience Program (PRP) grew out of research at the University of Pennsylvania influenced by cognitive-behavioural theories of depression. Central to PRP is the idea that 'people's beliefs about events mediate their impact on emotions and behaviour so students learn to detect inaccurate thoughts, to evaluate the accuracy of these thoughts, and to challenge negative beliefs by considering alternative interpretations'.[115] PRP also 'teaches a variety of strategies that can be used for solving problems and coping with difficult situations and emotions. Students learn techniques for assertiveness, negotiation, decision making, social problem solving, and relaxation'.[116]

PRP is typically delivered in 18 to 24 one hour lessons and within each lesson resilience concepts and skills are introduced and practised through role plays, short stories and cartoons that illustrate the core ideas and other practical activities. The PRP is now being introduced into the UK with 90 teachers trained in the summer of 2007 to deliver an adapted version of the PRP curriculum to groups of students in South Tyneside, Hertfordshire and Manchester local authorities. One of Alite's L2 Journey Schools, South Shields Community School, has been involved in the PRP pilot and will be teaching the course for the first time in the summer of 2009.[117] It will be interesting to see how the work done in PRP helps and supports the students and integrates within the learning to learn course already being delivered in the school.

Appendix I: Resources provided on CD

- Learner Preference Cards
- Superhero Top Trumps
- Memory posters
- Asking Great Questions Success Mat
- Billy Blunder cartoons
- Success stories
- Brain Facts activity cards
- Parents as Learners (PAL) Child Profile
- Parents as Learners (PAL) Activity Wheel

More resources are available at www.alite.co.uk

Appendix II: 4 stage cycle observation proforma

The 4 stage learning cycle	4	3	2	1
1. Connect				
▦ Provide a stimulus which engages the curiosity of the learners and begins to direct them towards the topic				
▦ Lead into a short activity or dialogue through which students explore what they may know or would wish to know about the topic				
▦ Utilise their existing experience of, and knowledge about, the topic				
▦ Model learning behaviours and high expectations through use of language, interaction with individuals and groups and through references to the learning process				
▦ Explore the way in which the learning will link what has gone before with what is to come				
Outcomes				
● Examine the learning outcomes in terms of content, process and benefits				
● Share what will be learned and any differentiation in outcome				
● Share how the topic will be or could be learned, outlining the methods to be used				
● Share how individuals will benefit in the immediate and longer term				
● Where appropriate, refer to the learner skills and attributes which will be developed				
cont.				

The 4 stage learning cycle	4	3	2	1
2. Activate				
■ Introduce the problem to be solved, the issue to be explored or the experience to be shared				
■ Structure learning activities around the problem, issue or experience which relate to the learning outcomes				
■ Provide any resources or additional sources of information				
■ Guide students into appropriate groupings and provide support and challenge				
■ Begin to draw attention to what is being learned and how it is being learned				
■ Build a positive climate and maintain students' motivation, concentration and application				
3. Demonstrate				
■ Allow students to demonstrate their own solutions to, or observations about, the problem, issue or experience using a variety of formats and media				
■ Allow students to evaluate and make improvements to their solutions				
■ Facilitate teacher, peer and self assessment processes to inform improvements				
■ Allow students to interrogate their solutions through the careful use of questions and thinking tools				
■ Ask, and encourage, challenging questions				
4. Consolidate				
■ Take time to examine what has been learned, how it has been learned and how we will secure benefits				
■ Where appropriate, refer to the learner skills and attributes which have been developed in the lesson				
■ Highlight the transferability of learning skills used to other lessons				
■ Preview and link work done in the lesson with future learning				

Appendix III: Our 5R's in detail

Our 5R's were first described in *The Alps Approach Resource Book* written by Alistair and Nicola Call in 2001. An attribute is a bit like a signature; it becomes more familiar and less susceptible to change as time goes on and as it is used again and again. Our aim is to develop the balance of attributes in the individual before they become too fixed to change.

Resilient

Resilient means 'sticking at it' especially when things get difficult. As a resilient learner:

- I persist.
- I have a positive attitude.
- I stay involved with my learning.
- I set targets and practise.

Responsible

Responsible means looking after yourself and others. As a responsible learner:

- I know right from wrong and make good choices.
- I manage myself.
- I help others.
- I think ahead.

Resourceful

Resourceful means knowing what to do and where to go when you get stuck. As a resourceful learner:

- I show initiative.
- I can learn using different methods.
- I ask good questions.
- I involve others, including the teacher, in learning.

Reasoning

Reasoning means making careful decisions. As a reasoning learner:

- I can explain my thinking.
- I consider all the evidence.

- I choose the best method or thinking tool.
- I take time.

Reflective

Reflective means learning from experience. As a reflective learner:

- I am curious.
- I can describe my progress.
- I listen to and learn from feedback.
- I learn from experience.

Appendix IV:
5R's progression specifications

Resilience	Bronze	Silver	Gold
I persist	☐ I can stick at some things for short periods of time. I ask for help when things get difficult and then will have another go	☐ I stick at most things and will have a go even when things are difficult. I usually finish what I start to a reasonable standard	☐ I stick at it until I've succeeded – if things are difficult I try different ways to succeed. I always finish what I start to a high standard
I have a positive attitude	☐ With some encouragement I give most things a go. Setbacks frustrate me but with help I find ways forward. I am learning to find positive things in whatever I do	☐ I enjoy a challenge when I think it's worthwhile. I am mostly positive about setbacks. I usually approach a task or challenge with a smile	☐ I always enjoy a challenge and get a lot out of it. I cope well with setbacks and always find ways forwards. I always remain positive throughout
I stay involved	☐ I can allow myself to be distracted. I may need someone to start me off and to check on my progress from time to time. I will do things if I really want to or am told to	☐ I use strategies to help avoid being distracted. With some initial support I can get on with things by myself. If I can see it's worth doing I'll get on with it	☐ I find interest in whatever I am doing and can become completely absorbed. I am a self-starter. I will happily get stuck in to most tasks
I set targets and practise	☐ I have begun to set myself targets and work towards them. I focus on what I am told. I am beginning to realise that practise is important and will practise when told to	☐ I set myself targets and can plan how to meet them. I focus on what I need to do. I usually decide for myself when to practise to meet my targets	☐ I set myself challenging targets and plan in detail the steps I need to reach them. I focus on where I want to get to. I practise regularly to meet my targets

Responsibility	Bronze	Silver	Gold
I know right from wrong and make good choices	☐ With help I understand the right and wrong way to act. When I am being influenced by others, I can recognise it when it is pointed out to me	☐ I have a sense of right and wrong and will usually make the right choices even when this is difficult. I am sometimes influenced by what others are doing but I can make choices for myself	☐ I have a strong sense of what is right and wrong. I make the right choices even when this is sometimes hard. I am independent and am not easily influenced by what everyone else is doing
I manage myself	☐ I bring most of what I need for learning. With encouragement I complete tasks on time. With help I deal with the important things first	☐ I usually bring what I need for learning. I complete most tasks on time. I prioritise the most important things and deal with them first	☐ I always bring what I need for learning. I complete all tasks on time. I am excellent at prioritising
I help others	☐ When asked to take my role in a group seriously I do so and can respond to others in a helpful way	☐ I can be a responsible group member. I usually play an active part and attempt to do my best for the team. I am sensitive to the learning needs of others and try to help them when I can	☐ I am aware of my responsibility to other members of my group. I am a positive asset, taking my own role seriously and not letting the team down. I actively help others in my group to learn and to move forward with their own tasks
I think ahead	☐ I sometimes jump into tasks without planning ahead. With guidance I can see the importance of thinking before I act and am practising some strategies to help to do this	☐ I usually plan ahead and am clear about what I need to do. I think before I act. I am aware that my actions have consequences for myself and others	☐ I always plan ahead and am certain about what I need to do. I realise that my actions have consequences for myself and for other people and I take time to think about what these are before acting

Resourcefulness	Bronze	Silver	Gold
I show initiative	☐ I sometimes try to find a solution and occasionally will ask for support	☐ I usually try to find a solution and am happy to check my understanding by asking the right questions	☐ I always work hard to find original solutions independently of anyone else. I think carefully beforehand about the questions I ask of my teacher
I can learn using different methods	☐ I know my preferred learning methods and can talk about how I learn best	☐ I know my preferred learning methods and I am beginning to practise learning in different ways	☐ I can learn using a number of different methods and adapt the methods I use to learn to different situations
I ask good questions	☐ I sometimes ask questions which help me get on with learning. I listen to the ideas of others in my group	☐ I ask good questions which help me and my group get on with learning. I usually listen to the ideas of others in my group and contribute my own	☐ I always ask good questions which help me and my group get on with learning. I build on the ideas of others in my group and contribute my own
I involve others, including the teacher, in learning	☐ I listen to information and instructions given to me by my teacher. I make use of learning material provided for me	☐ I listen carefully to information and advice from my teacher and make full use of learning materials provided. I add learning material I have found by myself	☐ I use my teacher as an important source of help. I search out the best learning resources. I can make reference to, and judge the worth of, several sources of information

273

Reasoning	Bronze	Silver	Gold
I can explain my thinking	☐ With help I can explain how I arrived at a decision. I can pick out similarities and differences between two or more things	☐ I can usually explain how I arrived at a decision. I can identify similarities and differences between two or more things and describe them	☐ I can always explain how I arrived at a decision. I am good at comparing and contrasting arguments and explaining. I can describe similarities and differences in detail without help
I consider all the evidence	☐ With help, I can choose evidence to support my argument or a decision	☐ I make use of more than one source of information to gather evidence. With some help I can sort relevant and irrelevant information	☐ I am able to collect and evaluate evidence from a number of different sources and explain the importance of doing so. I quickly see the difference between relevant and irrelevant information
I choose the best method or thinking tool	☐ I use advice given to me by my teacher about the best way to tackle a problem or task. I make use of a small number of thinking tools to sort or group information	☐ I can see a number of different ways to approach a problem or task and with help I select the best. I can use a range of thinking tools and can explain why I am using them	☐ I know there are always a number of different ways to approach a task or problem. I think around a problem, select the best method of tackling it and explain my choice. I independently use a range of thinking tools
I take time	☐ I sometimes rush into things but I am beginning to see the importance of thinking things through. With some guidance I plan the work I am going to do and review how well I am doing	☐ I usually take time out to think things through by myself or with a group. I can explain why this is important. I use planning sheets or thinking tools to help me with my planning	☐ I spend time thinking things through and consider the information I have been given. I will defer making a decision if necessary. I plan carefully, including deadlines and review times, and can adjust my plans

Reflection	Bronze	Silver	Gold
I am curious	☐ I sometimes find it hard to get interested in learning but I can learn well when motivated. Occasionally I enjoy it. Outside of school there are some things which interest me	☐ I am interested in learning but I need to be motivated to get fully involved. Often I enjoy what I do. Outside of school there are things which interest me and I am involved in	☐ I am very interested in learning and am soon motivated to get fully involved. I ask questions about what I am doing and why I am doing it. Outside of school I have lots of things which interest me and I am involved in
I can describe my progress	☐ I can describe my progress. I can say if I have been successful and link this to basic success criteria given to me by my teacher	☐ I can describe my progress and explain it. I can make reference to success criteria arrived at in discussion between myself and my teacher	☐ I can describe my progress and explain it in detail. I can make reference to success criteria I have arrived at by myself or with others with whom I am working
I listen to and learn from feedback	☐ I listen to feedback from my teacher and with support will respond to it and make some changes. I listen to advice from my classmates	☐ I respond to feedback from my teacher and make changes based on what is said. I listen to what my classmates say and act on their advice when necessary	☐ I respond to feedback from my teacher and incorporate this advice in changes. I seek out and listen to my classmates' views and will act on their advice as a valued source of feedback
I learn from experience	☐ With help from my teacher I can describe some things that have gone well and some things which did not go so well. Over time I learn from what didn't work so well. I try not to repeat mistakes	☐ With my teacher I reflect on what went well and what didn't work so well and agree suggestions for what I might do differently next time. I don't repeat mistakes	☐ I always find time to reflect on a project or process I have been involved in and ask important questions. I try to improve by learning from any mistakes

Notes

1 Butko and Movellan (2007).
2 Wilkinson and Pickett (2009).
3 DCSF (2009).
4 Future Foundation (2008).
5 Cited in Persaud (2005) p.359.
6 See Professor Michael Wesch, *An Anthropological Introduction to YouTube* (video MP4), June 2008.
7 See the exploding diner, Mr Creosote, in *The Meaning of Life* (1983), dir. Terry Jones and Terry Gilliam.
8 The workshop was organized by iNet, the international arm of the Specialist Schools and Academies Trust (SSAT) and the National Art Education Association (NAEA) with the support of HSBC bank.
9 Specialist Schools and Academies Trust (2006).
10 See Hill et al. (1996); Mortimore et al. (1988); Scheerens, Vermeulen and Pelgrum (1989); Willms (2000).
11 The 5R's of resilience, resourcefulness, responsibility, reasoning and reflection were first described in Smith and Call (2001), pp. 199–205. The authors drew from two of Guy Claxton's three R's which had been described in Claxton (1997). This was the first conception of the 5R's and preceded those used in Building Learning Power (resilience, reciprocity, reflection and resourcefulness) and by the Campaign for Learning (readiness, resourcefulness, resilience, remembering and reflectiveness). See Chapter 10.
12 Sodha and Margo (2008).
13 Werner and Smith (1992).
14 Newmann and Wehlage (1993).
15 Bransford, Brown and Cocking (2000); Gardner (2007); OECD (2002, 2007); Perkins (1993); Scardamalia (2001).
16 Marzano (2003); Marzano, Pickering and Pollock (2001).
17 Smith (2002).
18 Hattie (2009).
19 Hattie (2009), p. 22
20 Hattie (2009), p. 174
21 Weiner (1979).
22 See Kuhl (1984) and Heckhausen (1991).
23 Dweck (1999).
24 Choh and Quay (2001).
25 Dweck and Leggett (1988); McLean (2003).
26 Gary Hopkins online interview with Education World® Available at www.education-world.com/a_issues/chat/chat010.shtml# (accessed October 2009). © 2005 Education World.
27 Aronson (2002).
28 Hattie (2009), p. 40.
29 Cited in Rees (2008).
30 Sanders and Horn (1994) and Wright, Horn and Sanders (1997), cited in Marzano (2003), p. 72, from whom much of the material used in our arguments about effective teachers derives.
31 Haycock (1998).
32 Marzano (2000).
33 Hattie (2009), p. 109.
34 Hattie (2009), p. 124.
35 The OECD (2009) TALIS survey showed that across countries an average of 70 to 90% of lesson time in lower secondary schools is typically spent on teaching and learning. Between 5 and 17% is spent on administrative tasks and 8 to 18% on maintaining order. The international average for maintaining order is 13%. Brazil at 18% was the country where most time was taken up with maintaining order.
36 Cited in Hattie (2009), p. 4.
37 Sabers, Cushing and Berliner (1991).
38 Nagy and Herman (1984), cited in Marzano, Pickering and Pollock (2001), p. 124.
39 Scheerens and Bosker (1997); Kumar (1991); Hattie (1992, 2009); Marzano, Pickering and Pollock (2001).
40 Nuttall (2008), cited in Hattie (2009).

41   Johnson and Johnson (1999).

42   Hattie (2009), p. 95

43   Available at www.tascwheel.com

44   Office of Fair Trading (2009).

45   Collins (2001), p. 165.

46   Goldstein and Cialdini (2007), pp. 169–170.

47   Sourced from Wikipedia.

48   Moore (2008).

49   Fullan (1982), p. 102.

50   Facer and Pykett (2007).

51   Pollard, Groll, Broadfoot and Abbot, Primary Assessment Curriculum Experience II, 1993-1994 (PACE II), 1999.

52   Csíkszentmihályi (1998).

53   Shernoff Csíkszentmihályi and Schneider. (2003).

54   Csíkszentmihályi and Schneider (2000).

55   Dewey (1916).

56   Harris and Goodall (2008), quoted in Harris, Andrew-Power and Goodall (2009), p. 3.

57   Epstein (1991).

58   Fan and Chen (2001).

59   Graue, Weinstein and Walberg (1983).

60   Harris, Andrew-Power and Goodall (2009).

61   Feinstein and Sabates (2006).

62   Hart and Risley (1995).

63   Thanks to Doug Pettit of Cramlington Learning Village for providing this information and to the team at Cramlington for creating such a wonderful model.

64   See http://donaldclarkplanb.blogspot.com (accessed October 2009).

65   There are a total of 39 different PLTS skills, behaviours and personal qualities. By organising them in this way it is unclear which are skills (so may be more susceptible to development through teaching and through repeated use) and which are personal qualities (and so are less likely to be able to change). We also ask, do each have the same status? Some would appear to be social behaviours whilst others are cognitive skills. On face value it seems muddled and we are not reassured by the statement which says: 'The PLTS framework also reflects competency frameworks and skills taxonomies promoted through other initiatives such as Social and Emotional Aspects of Learning (SEAL), RSA Opening Minds and Futurelab's Enquiring Minds.' What does reflect mean and why this rather narrow group of initiatives?

66   Becta (2008).

67   Stross (2009)

68   Green and Hannon (2007).

69   Green and Hannon (2007), p. 37.

70   Information available at http://en.wikipedia.org/wiki/Sugata_Mitra, (accessed August 2009).

71   Illich (1996), p. 73.

72   Welsh Skills Framework available at www.wales.gov.uk/dcells/publications/curriculum and assessment (accessed May 2009).

73. Facer and Pykett (2007).

74   Curriculum for Excellence available at www.ltscotland.org.uk/curriculumforexcellence/curriculumoverview (accessed May 2009)

75   Curriculum for Excellence (see note 74).

76   Northern Irish Thinking Skills and Personal Capabilities Framework available at www.nicurriculum.org.uk/foundation_stage/skills_and_capabilities/ (accessed May 2009).

77   QCA outline of Assessment for Learning available at www.qcda.org.uk/4334 (accessed May 2009).

78   Opening Minds available at www.thersa.org/projects/education/openingminds (accessed May 2009).

79   Facer and Pykett (2007).

80   Duke of Edinburgh Award Scheme. Programme and Principles available at www.dofe.org (accessed May 2009).

81   Guide Association (2001).

82   Oxfam: Education for Global Citizenship – A Guide for Schools available at www.oxfam.org.uk/education/gc (accessed May 2009).

83   International Baccalaureate Organisation Programme available at www.ibo.org (accessed May 2009).

84   Facer and Pykett (2007).

85   Critical Skills Programme available at www.criticalskills.co.uk (accessed May 2009).

86   Critical Skills Programme (see note 85).

87   Philosophy for Children outline at www.sapere.org.uk (accessed May 2009).

88   Aude Education – Philosophy for Children available at www.aude-education.co.uk/philosophy (accessed May 2009).

89   Kestrel Consulting – Thinking Schools available at www.thinkingschool.co.uk (accessed May 2009).

90   A'Echevarria (2007).

91   Teacher Effectiveness Enhancement Project available at www.teep.org.uk (accessed May 2009).

92 Campaign for Learning Outline available at www.campaign-for-learning.org.uk (accessed May 2009).

93 Lucas (2001).

94 Futurelab Outline available at www.futurelab.org.uk (accessed May 2009).

95 Futurelab (see note 94).

96 Facer and Pykett (2007).

97 Claxton (2006).

98 Facer and Pykett (2007).

99 Hoskins and Fredriksson (2008).

100 Hoskins and Fredriksson (2008).

101 Education Council (2006) cited annex, paragraph 5, in Hoskins and Fredriksson (2008).

102 Goldspink (2008), p. 4.

103 Goldspink (2008), p. 4.

104 Department of Education and Children's Services (2004) p. 6, available at www.learningtolearn.sa.edu.au (accessed May 2009).

105 Goldspink (2008), p. 20.

106 The Project for Enhancing Effective Learning – About PEEL in Practice available at www.peelweb.org (accessed February 2009).

107 The Project for Enhancing Effective Learning (see note 106).

108 New South Wales Department of Education and Training (2006): About Quality Teaching available at www.det.edu.au/proflearn/qt/nsw (accessed February 2009).

109 New South Wales Department of Education and Training (2004): Professional Teaching Standards (see note 108).

110 Education Queensland: The New Basics Project available at www.education.qld.gov.au/corporate/newbasics (accessed February 2009).

111 The New Zealand Curriculum available at http://nz/nzcurriculum.tki.org (accessed October 2009).

112 The New Zealand Curriculum (see Note 111).

113 Habits of Mind available at www.habits-of-mind.net and www.habitsofmind.co.uk (accessed February 2009).

114 One school that has adopted Habits of Mind and the 5R's is St Peter's Church of England School in Exeter – contact L2 Champion Lyn Bourne for details at bourne@st-peters-exeter.devon.sch.uk

115 The Pennsylvanian Resilience Program available at www.ppc.sas.upenn.edu (accessed February 2009).

116 The Pennsylvanian Resilience Program (see note 115).

117 For details of how South Shields Community School have used the Pennsylvanian Resilience Program contact L2 Champion Karen Tones at ktones@sscschool.co.uk

Recommended websites

- www.alite.co.uk

Alite website for full details of programmes and the free newsletter

- www.sst-inet.net

Specialist Colleges Trust

- www.campaign-for-learning.org.uk

Learning to learn project

- www.ncsl.org.uk

National College for School Leadership

- www.innovation-unit.co.uk

The Innovation Unit

- www.transforminglearning.co.uk

The Hay Group

- www.demos.co.uk

Think tank

- www.ecls.ncl.ac.uk/l2l/

Newcastle University Learning to Learn project

- www.nifl.gov/nifl/cromley_report.html

US National Institute for Literacy report on Learning to Learn

- www.beyondcurrenthorizons.org.uk/learning-to-learn/

Examines the possible shape of learning in 2025

Bibliography

A'Echevarria, A. de (2006). *Thinking Through School* (London: Chris Kington Publishing).

A'Echevarria, A. de (2007). 'Thinking Through School: Building a Learning Community', *Learning and Teaching Update* (March 2007). Available at www.teachingexpertise.com/articles/thinkingthroughschool-building-a-learning-community (accessed May 2009).

Alexander, R. J. (2004). *Towards Dialogic Teaching: Rethinking Classroom Talk* (York: Dialogos).

Ames, C. and Archer, J. (1988). 'Achievement Goals in the Classroom: Students' learning strategies and motivation processes', *Journal of Educational Psychology*, 80: 260–267.

Anderson, L. W. and Krathwohl, D. R. (eds.) (2001). *A Taxonomy for Learning, Teaching and Assessing* (Washington, DC: Arts Education Partnership).

Aronson, J. (2002). *Improving Academic Achievement: Impact of Psychological Factors on Education* (San Diego, CA: Academic Press).

Barber, M. and Mourshed, M. (2007). *How the World's Best-Performing School Systems Come Out On Top* (London: McKinsey & Co). Available at http://www.mckinsey.com/App_Media/Reports/SSO/Worlds_School_Systems_Final.pdf (accessed October 2009).

Becta (2008a). *An Analysis of Emerging Trends Affecting the Use of Technology in Education* (Coventry: Becta).

Becta (2008b) *Harnessing Technology Schools Survey 2008* (Coventry: Becta). Available at http://partners.becta.org.uk/index.php?catcode=_re_rp_02&rid=15952&section=rh (accessed October 2009).

Bereiter, C. and Scardamalia, M. (2007). 'Beyond Bloom's Taxonomy: Rethinking Knowledge for the Knowledge Age', in M. Fullan (ed.), *Fundamental Change: International Handbook of Educational Change* (Dordrecht: Springer), pp. 5–22.

Black, P., Harrison, C., Lee, C., Marshall, B. and Wiliam, D. (2002). *Working Inside the Black Box: Assessment for Learning in the Classroom* (Swindon: NFER-Nelson).

Black, P. and Wiliam, D. (1998). *Inside the Black Box: Raising Standards through Classroom Assessment* (Swindon: NFER-Nelson).

Bono, E. de (2006). *Edward de Bono's Thinking Course: Powerful Tools to Transform Your Thinking* (London: BBC Active).

Bransford, J., Brown, A. and Cocking, R. (2000) *How People Learn: Brain, Mind, Experience and School* (Washington, DC: National Academy Press).

Brooks, R. and Goldstein, S. (2004). *The Power of Resilience: Achieving Balance, Confidence, and Personal Strength in Your Life* (New York: McGraw-Hill).

Buckingham, D. (2007). *Beyond Technology: Children's Learning in the Age of Digital Culture* (Cambridge: Polity).

Butko, N. J. and Movellan, J. R. (2007). 'Development and Learning', paper presented at IEEE 6th International Conference, 11–13 July 2007. Reprinted in *ICDL*: 151–156.

Choh, S. Y. and Quay, M. L. (2001). *Special Educators' Implicit Theories of Intelligence* (Singapore: Movement for the Intellectually Disabled of Singapore).

Claxton, G. (1997) *Hare Brain, Tortoise Mind: How Intelligence Increases When You Think Less* (New York: Fourth Estate).

Claxton, G. (2002): *Building Learning Power: Helping Young People to Become Better Learners* (Bristol: TLO).

Claxton, G. (2006). 'Expanding the Capacity to Learn: A New End for Education?', opening keynote address, British Educational Research Association Annual Conference, London, 6 September 2006.

Collins, J. (2001). *Good to Great* (New York: HarperCollins).

Commission of the European Communities (2006). *Modernising Education and Training: A Vital Contribution to Prosperity and Social Cohesion in Europe. Joint Interim Report of the Council and of the Commission on the Progress Under the Education and Training 2010 Work Programme* (Brussels: Education Council and European Commission).

Costa, A. L. and Kallick, B. (2000). *Habits of Mind: A Developmental Series* (Alexandria, VA: Association for Supervision and Curriculum Development).

Covey, S., Merrill, A. and Merrill, R. (1994). *First Things First* (New York: Simon & Schuster).

Csíkszentmihályi, M. (1991). 'Thoughts about Education', in D. Dickinson (ed.), *Creating the Future: Perspectives on Educational Change* (Aston Clinton, Bucks: Accelerated Learning Systems).

Csíkszentmihályi, M. (1998). *Finding Flow: The Psychology of Engagement with Everyday Life* (New York: Basic Books).

Csíkszentmihályi, M. and Larson, R. (1984). *Being Adolescent: Conflict and Growth in the Teenage Years* (New York: Basic Books).

Csíkszentmihályi, M. and Schneider, B. (2000). *Becoming Adult* (New York: Basic Books).

Dangwal, R., Jha, S. and Kapur, P. (2006). 'Impact of Minimally Invasive Education on Children: An Indian Perspective', *British Journal of Educational Technology*, 37: 295–298.

Deasy, R. J. (ed.) (2002). *Critical Links: Learning in the Arts and Student Academic and Social Development* (Washington, DC: Arts Education Partnership).

Department for Children, Schools and Families (2009). 'Breaking the Link between Disadvantage and Low Attainment: Everyone's Business', March 2009. Available at http://publications.teachernet.gov.uk/default.aspx?PageFunction=productdetails&PageMode=publications&ProductId=DCSF-00357-2009& (accessed October 2009).

Department of Education and Children's Services (2004). *Assessing the Impact of Phases 1 and 2 of Learning to Learn* (Adelaide: DECS Publishing).

Desforges, C. and Abouchaar, A. (2003). *The Impact of Parental Involvement, Parental Support and Family Education on Pupil Achievement and Adjustment: A Literature Review* (DfES Research Report 433) (London: DfES).

Dewey, J. (1916). *Democracy and Education* (New York: MacMillan).

Dweck, C. (1999). *Self Theories: Their Role in Motivation, Personality and Development* (Philadelphia, PA: Psychology Press).

Dweck, C. (2006). *Mindset* (New York: Random House).

Dweck, C. and Leggett, E. L. (1988). 'A Social Cognitive Approach to Motivation and Personality', *Psychological Review,* 95: 256–273.

Epstein, J. (1991). 'Effects on Student Achievement of Teachers' Practices of Parent Involvement', in S. Silver (ed.), *Advances in Reading/Language Research,* Vol. 5: *Literacy through Family, Community, and School Interaction* (Greenwich, CT: JAI Press), pp. 261–276.

Erlauer, L. (2003). *The Brain-Compatible Classroom: Using What We Know About Learning to Improve Teaching* (Alexandria, VA: Association for Supervision and Curriculum Development).

Facer, K. and Pykett, J. (2007). *Developing and Accrediting Personal Skills and Competencies: Report and Ways Forward* (Bristol: Futurelab).

Fan, X. and Chen, M. (2001). 'Parental Involvement and Students' Academic Achievement: A Meta-Analysis', *Educational Psychology Review*, 13(1): 1–22.

Feinstein, L. and Sabates, R. (2006). *Does Education Have an Impact on Mothers' Educational Attitudes and Behaviours?* (DfES Research Brief RCB01-06) (London: DfES).

Fisher, R. (2003). *Teaching Thinking: Philosophical Enquiry in the Classroom*, 2nd edn (London: Continuum).

Fisher, R. (2005). *Teaching Children to Learn*, 2nd rev. edn (Cheltenham: Nelson Thornes).

Fullan, M. (1982). *The Meaning of Educational Change* (New York: Teachers College Press).

Fullan, M. (1993). *Change Forces* (London: Falmer Press).

Future Foundation (2008). *Marketing to Children: Understanding the Changing Context of Children's Lives* (London: Future Foundation).

Gardner, H. (2007). *Five Minds for the Future* (Boston, MA: Harvard Business School Press).

Gilbert, C. (2007). *The 2020 Vision Teaching and Learning Review* (London: DfES).

Gilbert, I. (2007). *The Little Book of Thunks* (Carmarthen: Crown House).

Gilbert, J. (2005). *Catching the Knowledge Wave? The Knowledge Society and the Future of Education* (Wellington: NZCER Press).

Gladwell, M. (2000). *The Tipping Point: How Little Things Can Make a Big Difference* (London: Little, Brown).

Gladwell, M. (2005). *Blink: The Power of Thinking without Thinking* (London: Allen Lane).

Gladwell, M. (2008). *Outliers: The Story of Success* (London: Allen Lane).

Goldspink, C. (forthcoming). *Learning to Learn: Phase Three Evaluation Report* (South Australian Department of Education and Children's Services) (cited with permission).

Goldstein, M. and Cialdini, R. B. (2007). *Yes: 50 Secrets from the Science of Persuasion* (London: Profile).

Goleman, D. (2005). *Emotional Intelligence* (London: Bantam Books).

Graue, M. E., Weinstein T. and Walberg, H. J. (1983). 'School Based Home Instruction and Learning: A Quantitative Synthesis', *Journal of Educational Research*, 76(6)

Greany, T. and Rodd, J. (2003). *Creating a Learning to Learn School* (Stafford: Network Educational Press).

Green, H. and Hannon, C. (2007). *Their Space: Education for a Digital Generation* (London: Demos).

Greenfield, S. (2003). *Tomorrow's People* (London: Allen Lane).

Guide Association (2001). *The Educational Framework for Guiding* (London: Girl Guiding UK).

Hargreaves, D. (2004). *Personalising Learning: Next Steps in Working Laterally* (London: Specialist Schools and Academies Trust).

Harris, A., Andrew-Power, K. and Goodall, J. (2009). *Do Parents Know They Matter? Achievement through Parental Engagement* (London: Network Continuum Education).

Hart, B. and Risley, T. R. (1995). *Meaningful Differences in the Everyday Experiences of Young American Children* (Baltimore, MD: Paul H. Brookes).

Hattie, J. (1992). 'Measuring the Effects of Schooling', *Australian Journal of Education*, 36(1): 5–13.

Hattie, J. (2009). *Visible Learning: A Synthesis of over 800 Meta-Analyses Relating to Achievement* (London: Routledge).

Haycock, K. (1998). 'Good Teaching Matters … A Lot', *Thinking K-16*, 3(2): 3–14.

Heckhausen, H. (1991). *Motivation and Action* (Berlin: Springer-Verlag).

Henderson, A. T. and Mapp, K. L. (2002). *A New Wave of Evidence: The Impact of School, Family and Community Connections on Student Achievement* (Austin, TX: National Center for Family and Community Connections with Schools).

Higgins, S., Wall, K., Baumfield, V., Hall, E., Leat, D. and Moseley, D. (2007). *Learning to Learn in Schools Phase 3 Evaluation: Final Report* (London: Campaign for Learning).

Hill, P. W., Rowe, K. J., Holmes-Smith, P. and Russell, V. J. (1996). *The Victorian Quality Schools Project: A Study of School and Teacher Effectiveness. Report to the Australian Research Council*, vol. 1 (Melbourne: Centre for Applied Educational Research, Faculty of Education, University of Melbourne).

Hoskins, B. and Fredriksson, U. (2008). *Learning to Learn: What Is It and Can It Be Measured?* (Eur 23432 EN/JRC46532) (Luxembourg: OPOCE).

Howe, J. A. (1997). *IQ in Question: The Truth about Intelligence* (London: Sage).

Illich, I. (1996). *Deschooling Society* (London: Marion Boyars).

James, M., Black, P., McCormick, R., Pedder, D. and Wiliam, D. (2006). 'Learning How to Learn, in Classrooms, Schools and Networks: Aims, Design and Analysis', *Research Papers in Education*, 21(2): 101–118.

James, M., McCormick, R., Black, P., Carmichael, P., Drummond, M., Fox, A., MacBeath, J., Marshall, B., Pedder, D., Procter, R., Swaffield, S., Swann, J. and Wiliam, D. (2007) *Improving Learning How to Learn: Classrooms, Schools and Networks* (London, Routledge).

Johnson, D. and Johnson, R. (1999). *Learning Together and Alone: Co-Operative, Competitive and Individualistic Learning* (Boston, MA: Alleyn and Bacon).

Klem, A. M. and Connell, J. P. (2004). 'Relationships Matter: Linking Teacher Support to Student Engagement and Achievement', *Journal of School Health*, 74(7): 262–273. Originally presented at the Wingspread Conference on School Climate and Connectedness, Racine, WI, June 2003.

Kuhl, J. (1984). 'Volitional Aspects of Achievement, Motivation and Learned Helplessness: Towards a Comprehensive Theory of Action Control', in B. A. Maher (ed.), *Progress in Experimental Personality Research*, vol. 13 (New York: Academic Press), pp. 99–171.

Kumar D. D. (1991). 'A Meta-Analysis of the Relationship between Science Instruction and Student Engagement', *Educational Review*, 43(1): 49–56.

Lambert, N. and McCombs, B. (1998). *How Students Learn: Reforming Schools through Learner-Centered Education* (Washington, DC: American Psychological Association).

Langer, E. (2009). *Counterclockwise: Mindful Health and the Power of Possibility* (New York: Ballantine Books).

Leadbetter, C. (2004). *Personalisation through Participation* (London: Demos).

Lee, K. and Williams, C. (2005). 'Creating Learning Communities', *Curriculum Briefing*, vol. 3, no. 3 (London: Optimus).

Lucas, B. (2001). *Power Up Your Mind* (London: Nicholas Brealey).

McGregor, D. (2007). *Developing Thinking, Developing Learning* (New York: McGraw-Hill).

McLean, A. (2003). *The Motivated School* (London: Paul Chapman).

Margo, J., Dixon, M., Pearce, N. and Reed, H. (2006). *Freedom's Orphans: Raising Youth in a Changing World* (London: IPPR).

Marzano, R. J. (2000). *A New Era of School Reform: Going Where the Research Takes Us* (Aurora, CO: Mid-Continent Research for Education and Learning).

Marzano, R. J. (2003). *What Works in Schools: Translating Research into Action* (Alexandria, VA: Association for Supervision and Curriculum Development).

Marzano, R. J., Gaddy, B. B. and Dean, C. (2000) *What Works in Classroom Instruction?* (Aurora, CO: Mid-Continent Research for Education and Learning).

Marzano, R., Pickering, D. and Pollock, E. (2001). *Classroom Instruction that Works: Research-Based Strategies for Increasing Student Achievement* (Alexandria, VA: Association for Supervision and Curriculum Development).

Mitra, S. (2003). 'Minimally Invasive Education: A Progress Report on the "Hole-in-the-Wall" Experiments', *British Journal of Educational Technology*, 34: 267–371.

Mitra, S. (2005). 'Self-Organizing Systems for Mass Computer Literacy: Findings from the "Hole-in-the-Wall" Experiments', *International Journal of Development Issues*, 4: 71–81.

Mitra, S. and Rana, V. (2001). 'Children and the Internet: Experiments with Minimally Invasive Education in India', *British Journal of Educational Technology*, 32: 221–232.

Moore, R. (2008). *Heroes, Villains and Velodromes: Chris Hoy and Britain's Track Cycling Revolution* (London: Harper Sport).

Mortimore, P., Sammons, P., Stoll, L., Lewis, D. and Ecob, R. (1988). *School Matters: The Junior Years* (Wells: Open Books).

Mount, F. (2004). *Mind the Gap: Class in Britain Now* (London: Short Books).

Muijs, D. and Reynolds, D. (2001). *Effective Teaching: Evidence and Practice* (London: Paul Chapman).

Newmann, F. M. and Wehlage, G. G. (1993). 'Five Standards of Authentic Instruction', *Educational Leadership*, 50: 8–12.

Nuttall, G. A. (2007). *The Hidden Lives of Learners* (Wellington: New Zealand Council for Educational Research).

Office of Fair Trading (2009). *The Psychology of Scams: Provoking and Committing Errors of Judgement*, prepared by University of Exeter School of Psychology (London: OFT).

Organisation for Economic Co-operation and Development (2002). *Understanding the Brain: Towards a New Learning Science* (Paris: OECD).

Organisation for Economic Co-operation and Development (2006). *Think Scenarios, Rethink Education* (Paris: OECD).

Organisation for Economic Co-operation and Development (2007). *Understanding the Brain: The Birth of a Learning Science* (Paris: OECD).

Organisation for Economic Co-operation and Development (2009). *Creating Effective Teaching and Learning Environments: First Results from TALIS* (Paris: OECD).

Perkins, D. (1993). 'A Systematic Review of What Pupils, Aged 11–16, Believe Impacts On Their Motivation To Learn In the Classroom', *American Federation of Teachers*, 17(3): 28–35.

Persaud, R. (2005). *The Motivated Mind* (London: Bantam Press).

Petty, G. (2006). *Evidence-Based Teaching: A Practical Approach* (Cheltenham: Nelson Thornes).

Petty, G. (2009). *Teaching Today: A Practical Guide*, 4th edn (Cheltenham: Nelson Thornes).

Pollard et al. (2000). *Policy, Practice and Teacher Experience: Changing English Primary Education* (London: Continuum).

Pope, D. C. (2001). *Doing School: How We Are Creating a Generation of Stressed Out, Materialistic and Miseducated Students* (New Haven, CT: Yale University Press).

Prensky, M. (2006). *Don't Bother Me Mom: I'm Learning* (New York: Paragon House).

Rees, S. (2008), 'How Has the Introduction of a Learn To Learn Course Changed Teaching and Learning Since Its Introduction Into the School?', Master's thesis, University of Worcester.

Robinson, K. (2001). *Out of Our Minds: Learning to be Creative* (Oxford: Capstone).

Sabers, D. S., Cushing, K. S. and Berliner, D. C. (1991). 'Differences Among Teachers in a Task Characterised By Simultaneity, Multi-Dimensionality and Immediacy', *American Education Research Journal*, 28(1): 63–88.

Sammons, P., Hillman, J., and Mortimore, P. (1995). *Key Characteristics of Effective Schools: A Review of School Effectiveness Research*. Report by the Institute of Education for the Office for Standards in Education (London: University of London).

Scardamalia, M. (2001). 'Getting Real about 21st Century Education', *Journal of Educational Change*, 2: 171–176.

Scardamalia, M. and Bereiter, C. (2003). 'Knowledge Building', in J. W. Guthrie (ed.), *Encyclopedia of Education*, 2nd edn (New York: Macmillan Reference), pp. 1370–1373.

Scheerens, J. (1992). *Effective Schooling: Research, Theory, and Practice* (London: Cassell).

Scheerens, J. and Bosker, R. J. (1997). *The Foundations of Educational Effectiveness* (Oxford: Pergamon Press).

Scheerens, J., Vermeulen, C. J. A. J. and Pelgrum, W. J. (1989). 'Generalizibility of Instructional and School Effectiveness Indicators across Nations', *International Journal of Educational Research*, 13(7): 789–799.

Schwartz, M. and Fischer, K. (2006). 'Useful Metaphors for Tackling Problems in Teaching and Learning', *On Campus*, 11(1): 2–9.

Shernoff, E. S., Csíkszentmihályi, M. and Schneider, B. (2003). 'Student Engagement in High School Classrooms From the Perspective of Flow Theory', *School Psychology Quarterly*, 18: 158–176.

Sims, E. (2006). *Deep Learning* (London: SSAT).

Smith, A. (2002). *The Brain's Behind It: New Knowledge about the Brain and Learning* (Stafford: Network Educational Press).

Smith, A. and Call, N. (2001). *The Alps Resource Book: Accelerated Learning in Primary Schools* (Stafford: Network Educational Press).

Smith, A., Lovatt, M. and Wise, D. (2003). *Accelerated Learning: A User's Guide* (Stafford: Network Educational Press).

Sodha, S. and Margo, J. (2008). *Thursday's Child* (London: Institute for Public Policy Research).

Specialist Schools and Academies Trust (2006). 'G100 Communique: Transformation and Innovation: International Workshop for School Principals', 18 October 2006. Available at www.ssatinet.net/Docs/G100Communique_final.doc (accessed October 2009).

Stewart, T. (2001) *The Wealth of Knowledge: Intellectual Capital and the Twenty-First Century Organization* (New York: Doubleday Business).

Strang, J., Masterson, P. and Button, O. (2006). *ASK: How to Teach Learning to Learn* (Carmarthen: Crown House).

Stross, R. (2009). *Planet Google* (London: Atlantic Books).

Teddlie, C. and Stringfield, S. (1993). *Schools Make a Difference: Lessons Learned From a 10-Year Study of School Effects* (New York: Teachers College Press).

Townsend, T. (2007). *International Handbook of School Effectiveness and Improvement: Review, Reflection and Reframing*. Springer International Handbooks of Education series, vol. 17 (Dordrecht: Springer).

Thomas, W. and Smith, A. (2004). *Coaching Solutions* (Stafford: Network Educational Press).

Watkins, C. (2005). *Classrooms as Learning Communities: What's In It For Schools?* (London: Routledge).

Watkins, C., Carnell, E. and Lodge, C. (2007). *Effective Learning in Classrooms* (London: Paul Chapman).

Weiner, B. (1979). 'A Theory of Motivation and Some Classroom Experiences', *Journal f Educational Psychology*, 71: 3–23.

Wenger, E., McDermott, R. and Snyder, W. M. (2001). *Cultivating Communities of Practice: A Guide To Managing Knowledge* (Cambridge, MA: Harvard Business School Press).

Werner, E. E. and Smith, R. S. (1992). *Overcoming the Odds: High Risk Children from Birth to Adulthood* (Ithaca and London: Cornell University Press).

Wiggins, G. P. and McTighe, J. (2006). 'Examining the Teaching Life', *Educational Leadership*, 63: 26–29.

Wilkinson, R. and Pickett, K. (2009). *The Spirit Level: Why More Equal Societies Almost Always Do Better* (London: Allen Lane).

Willms, J. D. (2000). 'Monitoring School Performance for Standards Based Reform', *Evaluation and Research in Education*, 14: 237–253.

Wired for Health (2003). 'Literature Search on the Links between Emotional Wellbeing and Participation and Progression in Learning'. Available at www.wiredforhealth.gov.uk/Word/findings_updated_website.rtf (accessed July 2009).

Index